WHISTLEBLOWING IN THE SOVIET UNION

WHISTLEBLOWING IN THE SOVIET UNION

A Study of Complaints and Abuses under State Socialism

Nicholas Lampert

in association with the
CENTRE FOR RUSSIAN AND EAST EUROPEAN STUDIES
UNIVERSITY OF BIRMINGHAM
Schocken Books • New York

First American edition published by
Schocken Books 1985
10 9 8 7 6 5 4 3 2 1   85 86 87 88
Copyright © Nicholas Lampert 1985

Published by agreement with
The Macmillan Press Ltd,
London and Basingstoke

Library of Congress Cataloging in Publication Data
Lampert, Nicholas.
Whistleblowing in the Soviet Union.
"In association with the Centre for Russian and East
European Studies, University of Birmingham."
Bibliography: p.
1. Whistle blowing—Soviet Union   2. Corruption (in
politics)—Soviet Union.   3. Misconduct in
office—Soviet Union.
I. University of Birmingham.   Centre for Russian and
East European Studies.   II. Title.   III. Title: Whistle
blowing in the Soviet Union.
JN6529.W55L36   1985   354.47009'94   84-13975

Printed in Hong Kong
ISBN 0-8052-3951-0

To my father and to the memory of my mother

Contents

Acknowledgements   ix
Abbreviations   x
List of Tables   xi

1   INTRODUCTION
    1. Law, Lawlessness and Political Control in the USSR   2
    2. Abuse of Office and Citizens' Complaints   7
    3. Sources and Approach   9

2   ABUSE OF OFFICE IN SOVIET LAW AND PRACTICE
    1. Abuse of Office in Soviet Criminal Law   13
    2. Abuse of Office: Pressures and Temptations   21
    3. The Controllers   35
    4. The Legal Apparatuses   41
    5. The Party   46
    6. Law Enforcement: Some Variations   51
    7. Conclusions   59

3   WHISTLEBLOWING: SOME CASES
    1. Introduction   61
    2. Some Cases   69

4   WHISTLEBLOWERS, MANAGERS AND THE STATE
    1. The Whistleblowers   108
    2. The Management Response   116
    3. The Agencies of Appeal: The Local Party Apparatus   122
    4. The Tide of Complaints: The Response of the   127
       Party Leadership
    5. Petitioning and the Press   134
    6. Conclusions   144

5   SOVIET LAW AND THE SECURITY OF WORK
    1. Soviet Labour Law and Work Disputes   147
    2. Management Attitudes and the Security of Work   149
    3. The Role of the Trade Unions   158
    4. The Role of the Courts   161
    5. Other Channels of Appeal   172
    6. Conclusions   175

6 CONCLUSIONS

1. A Brief Summary 177
2. Abuses and Complaints: a Round-table Discussion 179

Appendix 190
Notes and References 191
Bibliography 204
Index 207

Acknowledgements

I would like to thank several people for their interest and assistance at various stages in the writing of this book. Gabor Rittersporn inspired me by his shared concern with the issues and by his great knowledge, while Steve Shenfield and Mike Clarke in different ways encouraged me by discussing a number of aspects of the research. Vladimir Andrle's work on the Soviet power structure has served as a catalyst over the years, and its influence will be seen even where it does not make an explicit appearance. I owe special thanks also to Phil Hanson, who pointed me in the direction of new material. I benefited from the comments of Aron Katsenelinboigen and Stash Pomorski, and from the ready assistance of Mike Berry with some translation problems. As general editor of the series, Bob Davies read the whole of the first draft and, as always, had valuable things to say. I was lucky to be able to take them into account in writing the final draft.

In the spring of 1981 I spent a month at the Department of Labour Law, Moscow State University. My thanks are due to colleagues there who assisted me with problems of Soviet labour law, with which the research began. They should not, though, be held responsible for any of the arguments in the book.

In January 1983 I paid a visit to Israel to conduct some interviews with former Soviet citizens. This could not have been done without the expert guidance of Konstantin Miroshnik. I would like to thank him for his help and hospitality, and also the Centre for Russian and East European Studies at Birmingham University for a generous contribution towards the cost of the trip.

Finally, there are several friends in the Soviet Union, who shall remain nameless, who contributed to the study in numerous ways. One in particular gave me a powerful impetus by telling me about his tireless efforts in pursuit of justice.

Part of Chapter 2 appeared in *Soviet Studies*, vol. xxxvi, no. 3 (July 1984), and part of Chapter 4 in a contribution to M.C. Clarke (ed.), *Corruption* (London: Frances Pinter, 1983). I am grateful to the editors and publishers for permission to use this material.

Abbreviations

BVS SSSR	Byulleten' Verkhnogo Suda SSSR (Bulletin of the Supreme Court of the USSR)
CDSP	Current Digest of the Soviet Press
Gorkom	Gorodskoi komitet (city party committee)
Lit. Gaz.	Literaturnaya Gazeta (Literary Gazette)
OBKhSS	Otdel dlya bor'by s khishcheniem sotsialisticheskoi sobstvennosti (police department for the struggle against theft of socialist property)
Obkom	Oblastnoi komitet (province party committee)
Raikom	Raionnyi komitet (district party committee)
Sots. Ind.	Sotsialisticheskaya Industriya (Socialist Industry)
Sots. Zak.	Sotsialisticheskaya Zakonnost' (Socialist Legality)
Sov. Gos. i Pravo	Sovetskoe Gosudarstvo i Pravo (Soviet State and Law)
VTsSPS	Vsesoyuznyi Tsentral'nyi Sovet Professional'nykh Soyuzov (All-Union Central Council of Trade Unions)

List of Tables

2.1 Penalties for different types of abuse of office. 53
2.2 Penalties for abuse of office, by sector. 55
3.1 Letters to the CPSU Central Committee. 63
3.2 Letters to Soviet newspapers, 1952–81. 64
5.1 Stated reasons for dismissal in cases before the courts, 1975. 153
5.2 Management response to complaints by employees about abuse of office. 155

1 Introduction

After November 1982, when Andropov took over as leader of the Soviet communist party, the Soviet authorities and media devoted a great deal of attention to the problem of social order and discipline in the USSR. It was insistently suggested that the current level of lawlessness and disorder in social life should no longer be tolerated. Soviet citizens must learn to work in a disciplined way, public order must be improved, and officials at all levels must observe the law and not use their positions in the pursuit of personal and local ends. The beginning of the law and order campaign was signalled by Andropov at a meeting of the party central committee in November 1982, when he appealed to the party and to the people as a whole to 'carry out a more decisive struggle against all violations of party, state and labour discipline'.[1] The campaign was accompanied by much comment in the press from Soviet citizens, expressing great concern about the state of public order, discipline and legality.

The campaign was not a new element in Soviet policy. It was, rather, the latest in a long series of such attempts through central initiative and public propaganda to strengthen law and order at all social levels. Such campaigns testify to a stubborn gulf between the edifice of formal rules and the rules that actually govern social practice. On the one hand, there is in the USSR a large and intricate body of law that has been established to regulate social behaviour. The rights and duties of Soviet citizens are laid down in the greatest detail by a state which wants to ensure a wide-ranging supervision over the activities of the population. Yet, in a wide variety of settings, the law is regularly flouted, creating the impression that to a large extent the formal rules do not count. The central purpose of this book is to examine the causes and consequences of this gulf between rules and behaviour in relation to one set of law and order problems, which I shall call 'abuse of office'. Abuse of office is an umbrella term that refers to a number of managerial and official practices that are prohibited in Soviet criminal law. They include a variety of phenomena: for example, deceiving the state about the results of an

1

organisation's activities, appropriating state property, taking or giving bribes, deceiving customers, dismissing people for reasons of personal hostility, giving unauthorised special rewards to favoured employees, and engaging in illicit exchanges with the managers of other organisations. The common element in the variety is that people are using the resources or powers of an office in illegal ways. I shall try to draw a picture of the conditions under which this problem arises, to get an idea of the pattern of law enforcement, and to draw some conclusions from this pattern about the extent and limits of central political control. A large part of the book will be exploring these issues from a particular vantage point, focusing on attempts by Soviet citizens to bring complaints about abuse of office in various organisational settings. Hence the title of the book. I shall suggest that by examining the origins and outcome of 'whistleblowing' – that is, attempts 'from below' to expose management illegality – one can throw much light on the conditions which encourage or inhibit such breaches of law. At the same time, by adopting this angle of vision one can get some clues about why it is that abuse of office becomes a problem not just for the state, but also for the Soviet public.

In this introductory discussion I shall give an outline of the main ideas that lie behind the argument of the book, and say something about the sources and approach used in writing it.

1 LAW, LAWLESSNESS AND POLITICAL CONTROL IN THE USSR

In recent years there has been much official propaganda in the Soviet Union directed at the problem of managerial and official illegality, and at the problem of legality in general. In itself this may not be worthy of special comment. After all, the existence of a gap between law and social behaviour is not peculiar to the USSR. However, this gap takes on a particular significance in the Soviet Union and in other state socialist societies, because of the very ambitious character of political control. The Soviet Union has a highly centralised political system in which attempts are continuously made to draw up and implement central plans for the production and distribution of goods, and more generally to establish an encompassing form of political management over social life. Such a form of management can only work well if there are well-understood and more or less stable rules which are taken seriously by the citizens. It is this that makes possible the predictability on which effective central control must rest. In particular, it is important that people occupying positions of authority and responsibility should have a clear set of duties and abide by them. It is not therefore surprising to find that there are elaborate rules and norms laid down for managers and officials in the USSR, who have been given a special responsibility as executives on behalf of the state.

But the Soviet leadership seems to be faced here with a major dilemma. In order to secure effective political control the Soviet rulers need law and legality – stable rules and clearly specified rights and duties for individuals and organisations. Yet the Soviet form of political management itself helps to create an environment in which illegal practices flourish. To some extent, it could be said, this is simply the consequence of the very broad scope of reference of Soviet law, and criminal law in particular. Since managerial and official practices are surrounded by so many laws and regulations, abuse of office is created by the law itself. But there are more substantive issues involved as well. In the first place, because the mechanism of directive planning is highly imperfect, the managers of economic units feel obliged regularly to break the law in order to meet their targets in the face of constant difficulties with the supply of needed goods and materials. In this way 'unofficial' practices become part and parcel of 'official' production and exchange. Secondly, the highly centralised character of management over all types of organisation nourishes a pervasive tendency to indulge in false reporting about the organisation's performance. Finally, one can argue that the form of Soviet centralised management is itself a major source of widespread shortages of goods and services, which encourage people to use their public positions for private gain. It assists theft, and allows people who control the distribution and allocation of goods and services to reward favourites and to extract extra benefits by taking gifts and bribes.

If these assertions are true, or partly true, then the problem is that the political structure itself helps to generate the illegalities that regularly preoccupy Soviet party leaders and law enforcement agencies. It can be argued too that the dilemma gets more serious the more complex Soviet society becomes. On the one hand, the greater the complexity of the system that is to be managed, the more important it is to ensure a basis of behaviour in stable rules: law becomes more critical. On the other hand, the more complex the goals to be achieved, the more difficult it is to draw up and implement coherent plans for the whole of society, and the more problematic it becomes to achieve the sort of wide-ranging legal regulation which the political leaders consider desirable.

To say this is not to suggest that the problem of managerial and official illegality is 'worse' in the Soviet Union than in advanced capitalist countries or in the Third World. There are special problems that arise with a form of state management of the Soviet kind, and political lessons can be learned from that. But it is not an aim of the book to contrast the USSR with other types of political system, with a view to showing how awful the phenomenon is in the Soviet case. It should be stressed at the outset that this is not a comparative study. A comparative analysis would indeed be valuable in assessing the validity of statements about the relationship between abuse of office and political structure. But that is a task for another study. The present research might make a contribution to a comparative analysis, but does not itself attempt to do it.[2]

There is, then, no underlying suggestion that abuse of office is a greater problem, or has more destructive consequences, in the Soviet Union than in other societies. But the issue is, plainly, a significant one within the Soviet context, and its significance does not have to be demonstrated by reference to comparisons with other political systems. In the first place, the Soviet authorities are preoccupied with abuse of office as one type of law and order problem: this in itself makes it an issue. That preoccupation is in turn based on a reaction to the disruptive consequences of management illegality for the planning mechanism, and more generally for the mechanism of political control – even if some types of abuse are indeed 'functional' for the workings of the economy. But also, Soviet official norms share with all modern bureaucratic cultures the idea that, for reasons of morality as well as efficiency, the incumbents of offices should stick to the rules and that offices should not be used for personal ends. The assumption is that lawlessness in the sphere of management and official practice has a morally corrosive effect for the whole society, as well as undermining the efforts at central political direction. Indeed, these two things are closely related, because effective political management depends on a definite degree of social unity based on shared norms and purposes. If the laws are broken with impunity by people in responsible positions, this is likely to lead to a nihilistic attitude towards official values in general, which threatens to undermine that unity.

This point leads on, though, to a second warning that should be issued early on. To say that abuse of office is an important social problem is not to say that such forms of illegality are in some absolute sense intolerable for the Soviet political system, that the Soviet state is about to collapse under the weight of the contradiction between legal norms and actual practices. There is nothing to suggest that this is so, and it is quite possible that the Soviet political leadership is prepared to live with these problems indefinitely, especially if they do not interfere with the achievements of priority goals. The Soviet leaders are well aware of widespread breaches of law, and are surely aware of the connection between abuse of office and defects in the system of central management. But from their point of view it is no doubt preferable to live with such problems than to embark on radical changes in the economic and political structure that might reduce their ability to pursue the priority objectives, and bring other unwanted social problems as well.

There are, none the less, signs that the tension between law and social practice has become a more pressing issue in recent years. This is suggested by a heavy stream of support in favour of legality, and pressures towards greater legal regulation in the past ten to fifteen years. One manifestation of that has been a trend towards greater codification of law in all areas.[3] Secondly, there has been much propaganda in support of the civil rights of Soviet citizens, an aspect which received especially heavy coverage in connection with the new Constitution of 1977. Third, there has been much talk and some action in relation to training in law for citizens and activists, as part of a general effort to raise the level of law consciousness among Soviet citizens. That has been accompanied too, in the 1970s and early 1980s, by a spate of academic writing on the role of law in society and on the concept of legal consciousness.[4]

Some of these trends were reflected in a speech by Brezhnev to the 26th Party Congress, in which he referred to the importance of the 'renewal of Soviet law':

New laws will allow a more exact and detailed regulation of the various aspects of social relationships. Work on the improvement of the law will continue. Three directions are especially important: the management of the national economy, the realisation of the constitutional rights of citizens and social organisations, the publication of an all-Union code of laws.[5]

The improvement of legal norms, he went on to say, was an 'objective demand of the times', economically vital because the law was a means to 'increasing the efficiency and quality of production, and strengthening state and labour discipline', and politically important because a 'true people's democracy' was impossible without respect for the legal order. Without that one would have a condition of 'anarchical arbitrariness'.[6]

Alongside this emphasis on legal regulation and codification, 'law and order' propaganda has been much in evidence as well. By this I mean propaganda directed at (a) law-breaking by people in official and managerial positions, (b) workplace offences (especially petty theft), (c) public order on the streets, mainly in connection with drunkenness and crimes of violence. Some of these law and order worries were expressed in a Central Committee resolution of May 1979, which included the following appeal:

> A systematic, purposeful and uncompromising struggle should be waged, using all means of propaganda and education ... to eradicate ... the ugly vestiges of the past ... such as money grubbing and bribery, the desire to grasp whatever one can from society without giving it anything in return, mismanagement, wastefulness, drunkenness, hooliganism, red tape, a callous attitude towards people, and violations of labour discipline and public order. It is necessary to use both verbal persuasion and the harsh force of law in the struggle against these phenomena.[7]

In these and many other similar official pronouncements, the demands of effective management and the rhetoric of civil rights have converged with the appeals for more order and discipline to heighten the emphasis on respect for law. This emphasis reflects an awareness of the growing importance of legal regulation as the socioeconomic structure to be managed becomes larger and more intricate. The appeal for legal restraints on managers and officials is a part of that wider emphasis. Yet the dilemma is that this same structure has generated a set of political relationships that constantly inhibits the ostensible efforts of the authorities at the centre to curb illegal practices. This seems to be reflected in the following state of affairs. On the one hand, the central authorities issue a stream of injunctions instructing the law enforcement agencies to put a stop to illegal activities by management and local officials. On the other hand, the representatives of the centre constantly protest that these agencies are unwilling to act vigorously; that illegal practices are condoned and often encouraged by administrative superiors and local controllers; that investigations into malpractice are superficial and punishments too light. The pursuit of personal, local and departmental interests seems to be in endemic tension, then, with the stated central ambition to defend the general social interest against the corrosive effects of disrespect for the law.

If this is so, then the very existence of a strong political centre comes into question, if by political centre one means a central source of power able or willing to mobilise the agencies of the state against breaches of law. To be sure, the party leadership can launch periodic campaigns against particular forms of law-breaking, thus producing a shift in the climate of law enforcement. But such campaigns cannot in themselves be expected to tackle the underlying problem, because the relationships of patronage and protection are too strong. They are too strong between higher and lower levels of administration, between local party officials and offending managers, and between higher and lower levels of the party hierarchy. If the legal agencies, especially the procuracy (the main investigative organ) and the courts, had greater political independence they could cut through some of this protection. But they cannot act without reference to local political interests. This is shown by the pattern of law enforcement, which reflects the power of the local political authorities in the face of central demands and appeals.[8]

Soviet political officials have established a high level of security, not to say complete immunity, even in the face of exposure for condoning violations of criminal law. That security reflects a general stabilisation in the position of officialdom in the post-Stalin period. The relationship between the higher and lower levels is, it seems, one of mutual support and mutual dependence. Elements of tension remain, and these are revealed by the effect of regular pressure from the centre to ensure that law enforcement agencies clamp down on abuses. But the teeth of such pressure become severely blunted by the fact that at each level of the hierarchy there is a reluctance, except in a token way, to make the people lower down answerable for their actions. The extent and limits of that tension, and the pattern of protection, emerge in a particularly concrete way if one looks at what happens to complaints by Soviet citizens about abuse of office.

2 ABUSE OF OFFICE AND CITIZENS' COMPLAINTS

A striking feature of the Soviet system is the extent to which the political leadership has attempted to draw ordinary citizens into the process of law enforcement. One of the ways in which the Soviet authorities try to keep abuses in check is by encouraging individual citizens to uncover illegal practices, to blow the whistle on wayward managers and officials. The state appeals to the citizen to act as an assistant in the law enforcement process, to defend his or her rights in law and to expose attempts by people in official positions to use their offices for illegal ends. There are considerable pressures acting against such initiatives, especially if they involve an employee taking a complaint about management outside the organisation. Yet it is by no means uncommon for employees to lodge complaints of this kind. They form one element of the wider, and politically very important, phenomenon of petitioning. Petitioning is the procedure in which individual citizens make written or oral submissions to agencies that are responsible for ensuring that the laws are observed and the rights of individuals upheld. For example, Soviet citizens can appeal to a higher administrative authority, to the party organisations, to the legal agencies, the soviets and the trade unions, either in the pursuit of personal grievances, or in the more disinterested attempt to uncover illegalities in the organisations where they work. The press also plays a vital role in the petitioning process, acting as a defender of wronged individuals, and putting pressure on other agencies to act against injustices.

The phenomenon of petitioning is not of course unique to the Soviet Union. In all societies in which the state has extended its role and its area of intervention and in which therefore administrative decisions impinge to an increasing extent on individual citizens, complaints procedures have tended to become more important. The citizen is given at least some form of redress against official malpractice. This trend has been reflected, for example, in the role of the Ombudsman in several Western countries.[9] But in the Soviet Union the petitioning procedure plays an unusually important role, and is used by Soviet citizens to an enormous extent. The mechanism is important partly because it is a source of information and helps law enforcement. But it is also significant as an ideological force, as a source of potential unity between the concerned citizen and the would-be guardians of the general interest at the centre.

Whistleblowing is one form of submission from below. In blowing the whistle, an individual acts in accordance with Soviet official ideals and in accordance with official moral injunctions to the population. But if people lodge complaints about abuse of office they are likely to face immense difficulties. This too is not an unfamiliar phenomenon in the West: employees who spill the beans on malpractices in corporations or government agencies are not likely to be thanked for it.[10]

The difference is that in the Soviet Union whistleblowing has become more regularised and plays a more accepted part in the overall process of law enforcement. This provides some degree of protection for the complainants, but the problems of making a complaint stick are still very great. The reasons for this difficulty arise from the same set of conditions as those which tend to blunt the impact of law enforcement in general in relation to abuse of office. The course of a complaint reveals some elements of tension between central and local political power, but also gives a clear picture of the symbiosis between them. A complaint about abuse of office will typically be ignored or resisted by political and legal agencies at the local level, thus producing a strong tendency to take a complaint higher in the attempt to get something done. This process is occasionally successful, but fraught with difficulty and uncertainty. The upshot is that people who appeal to official values in pursuit of their claims are likely to pay much more heavily for their efforts than those they seek to criticise.

Meanwhile, another important problem arises, because whistle-blowers will typically be penalised – often dismissed – as a result of their efforts. In order to vindicate themselves they will therefore often have to make appeals for redress or reinstatement under the provisions of labour law. This raises important questions about the degree of job security offered to Soviet employees by the law.

There is some evidence that the party leadership has become increasingly preoccupied with the question of petitioning in general, and complaints about abuses in particular. Just as the leaders have shown growing concern about lawless behaviour on the part of managers and officials, so they have expressed some disquiet about the great volume of complaints from Soviet citizens which in one way or another attempt to redress grievances against people in responsible positions. The basic response of the party leadership to this problem has been to summon the local controllers to act more decisively and to pay more attention to the citizens' demands. But such appeals tend to founder on those relationships of patronage and protection to which I have already referred.

3 SOURCES AND APPROACH

The reader may find the proposed theme interesting, but may also think that it is naive to believe that it could be adequately investigated by a Western observer. It might be thought that subject matter of this kind would fail to get any serious coverage in Soviet published sources. The secrecy might not be as great as in the case of military information, but sufficient to make any serious inquiry impossible. In fact this is not so. The political apparatus, the legal agencies and the press (which acts as an ideological arm of the apparatus) are engaged in a continuous effort to enforce the law, to publicise violations and to establish some link with the aggrieved citizen who wants to lodge a complaint about breaches of law. This effort is a partial and selective one, but in performing those functions the agencies of the state must keep their eyes open, and the press must provide material offering instructive examples to show the importance of sticking to the rules. Public exposure serves constantly to restate the boundaries between the permissible and the impermissible, and to give expression to a real or wished-for social unity in the face of transgressors. In this respect the moral meaning of law and order reporting in the USSR seems to be similar to the meaning of such reporting in much of the Western press – with the difference that in the Soviet Union the message is less sensationally presented and more explicitly stated.[11] In any event, the Soviet press regularly gives a lot of coverage to law and order issues of all kinds, including abuse of office, often with considerable detail about particular situations and organisations. I have therefore relied greatly on such 'investigative' reports, in conjunction with legal sources which provide accounts of law-breaking and law enforcement for a narrower specialist audience.

If the Soviet press is heavily censored, and very selective in its choice of material, this does not then mean that it obliterates all 'awkward' information. Still, the fact that a lot of information is published about breaches of law does not in itself get one very far. The task remains to interpret such material, and to glean from the form of the narrative, as well as from its content, the character of the events and relationships involved. This is not so much a problem of 'reading between the lines', in the sense that the real intentions of the author must be decoded. It is rather the problem of having no direct experience of the situations described. The difficulty is not peculiar to Western students of Soviet society. It is an obstacle in the study of any 'other' culture, and indeed in the study of parts of one's own culture, and at another level a problem with all academic knowledge. But the distance that has to be bridged for Western observers of the Soviet Union – it is a serious physical distance as well as a cultural one – magnifies these difficulties.

The job then is to transcend the gap that is created by these distances, and to think oneself as far as possible into the social roles and situations described. This is not easy, but it is a necessary condition for an adequate analysis. To assist in this task, the published sources have been supplemented by discussions with colleagues and friends in Moscow and Leningrad, and by a series of interviews with Soviet émigrés in Israel, people who had worked in the USSR as managers, lawyers or journalists.[12] The purpose of the interviews was to try out some of the ideas I had been working with, and to gain additional illustrative material, by questioning people who had experience on the ground of the kind of situations reported in the press. Such meetings are hard for Western researchers to arrange in the Soviet Union, and would be difficult to conduct with the necessary degree of openness. There are of course familiar reservations about the use of émigré sources: those who have left the USSR for more or less political reasons may have a systematically slanted view of events. This is a pertinent point in some contexts, especially if one is doing a study of Soviet political attitudes. But in the present context it is not a weighty objection. The interviews were concerned only with concrete events and organisations, not with general views about the nature of the Soviet system. I should add too that in the event, the interviews have been used only as a supplementary source of illustrative material. They did not change any substantive argument that emerged from a study of published sources. This may be of some comfort to would-be students of Soviet society who are sceptical about the chances of getting to know anything from the public images that the Soviet Union presents to its own citizens and to the world.

Finally, a few words about the way the book was conceived and written, which may help to explain the apparently peculiar mixture of elements within it. Neither the structure of the book, nor indeed the substantive themes, were clearly envisaged at the beginning. They emerged in the course of the research itself. At the outset my intention was to investigate the character and causes of work disputes in Soviet organisations. It became evident rather quickly that the most serious disputes arose in situations where an employee was protesting about one or another form of illegal practice by the management of the organisation. This protest had arisen either out of the pursuit of a personal grievance or else in the more disinterested defence of law and morality. In order to pursue this protest the employee had lodged a complaint (or several complaints) with party or state agencies, and had appealed to the national press for assistance. Very often such whistle-blowers had suffered serious consequences at work, incurring penalties from management (often leading to dismissal), penalties which were allowed for in labour law but which were designed as weapons against unproductive workers, not against people who had become an embarrassment to the organisation.

The press was full of reports about situations of this kind. In order to understand how such conflicts had arisen, it was necessary to examine *what* the complainants were protesting about, *why* they had taken the step of going outside the organisation, and *how* they were able to use the Soviet complaints procedure in their efforts to get something done. A study that had begun as an investigation of work disputes quickly developed into a study of a particular type of citizens' complaint, which formed part of the wider phenomenon of petitioning.

Finally, in order to understand the fate of such a complaint, and the chances of the law being enforced in a situation of this kind, it was essential to examine why the breaches of law arose, how firmly entrenched they were, what sources of protection were available to managers in relation to whistleblowers, and how all these pressures affected the pattern of law enforcement. The key to the course of the dispute had to be sought in the circumstances leading to abuse of office, and in the attitude of the political and legal agencies towards it.

The exposition in the book is in reverse order to the order I have outlined. The research began from a concrete social problem (work disputes arising from 'criticism from below'), and worked outwards from that. The presentation works inwards towards the starting point. It begins, in Chapter 2, with a discussion of the basic problem of law and lawlessness in the context of abuse of office, and examines the character of the political relationships that might account for the pattern of law enforcement. In Chapters 3 and 4, I go on to illustrate and examine the character, causes and consequences of whistle-blowing, arguing that what happens to complaints of this type high-lights the tensions between law and lawlessness, and the political relationships in which the process of law enforcement becomes embedded. In Chapter 5 I come to the question of work disputes, focusing especially on those which involve dismissals and appeals for reinstatement. The fate of a whistleblower depends to an important extent on the degree of job protection provided by Soviet labour law. The purpose of the chapter is to assess the extent and limits of that protection, and on what it depends. The final chapter ties some of the threads together again, and considers some political conclusions that might be drawn from the problem of abuses and complaints in the USSR.

2 Abuse of Office in Soviet Law and Practice

Abuse of office, in the broad sense in which it is defined in this book, provides a major focus of concern for the political leadership, for the law enforcement agencies and for the media in the Soviet Union. The reasons for this are readily understandable. The Soviet system is based on an encompassing form of state management. This has led to a proliferation of rules surrounding the activity of all officials. Such rules are vital for any form of political and administrative control in any political system. But in the Soviet Union the great scope of state activity has increased the compass of legal regulation. In particular, it has given the criminal law a very broad scope of reference in relation to all organisational activity. At the same time, the attempt by a central authority to formulate and implement such rules has brought manifold problems of evasion. As a result a wide gulf has opened up between officially declared legal norms and moral values on the one hand, and managerial practice on the other. In this chapter I shall try to illustrate this state of affairs and to trace out some of its implications. In section 1 I give a brief account of the main forms of abuse of office as defined in Soviet law. Section 2 will look at some of the pressures and temptations that might explain the persistence of such abuses. Then in sections 3-6 I shall try to draw a picture of the pattern of law enforcement, and to link that picture with the pattern of political power as a whole.

1 ABUSE OF OFFICE IN SOVIET CRIMINAL LAW

Throughout this book the term 'abuse of office' will be used in a broad way, to cover a range of practices prohibited in Soviet criminal law. These practices are defined in three different sections of the criminal codes: 'crimes against socialist property', 'economic crimes' and 'official crimes'. But what all the varieties of abuse of office have

13

in common is that they involve people in positions of responsibility making use of the powers or resources at their disposal for illegal ends.

The scope of those parts of the criminal law that relate to abuse of office is very wide. This reflects the primacy of state property in Soviet law and the 'total' character of Soviet political management over organisational life. Indeed the regulating role of criminal law extends, at least in principle, to the production process itself, since mismanagement, negligence, waste and poor-quality products are in certain circumstances defined as criminal offences.[1] This marks an important contrast between state socialist and capitalist economies, since in the latter the main sanction against waste is failure in the market place.[2]

The broad scope of Soviet law in relation to abuse of office is not only due to the political management of production. Anybody with authority in any recognised organisation in the Soviet Union is a 'servant of the state', even if the organisation (say a trade union) is not officially regarded as a 'state organisation'. Any holder of office is responsible to the political authority and his or her obligations to the state are defined by criminal law as well as administrative rules. What then are the main forms of abuse of office as described in the criminal codes? The list that follows is not an exhaustive one, but it will be sufficient to set the scene for later discussion. All references are to the Criminal Code of the Russian Republic (RSFSR). The codes of the other republics differ in some details from the RSFSR Code, but not in substance.

Embezzlement

The term embezzlement will be used to refer to some of the offences included under article 92: theft (*khishchenie*) of state or social property. The theft of state property is authoritatively described as

the most dangerous type of infringement of socialist property. Its social danger lies in the fact that material values, which are national property and are allocated for the fulfilment of the needs of society as a whole, are withdrawn without compensation from disposal and control by government and social organisations, and are illegally transferred to the personal use of individuals.[3]

Embezzlement refers to theft of state or social property when carried out by someone occupying an 'office', as opposed to theft by those who do not hold offices – for example, theft of materials by factory workers or diversion of goods in transit by rank and file road or rail transport employees. Both the latter are common offences in the Soviet Union, but they fall outside the scope of this study. Embezzlement may mean the appropriation of money, materials or goods for personal use (*prisvoenie*), or the appropriation of materials or goods so as to dispose of them for private gain (*rastrata*).

False Reporting

False reporting can take different forms, which it is important to distinguish. The first is covered by article 152, headed 'Report-padding (*pripiski*) and other types of false reporting in connection with the fulfilment of plans'. This type of misinformation, which is often dubbed 'eye-wash' (*ochkovtiratel'stvo*), is designed to overstate the performance of an organisation. *Pripiski* have been described in a legal commentary as

> anti-government actions of people in official positions, aimed at concealing the results of unsatisfactory economic activity and colouring the true position with the fulfilment of plans; they take the form of padding reports presented to the state and wilfully distorting accounting data. Such actions are usually dictated by careerist motives or by other motives of personal gain. Trying to pass themselves off as good managers, or in order to get bonuses or in the expectation of other rewards, some executives of enterprises, organisations and establishments disregard the interests of the state, engage in criminal activity and thus do great harm to the national economy.[4]

In similar vein, a review by the USSR Supreme Court describes the typical reason for this kind of false reporting as 'the illegal formation of economic incentive funds, bonuses, wages and other material rewards'.[5]

It should be noted that the receipt of illegal bonuses or other payments is treated in Soviet law as a form of theft, so that report-padding, according to a strict interpretation, will often involve embezzlement as well – although it must be shown that the intention behind the report-padding was some kind of mercenary gain. As a commentary by the USSR Supreme Court explains:

> If padding [*pripiski*] in state accounts and the presentation of other intentionally distorted statistical data on the fulfilment of plans are accompanied by the subsequent ... appropriation of material resources by oneself or by others, the action must be qualified according to the articles of the criminal code making provision for responsibility for report-padding [*pripiski*] and for theft of socialist property, taking into account the whole sum ... both the part received by the official carrying out the report-padding, and the part transferred to other individuals in the form of bonuses or other payments.[6]

A second type of false reporting is connected with illegal wage payments, and involves misinformation about the amount of work done, thereby paying workers more than they are entitled to. One should include here also the notorious phenomenon of 'dead souls', which means having people registered on the payroll who are not in fact working in the organisation. It is a way of expanding the wage fund and giving management extra financial flexibility. This kind of false reporting is not covered by article 152 because it does not involve false accounting data in relation to plan fulfilment. It could in principle by covered by articles 175 or 170 – these will be discussed below. If the illegal extra payments are wholly or in part appropriated by management for personal use, then theft of socialist property will be involved as well.

Finally, there is the type of misinformation which is designed to understate the resources at the disposal of the organisation in order to cover up losses that have occurred through negligence or theft. For example, materials or products may be written off in order to conceal their appropriation. In this case the main offence is of course theft, not the misinformation itself.

Forgery

Article 175 defines forgery as 'the inclusion by an official for mercenary ends or other personal motives of deliberately false information, falsifying, rubbing out or changing a date, and drawing up or giving out deliberately false statements or including a deliberately false written report'.[7] It is clear that this offence is closely akin to 'false reporting' in article 152. Indeed, if an organisation is not directly involved in 'material production', its officials are not supposed to be charged under article 152, but under article 175.

Bribery

In article 173, bribe-taking is defined as 'the receipt of a bribe in any form whatever by a person in an official position, for the purpose of carrying out or not carrying out in the interests of the bribe-giver any action which the official should have carried out by using his official position [*sluzhebnoe polozhenie*]'.[8] Bribe-giving (article 174) is also a criminal offence, unless it is a case of extortion, or unless the bribe-giver volunteers information after the event.

In the case of abuse of office, bribery is more likely to mean bribe-taking. But bribe-giving may also occur as an official crime, for example where supply officials are bribed to provide scarce materials, or where law enforcement agents are paid off to keep quiet about some form of illegality.

A USSR Supreme Court judge has described bribery as 'one of the crimes most alien to Soviet morality. It undermines the authority of the state apparatus and discredits its activity.'[9]

Deceit of Customers and Clients

Article 156 describes this as 'False measurement, false weighing, short-changing, charging more than official retail prices, or more than official prices and scales for everyday and communal services provided to the population, or other forms of deceit of customers and clients in shops and other trade enterprises or in public catering, in everyday services for the population and in municipal economy.'[10]

This description seems to make for a blurred boundary between deceit and bribery, and also between deceit and theft. For example, if a shop assistant or manager is paid over-the-odds for a product that is in short supply, it is not immediately clear if this deserves the title of a bribe. Similarly, if an employee in a restaurant waters down the wine and appropriates the extra takings, it is not clear if theft is also involved. This is one area of the law – by no means the only one – where some ambiguity remains.

Two forms of 'deceit' were only recently (in September 1981) added to article 156. One concerns the practice of selling goods direct from wholesale outlets or selling under-the-counter in retail organisations. The other relates to the apparently pervasive practice of paying extra to rank and file employees (not 'officials') for goods and services that are in high demand.[11] Before the change in law, a Supreme Court judge commented:

> in the recent period cases of illegal levies from citizens have become widespread, especially on the part of employees in trade and services, whereby they obtain rewards for actions which they could or should have carried out in the course of their duties ... The actions of such people, not covered by the Criminal Code, seriously violate the rights and lawful interests of citizens, and have a corrupting effect on the morally unstable part of the population.[12]

Private Enterprise

Article 153 outlaws 'private enterprise activity through the use of state, cooperative or other social forms'. A legal commentary clarifies the term private enterprise as follows: it entails

> the organisation and management of the work of a private enterprise of a non-socialist type. Such enterprises cannot legally exist in socialist society, so their setting up and activity appears outwardly as legal economic activity by a socialist organisation, while giving the offender at the same time the possibility of extracting a private profit.[13]

The same article also outlaws 'commercial mediation', described as 'assistance to individuals in obtaining goods in short supply and in the sale of goods', while article 154 bans 'speculation', that is, 'the buying or selling of goods or other items for the purpose of making a profit'.[14] These provisions, among others, reflect the very restrictive attitude towards private production and exchange contained within Soviet law. Some forms of private activity are legal, and in agriculture are officially recognised as indispensable to the economy as a whole.

But in general the law remains highly antipathetic to private initiatives.

Some Other Offences

The list above is a selection from the offences that are given special mention in the Soviet criminal codes, and which could be included under my umbrella term, 'abuse of office'. In addition, there are many common offences which are not specifically mentioned, which would be typically covered by article 170, entitled 'Abuse of power or official position'. This is defined as:

> the wilful use by an official of one's position in a manner contrary to the interests of service, if this is done for mercenary motives or other reasons of personal gain, and if it causes significant damage to state or social interests, or to the rights and interests of citizens that are protected by law.

It is further explained that an official (*dolzhnostnoe litso*) is:

> a person acting permanently or temporarily as a representative of authority, or a person permanently or temporarily carrying out duties in state or social institutions, organisations or enterprises related to the performance of organisational–executive or administrative–economic tasks . . . [15]

'Abuse of power or official position' is so broad a category that it could in principle include all the forms of abuse of office that I shall be concerned with in this book. In practice, it is used to cover offences that are not given a particular description elsewhere in the criminal code. Very often what is involved is one form or another of illicit use of resources over which an official has administrative control. For example, if managers allocate housing or bonuses or other benefits over which they have administrative control to favoured employees, and not to people entitled to those benefits, this is 'abuse of power'. Other examples might include: managers making personal use of the resources or personnel of the organisation (for example, the use of construction materials for private building, or the repair of personal cars in official work time); entertaining visiting officials with funds not allocated for that purpose; sending gifts to important contacts (e.g. planning officials or suppliers); barter exchange between enterprises; spending safety funds on capital repairs; illicit hiring of private construction workers.

In addition to practices of this kind, which involve the use of the resources of an organisation for illicit purposes, a variety of other practices would come under article 170. If an official turns a blind eye to illegal practices by other officials, if a party or government official fails to respond to a citizen's complaint, if a manager hires an employee nepotistically – all these are abuses of power. Finally, it should be noted that certain violations of law relating to conditions of labour are criminal offences. For example, dismissing an employee for reasons of personal hostility, or failing to observe safety regulations, will under the appropriate conditions incur criminal liability. These provisions are to be found in two other sections of the criminal code: one dealing with the 'political and work rights of citizens', the other with 'social order and public health'.

Penalties

The criminal codes stipulate a variety of punishments for these offences, and the maximum penalty allowed gives a good idea of how seriously the different forms of abuse are regarded in law. The most serious offences are embezzlement and bribery. Embezzlement in 'especially large amounts', or bribe-taking in particularly aggravating circumstances, can both carry the death penalty; custodial sentences for embezzlement range from four to fifteen years, and for bribe-taking from three to fifteen years, depending on the amounts involved and the circumstances (for example, whether they were individual or collective offences, or whether the offence is held to have led to 'serious harm to state or social organisations'). Bribe-giving can incur a custodial sentence of three to fifteen years; deceit of customers, two to seven years; abuse of power, three to eight years; private enterprise, up to five years; report-padding, up to three years. In some cases additional penalties are allowed for: confiscation of property, or deprivation for a certain period of the right to hold particular positions. Non-custodial sentences are provided for in less serious cases of embezzlement, deceiving customers and abuse of power: offenders may incur only dismissal or 'corrective labour', which is in effect a fine, involving the deduction of up to 20 per cent of one's salary for up to two years.[16]

2 ABUSE OF OFFICE: PRESSURES AND TEMPTATIONS

A Preliminary Note on the Scale of the Problem

It would be widely agreed that many of the forms of illegality outlined above are endemic in Soviet managerial practice, in one or another type of organisation. But it is very hard to say how widespread these practices are, because such calculations are inherently difficult to make, if not impossible in principle. One approach would be to attempt to measure the size of the so-called 'second economy', a term which in the Western literature conventionally refers to the unofficial (hence illegal) production or exchange of goods and services. If such a measurement were possible it would be of interest and would provide a *partial* indication of the impact of 'economic', 'property' and 'official' offences.

The second economy can be understood to include: (a) all forms of illicit production (for example, home-distilled vodka at one end of the spectrum, and at the other end, private production of mass-produced goods under the cover of a state enterprise); (b) buying and selling goods for private profit; (c) the illegal provision of private services (for example, house repairs and building, transport facilities, educational and medical services, car repairs); (d) all forms of 'extra' payment, whether in money or kind, for goods and services provided by people in state or social enterprises. This would include the payment of 'tips' to shop assistants for deficit items, and all manner of inducements to gatekeepers who control the provision and allocation of consumer and producer goods. The concept of exchange could also be broadened to include the payment of a bribe in return for a benevolent attitude towards a dubious set of accounts.

The Western literature on the Soviet second economy has not generally attempted to quantify it. Simes states that 'this market [i.e. the parallel market] annually accumulates billions of rubles', but that 'precise figures are unknown'.[17] Grossman concludes in one article that 'not even an educated guess of size can be attempted by an outside observer',[18] and in another that for the time being it is better to stick to vague generalisations than to provide specious figures.[19] Typically it has simply been assumed, on the basis of a massive amount of personal testimony and anecdotal evidence in Soviet published sources, that unofficial forms of economic activity do indeed play a vital – though yet to be measured – part in the Soviet economy. Attempts have then been made to describe, classify and explain these forms. One systematic effort has, however, been made to estimate the impact of second economy activities, by calculating the proportion of incomes of Soviet citizens derived from private sources and the proportion of all consumption expenditures made to private recipients. The study, by Ofer and Vinokur, is based on a survey of about 1000 émigré families in Israel. Both legal and illegal private exchanges were included, but since the study covered only urban families, it can be assumed that most of the activities involved were illegal. With all the appropriate warnings about the data, the authors conclude that 10 to 12 per cent of total incomes were derived from private sources and 18 per cent of consumption expenditures made to private recipients. It was estimated on this basis that unrecorded private activity might add 3 to 4 per cent to existing estimates of GNP.[20]

The second economy, as defined above, connects closely with *some* of the activities covered by the term abuse of office. The illegal provision of goods and services relies to a large extent on the theft of state and social property, and people in managerial positions are partly responsible for this. Theft in turn is connected with certain types of false reporting. The legal concept of bribery covers some of the illegal inducements for the provision of goods and services – if they are given to an 'official', and if they are in money form (if the inducements are in natural form, the legal position is not so clear). Again, certain kinds of private production are abuses in the definition that I am using. To this extent, Gur and Ofer's assessment of the second economy should provide a warning against inflated estimates of the overall economic impact of illegal practices. However, such an assessment cannot adequately reflect the significance of the phenomena with which I am concerned. The concept of abuse of office is both broader and narrower than the second economy. It is broader because it does not necessarily involve illegal exchange – even in a broad sense of exchange. For example, some kinds of false reporting, the allocation of housing to favoured employees, nepotism, the 'turning of a blind eye' by law enforcement agents, criminal infractions of labour law, systematic failure by an official to respond to a citizen's complaint – all these refer to a broader set of actions than is suggested by the idea of the second economy.

Abuse of office is also, though, a narrower concept, because it excludes people who are not 'officials'. It can well be argued that the majority of the Soviet population, as buyers or sellers of goods and services, are involved in the second economy. But abuses refer by definition to offences committed only in certain occupational settings.

There are great problems, then, in measuring the extent of illegality in the context of abuse of office. Without hoping to do so, I shall make the same working assumption as many Soviet leaders and law enforcement agents: the assumption that abuse of office is indeed a significant and persistent phenomenon which has some important political and moral effects. With this in mind, one can turn to consider why it is that the types of illegality outlined above have become widespread. An answer to this question needs a response at many levels. I shall start by looking at some of the pressures and temptations that incline managers towards breaches of law, and then go on to examine the role of agencies that have been made responsible for enforcing it.

Meeting Targets

Many forms of managerial illegality in the Soviet Union, especially perhaps those which would be regarded as 'abuse of power' in the criminal code, are conditioned by the peculiar economic environment in which Soviet organisations work. The condition of success is to meet plan targets. This is fundamental because 'making the plan' determines the prospects and prestige of the managers and of those to whom they are responsible: that is, their superiors and the local political officials in whose domain they find themselves. It is important too because it determines the level of bonus payments for the members of the organisation.

In an environment of tight planning, with systematic problems in the distribution and supply of raw materials and intermediate goods, together with widespread shortages of labour (however these shortages are conceived), many forms of managerial malpractice can be seen as ways of creating the conditions in which an organisation can survive and prosper. The requirements of the ever-looming plan confront Soviet managers with a struggle for survival that cannot be fought without regular breaches of law. For example, sending gifts and bribes to suppliers and higher officials, the illicit use of enterprise funds for entertaining, setting aside scarce goods for 'important' people who will be useful to the organisation, barter exchange between enterprises, private contracts for construction work – all these can be seen as measures that help to create the necessary conditions of success, that help to overcome a series of ever-present constraints. In a similar way, Soviet managers might argue that illegal wage payments, together with management favours to selected employees in the allocation of various benefits, should be seen ultimately as means towards the same goal, because they help to strengthen the loyalty of valued members of the workforce.

The imperfections of the Soviet system of central planning and distribution have, then, encouraged the emergence of a pervasive network of informal contacts and exchanges. Soviet criminal law is based upon the assumption of a completely rational process of planning and distribution, in which there is no room for such exchanges. But without these relationships Soviet managers could not survive in the environment in which they work. The upshot is that directive planning actually needs the oiling mechanism of unofficial forms of exchange. Without it the economy would grind rapidly to a halt. The 'unofficial' distribution of resources becomes part and parcel of the 'official' structure, because it is a necessary condition for the more or less successful fulfilment of plans.

Such a picture is by now very familiar. It has been vividly described by a number of Western observers,[21] and a wealth of anecdotal material in Soviet sources testifies to its accuracy, at least in broad terms. This does not mean that the difficulties confronting Soviet organisations affect all sectors in the same way or to the same degree. The more privileged the organisation in a hierarchy of planning priorities, the less necessary will it be for its managers to wheel and deal, solicit and bribe other organisations on which it depends. Production for defence is at one pole. Even if not immune from some of the problems that afflict Soviet industry in general, it is none the less highly privileged in the supply of materials and workers. The pressure towards breaches of law must surely be relatively weak for this reason.

Somewhere near the other pole one might find problems of the kind described by the former head doctor of a sanatorium. He explained that, although there were few problems with the central supplies to which the sanatorium was entitled (for example, drugs and food), other matters provided a constant headache:

> If [as a manager in the Soviet Union] you use only correct methods, you are scarcely likely to keep your job for more than a year. You will simply not cope because of serious objective difficulties ... Let us take, for example, sanatoria ... The sanatorium where I worked

was a separate settlement. There are buildings for patients, houses for staff. In these buildings the water, electricity and sewage systems must work ... and be maintained. Families grow, you need more houses, you need to expand the sanatorium. So you always need building materials, you need contractors who are going to build all this, you need to know how to obtain money to pay for it, and money ... is mainly non-cash, everything is signed for through the bank. This also creates difficulties, because the bank doesn't always want to pay. It is very difficult to do all this in legal ways. It is difficult to get yourself put into the plan and get a contractor who will build all this; it is very difficult to get hold of the necessary funded [*fondovye*] building materials, even if there is the money for them and you order them year after year – you won't get them. All this you literally have to get hold of, and to get hold of it you must ask and demand, and humble yourself and get it by hook or by crook [*vsemy pravdami i nepravdami*] ... I look for a contractor, and I have been assigned money for this ... But the contractor's plan is already full ... they say they can't take me into their plan ... they already have a full schedule. They haven't got the materials. That means that I must obtain the materials for them as well. And to overcome these complications *spirit* has a great significance. If I had a cistern of spirit, I could build another whole sanatorium next door to mine, to the cost of several million rubles ... Pure spirit, it's better than vodka ... The money that I was allocated for this construction is money only on paper ... If [the construction people] are going to take on extra work over and above their plan, one must reward them in some way. Well what can I give them, I don't have anything. But since they know that I am ... the head doctor, that I have spirit, they demand it ... Spirit is my key ...[22]

Soviet executives are clearly faced with a Catch-22. If they put themselves 'above the law' in the course of their duties, they open themselves, at least as a possibility, to unpleasantness from law enforcement agents. But the higher law is to make a success of the job, to fulfil the plan. No manager, if she wants to succeed, can put herself 'above the plan'. This problem is simply by-passed by Soviet legal commentators. For example, one authoritative source explains:

an official acts contrary to the interests of service when an action that he takes or fails to take contradicts the tasks [*zadachi*] of the establishment or enterprise, or the interests of the state as a whole. Officials ... cannot justify the violation of state discipline by reference to the interests of 'their' institution.[23]

But from the standpoint of Soviet managers, the trouble is that to meet 'the interests of the state as a whole', i.e. to fulfil the plan, they must pursue the interests of 'their' institution and break numerous rules and regulations, and often the criminal law, in the process. It is a question of choosing the smaller evil and the smaller crime. This was clearly expressed by the former manager of a large transport organisation (it should be noted that he makes a non-legal distinction between 'violations' and 'crimes' – in Soviet law, all the things he mentions are defined as criminal):

> I always said to my employees, to my supply people ... that they should remember that there are crimes [*prestupleniya*] and there are violations [*narusheniya*]. For violations you are penalised, for crimes you are locked up ... a crime is when you have done something that involves spending a lot of money, with theft, with all kinds of affairs [*afery*], etc. But a violation is when you are obliged to do it ... for example, I buy some part or another, and I put it in the vehicle, which is in use again after a couple of hours. Or else I don't buy the part, I refuse to break the rules, the vehicle stays idle. In the first place I have to pay the driver ... this is already a crime, because I can pay out for one or two hours or for a day, but not for a month. Secondly, whether you like it or not, the mechanic will strip it [*raskulachivaet*], because he has to put another vehicle in working order ... I consider that it is better to violate than to commit a crime, because the result of refusing a small violation leads to a crime ...[24]

In the light of these pressures it is appropriate to interpret some typical abuses as 'organisational' rather than 'individual': the purpose of illegal practices is to further the overall aims of the organisation, not the personal interests of individuals within it.[25] As Soviet managers have been known to say when under criticism for breaking the law: 'We weren't doing it for ourselves!' (*Ne dlya sebya staralis!*).[26]

Some such distinction is surely necessary. But the line is also blurred, for several reasons. To begin with, organisational success will be accompanied by individual material and moral rewards. Second, 'individual' offences may be justified (or rationalised) in organisational terms. Finally, different forms of illegal activity may be involved in a single act: an action which is an organisational abuse for one party may be individual for the other party (for example, I may give a bribe for selfless reasons, but does the other person *take* a bribe for selfless reasons?). I shall return to these points later on in the discussion.

Keeping up Appearances

One set of conditions leading to breaches of law, as we have seen, relates to the particular form of struggle for survival that the managers of Soviet organisations are engaged in. A second set of pressures, closely related to this struggle, but requiring a separate treatment, arises from the perceived need to keep up appearances. It is this which leads to report-padding (*pripiski*), to overstating the results of the organisation.

This phenomenon is not unique to state socialist societies. Capitalist firms may engage in their own form of false reporting for the purposes of public relations and advertising, and direct analogies might be found in the reporting of results by managers of sub-units within large private conglomerates and within nationalised industries in the capitalist world.[27] However, problems of report-padding are likely to be especially marked in a system of directive planning, where the rewards of most organisations depend on the submission of satisfactory reports on plan fulfilment to a higher administrative or planning authority. This constraint applies to all types of organisation, and not just to those involved in economic activity. If plan targets are not met, there will be a strong temptation to cover up for failure by exaggerating achievements. Unless managers do so, they will 'let down' the collective, themselves, their superiors and the local party officialdom. Thus the head of a construction organisation, prosecuted in connection with report-padding, justified himself in court with the following phrases: 'the column did not receive enough materials'; 'we had to make up for omissions'; 'it was embarrassing to let down the higher organisations'.[28] In similar vein, another director was reported as saying:

The position was difficult. Equipment was out of repair. From lack of experience, I did not know how to carry out capital repairs. Raw materials were not being supplied. The plan was under threat. And since we must by law fulfil the state plan, we decided to resort to report-padding. I could not go and say that I was no longer capable of managing the factory. Demands were made on me, and I made demands on others ... I could not let down the district and the city.[29]

By all accounts, report-padding is a widespread phenomenon. But this does not mean that it is rife in every area of activity, nor that it always takes the same form. The possibilities vary, depending on the character of the organisation. For example, in construction and agriculture there is greater scope for falsifying the amount of work done. There are therefore more possibilities both of overstating achievements and of understating them (to cover up spoilage or theft).[30]

Report-padding may take different forms. Often *pripiski* will involve little more than a report, a few days premature, that such-and-such a quantity of goods has been completed. The enterprise or a sub-unit of the enterprise will then finish off the work in the first few days of the next month. One informant, who worked for many years as shop manager in a large radio plant, explained how this might happen:

The month finishes, the stores have limited room. The plan period has ended. The store manager says: I'm full up to here, I've nowhere to put the goods, you keep them in the shop. So then ... he gives me an invoice for the goods, which haven't been released, and I give him a receipt, saying that such-and-such a quantity of goods are in the safe keeping of the shop. That's all. I have some things to finish off ... so I work for the first 3–4 days and deliver the goods to the stores ...[31]

But *pripiski* may take on more elaborate forms than this, leading to a highly falsified set of indices that builds up over time. An informant who worked as a legal consultant for a wholesale trade firm described one situation that arose in her organisation (it led eventually to a criminal investigation, but the charges were dropped):

In order for the organisation to receive the 13th pay packet ... the quarterly bonus, in order that it should be somewhere on the board of honour, and in general for the organisation to be acknowledged ... it had to have a number of excellent financial indicators. In particular, it had to show good profitability ... naturally, our base didn't have these excellent results in reality ... Our chief accountant drew up a double balance ... She had her main book, in which she entered her accounting indices. She exaggerated the profit ... year after year. Furthermore, the head of the base could not have been ignorant of this ... she gave this balance to the *glavk*, but presents flowed in that direction as well ... Then one day the USSR Ministry of Trade received a report from the USSR State Bank that there was some sort of rift between the indicators and the actual figures ... It was revealed that the balance was inflated by 11 million rubles over 15 years ...[32]

Two other informants stressed the importance of distinguishing between variants of *pripiski*, and judged these variants differently from a moral point of view. The first, a very successful former manager of a large construction firm, had this to say:

One type of *pripiska* consists in the fact that ... although at the end of the month I laid 100 cubic metres of concrete ... I needed 120. So I write down 120. I will finish it not by January 1st, but by the 5th ... In principle this is not theft, nobody will suffer a loss as a result ... [But there is] a second type: I laid 100 cubic metres ... I wrote that the depth of the foundations was minus 120, when it was really minus 115, so that in fact this was theft from the state. I simply didn't do it, that means that somewhere the cement, sand, metal and workforce are left over ...[33]

Another informant, the former manager of a transport organisation, was even more emphatic about the moral distinctions. To 'make up' the plan in the first few days of the succeeding monthly period and to even out the performance over a longer plan period was unobjectionable. But with full-blown padding 'you are forging the state plan'. Speaking of the latter situation he said:

A person should be punished for this. It shows an inability to manage [*rukovodit'*]. If he can't do it, he should drop out of the game. That is my view. What is a *pripiska*? It's like card playing. You sit down to play, you start to lose, and again and again, you get into a rage. A person who engages in *pripiski* – this becomes an illness, a terrible illness. And then it accumulates over many years, and you can't get out of it.[34]

The type of false reporting which sometimes occurs in connection with the payment of wages has a somewhat different purpose to the one illustrated in the examples I have given so far. Here the books are indeed cooked to keep up appearances, but with the aim of topping up wages rather than 'deceiving the state' about plan fulfilment. This form of offence is particularly common in the building industry. This is partly to do with the unusual difficulties with the supply of materials in this sector, so that workers are often paid for idle time. But another reason is that it is especially difficult in building work to detect how much work has gone into the final result. One informant explained the 'necessity' of this kind of false reporting to keep on the right side of the workforce:

> The workers get paid according to a work roster. If you pay them according to the work norms they will get a very small sum, the work norms are very tight, they are drawn up in ideal conditions . . . the real conditions are quite different . . . There is a delay in getting materials . . . this isn't the worker's fault, but he must earn his 160 or 180 rubles. So the report-padding begins . . . This is false reporting that I would classify as unavoidable . . . The driver (for the transport department) must get his wages as well, some minimum, or else he won't work. Let's suppose that he brought in sand in three trips, they write down four, this is a kind of product that you can't account for.[35]

To some extent it would be legitimate to regard report-padding as an organisational abuse – to the extent that it is designed to give the organisation a good name or to keep the members of the organisation content. But the distinction between organisational and individual becomes very slippery here, because report-padding also tends easily to become a source of personal gain. In many cases it leads to the receipt of unearned bonuses, while in the case of phoney work rosters, false reports can become a source of private gain for management as well as workers. As one former manager commented:

> . . . the construction foreman is obliged more than anyone to break the rules. But if he carries out a necessary violation, then often he doesn't forget about himself either. He considers that in order that production should not suffer, in order to keep workers, they must be sure of receiving their wages . . . and he considers that if he committed a violation and added 1000 rubles, then he can make 500 for himself . . .[36]

Public Office and Private Gain

The conditions discussed so far suggest that to a large extent breaches of law are seen as necessary for the organisation to succeed, or at least to present the appearance of success, and thus to satisfy those to whom the management is answerable that it is doing a good job. But there are other breaches of law that look much more clearly 'individual', and that fit more unambiguously into a conventional notion of 'abuse of public office for private gain'. In a less serious category, there is the use of public resources and personnel for the satisfaction of personal comforts. This might involve, for example, making use of building materials without obtaining them through the proper channels, or employing workers to do private jobs in enterprise time. Such practices are apparently very common, and are commonly exposed in Soviet investigative journalism. One has the strong impression that they are generally regarded as perks of the job – not dissimilar in principle from manipulation of expense accounts by employees of capitalist firms. But they are of course violations of criminal law in the Soviet Union, and in appropriate circumstances law enforcers might take a hard look at such activities.

In the more serious categories are embezzlement and bribery, which are both prominent as objects of attention by Soviet law enforcement agents and which, as we have seen, are regarded in law as the gravest offences that are covered by the general concept of abuse of office.

At the outset it has to be said that in practice 'individual' offences are sometimes explained and justified in organisational terms. One example of such a justification was given by a former legal consultant with a large import–export firm:

There are no separate violations, everything is connected. For example: in order that we could get our bonuses and in order that our organisation would come out somewhere on top, we had to fulfil the plan. [Suppose] it was impossible to fulfil the plan ... That meant we had to change the plan at the end of the plan period. How was this done? You had to go to the ministry, to some Maria Ivanovna or other, and bring her a nice present: either a beautiful fur, or an expensive gold chain, or something of this sort. Tell me, who is going to afford that out of their own pockets? So you need money ... this is how it starts ... A wagon load of goods arrives. We have many warehouses. Someone comes along and says that the boss is going to Moscow, they need such and such a sum of money. They say this to the warehouse manager, but to do this you need to have someone in the job who can be trusted ... Well, how is the warehouse manager going to get hold of this money? After all, he doesn't print it, he gets a salary ... So a wagon arrives, he takes this one little wagon load from the whole train and sells it to someone on the side.[37]

In this case an apparently individual offence (embezzlement) is closely connected with the perceived need to make payments in order to satisfy the interests of the organisation. No doubt such situations are common. Still, there is plenty of illegal activity which has the character of unambiguous private gain. There are many pressures and temptations, traditions and perceptions involved. It would take a lengthy study in itself fully to examine the conditions underlying embezzlement and bribery. But I shall venture a few comments.

Since embezzlement takes place typically for the purpose of sale through illegal channels, it is evidently made possible, at one level, by the demand for the goods in question. Pervasive shortages and a very deficient system of distribution provide a set of favourable underlying conditions. No less important is the technical possibility of concealing the theft from controllers and legal agents. These factors taken together seem to explain why embezzlement is especially prevalent in the building industry and in agriculture. On the one hand, the materials and produce in these sectors are in great deficit in the Soviet Union. On the other hand, detection is more difficult. There is relatively greater scope for writing off losses, and much legal comment and anecdotal evidence suggests that this is closely linked with the level of theft, and not just with a negligent attitude to storage.[38]

Theft is assisted also by the widespread perception that official wages and salaries are not enough to live on. Legitimate sources of income cannot cater for the life-style that people have come to expect, and gaining extra rewards through the use of one's office seems to have become, to a greater or lesser extent, an informally accepted way of boosting one's formal earnings. There is a much quoted curse, said to have originated in Odessa: 'May you live on your wages alone!'[39] which reflects a widely shared view of things.

Finally, theft is encouraged by a particular attitude towards state property, which treats it as, to some extent, 'up for grabs', because of the sense that nobody is concretely harmed by removing some of the state's resources away from official channels of distribution. Pomorski (1977) traces this attitude to a double response. On the one hand social experience teaches citizens that they are not 'possessors' of state property; on the other hand Soviet ideology insists that property belongs to the people. As a result, 'the individual experiences neither feelings of identity, characteristic of an owner or co-owner, nor respect for the autonomous rights of another'.[40] This analysis seems to me plausible, though it may be more relevant to shopfloor perceptions than to those of management. It is a dimension that would merit a closer study.

Some of the conditions I have mentioned in relation to embezzlement are relevant also to an investigation of bribery. As in the case of embezzlement, shortages and low wages provide a basic set of conditions, justifications and rationalisations.[41] Bribery and gift-giving enter into a wide set of social relationships. These include, as we have seen, relations between socialist organisations, because of the ever-present problem of deficit supplies. According to one Soviet supply agent, quoted in the press, 'nowadays to go on a business trip without a box of sweets or a bottle of high quality wine, is like going to a ball without tails. It would be better to stay at home.'[42]

There are also widespread opportunities for bribery in the relationship between individual consumers and service personnel, as well as between criminal offenders and controllers or law enforcement officers. The possibilities and pressures are especially great in the trade network. Trade personnel take bribes from customers (in law they are not always bribes, but 'deceit', since shop assistants cannot commit 'official' crimes); kickbacks may then be paid to management, which may in turn make payments higher up. As one Soviet observer comments:

> The buying off of officials, established in the course of a considerable period, can turn into a definite system, in which there is established a particular hierarchy in the transfer of bribes. People with access to material values give bribes to their immediate superiors, to the inspectorate, to employees of the control organs.[43]

It is not, however, the trade network alone that creates such opportunities. Any 'gatekeeper' role, from the most modest (say, the doorkeeper in a restaurant) to the most exalted (say, an official who makes decisions on the allocation of flats or cars) gives the incumbent opportunities for illegal gain. People who provide desired services are also often in a position to take inducements. For example, there are frequent commentaries in the Soviet press about bribery in educational and medical establishments.

In the light of these brief comments, it could be said that both embezzlement and bribery are grounded in the experienced shortages of goods and services, and in low earnings. The material expectations of both buyers and sellers have led to a partial decentralisation of distribution and allocation. But given the state monopoly, and the nature of Soviet law, the market relationships have come in through the back door, in a criminal guise. These conditions seem to create a definite dynamic, which makes embezzlement and bribery solidly entrenched. The demand is there and people are prepared to pay considerable extra amounts for deficit goods and scarce services. But this intensifies the pressure to earn illegal income in order to make these payments. It is possible that some such dynamic lies behind the popular impression in the Soviet Union itself that the level of corruption and of illegal forms of exchange has considerably increased over the past ten or twenty years.

Even highly placed people within Soviet officialdom, who have access to deficit goods and services as of right (though these rights are covert), may be tempted to increase their possessions illegally, partly perhaps so as to insure themselves against future loss of position. Material wealth in the USSR attaches to the job, and cannot be converted into capital. In this sense, material privilege retains a definite element of insecurity. Accepting gifts and building houses is one way of making these privileges more permanent.

The new – or not so new – Soviet consumerism has often been officially castigated, and signs of moral concern are frequently expressed in the media. A few years ago Aliev, then first secretary of the Azerbaidzhan republic party committee, gave an interview in which he bemoaned the new ethos. He was speaking about Azerbaidzhan, but the interview was published in *Pravda*, and no doubt was thought to have a wider relevance. He referred to:

[the desire to] shine, to stand out from others not with generosity and beauty of one's soul, not with creative work, but with consumerist zeal, 'useful' acquaintances and contacts, the ability to 'set someone up' somewhere, to 'get' a posher flat, a 'more deficit' good. And already, you notice that a two-storey country house, or a car become for some people a measure of life success, the sun in the skies. And already for the sake of this one can do a deal with one's conscience, accept an expensive 'present', 'not notice' how under your very nose scoundrels are running the show . . . [44]

This homily must have seemed a bit hollow to the millions of *Pravda* readers if they saw it: party leaders are themselves not noted for their asceticism. But such comments give some idea of the material expectations that underpin the use of public office for private gain.

The considerations I have focused on go some way towards under-standing the more venal forms of abuse. But they do not provide a full explanation. There is a definite danger of economistic bias in the way that the issue has been presented so far, since nothing has yet been said about cultural influences that might affect the character and extent of breaches of law, independently of 'objective' economic pressures. One way of getting at this problem would be to try to look closely at the pattern of economic, official and socialist property crime in the different cultural milieux that are to be found in the USSR. In the Transcaucasian republics especially (of these, Georgia has acquired the most notoriety), a number of influences have led to a systematic disregard for the law at certain periods. The strength of family ties, the role of the gift, the importance of 'macho' displays of material wealth, and perhaps the strength of entrepreneurial traditions, have helped to create a number of enclaves in which certain types of abuse have flourished to a degree that has seemed astonishing to the outside world.[45] In the 1960s and early 1970s it began to look as if the writ of Moscow did not run in Georgia, Armenia and Azerbaidzhan. Since then it has been at least partially reestablished, but these republics, together with the Central Asian republics, continue to produce some of the more glaring cases of abuse. None of this can be explained without an analysis of the peculiarities of the cultural milieu.

3 THE CONTROLLERS

I have examined certain of the pressures and temptations facing Soviet executives, which could help to explain some typical forms of abuse of office. But the opportunities and the risks will depend also on the law enforcement agencies. I shall use the term 'law enforcement agency' in a broad way, to include not only the legal apparatuses but all those agents that have been given some kind of direct responsibility for ensuring that managers and officials abide by the law. I shall call these agents the controllers, the legal apparatuses and the party. The *controllers* can be found both within and outside organisations. The most important controllers 'within' are the chief accountants. Legal departments have also become important in recent years, with some controlling functions. Controllers outside the organisation include: (a) superiors within any administrative hierarchy who are responsible for carrying out periodic inspections and audits of the enterprises subordinate to them; (b) financial agencies, especially the Ministry of Finance and the State Bank; (c) the Committees of People's Control, which are assisted by volunteer groups within organisations. To this list could be added the trade unions, which have a supervisory role in relation to the observance of labour law. The *legal apparatuses* are the procuracy, police and courts. The *party* refers to central and local party organs which are responsible for overall supervision of all the institutions within their domain, including the legal apparatuses themselves. In addition the press is an important agent of law enforcement in the broad sense: acting as one arm of the party, it publicises many instances of abuse, comments favourably or critically on the activities of other law enforcement agencies, and tries to put pressure on them if they are seen to be failing in their duties.

I shall not try to give a proper account of all these numerous possible sources of intervention. I shall make some brief remarks on the controllers in this section, and then go on to focus more closely, in sections 4–6, on the legal apparatuses and the party. The role of the press will be discussed in Chapter 4, and the trade unions in Chapter 5.

Control from Within

The main controllers inside an organisation are the chief accountants. They are in a strategic position because all monetary transactions pass through their hands, and few manipulations with accounts can occur without their acquiescence. For this reason they have been given special responsibility by the state to refuse to carry out illegal orders. But chief accountants and other financial specialists are under great pressure to submit to management demands.[46] One clear form of evidence for this is the fact that when illegalities involving financial abuse are penalised, accountants often appear alongside directors as offenders. There are some important exceptions to this rule, as we shall see later: financial controllers do on occasion decide to blow the whistle on malpractices. But on the whole they evidently feel compelled to go along with the management. To do otherwise would be to 'let everybody down', and is likely to be fraught with personal unpleasantness.

Consultants (*yuriskonsul'ty*) in legal departments form another 'internal' extension of law and order within enterprises. They have been set up in an increasing number of organisations, reflecting the growing emphasis on legal regulation. They have no direct responsibility for financial matters: their main job is to ensure that all contracts with supplying and client organisations, and all relationships between management and employees, are legally above board, and to assist in disputes that may arise in these areas. The job is therefore less risky than that of the financial controller.

Legal consultants, like chief accountants, have potential disruptive power: they can refuse to sign dubious documents, and can threaten to expose their superiors. But there is no evidence that they are generally inclined to use their influence in this way. They may, though, insist that the documentation is correct, thereby helping management, and satisfying certain professional standards. This was how one former legal consultant (the head of the legal department of a large trade firm) described her function. She was emphatic that she kept away from direct involvement in anything illegal, but acknowledged that she played a contributory role:

> ... [the management] couldn't quarrel with me. It was essential for them that the [legal] department should represent their organisation to the world outside in the way they wanted, so that the organisation should be respected ...
>
> If I received clearly fictitious documents, if I saw ... that they were badly drawn up, I phoned up and said: If you're going to do this then draw it up so that it's all fixed to a 'T'.[47]

Control from Outside: Administrative Superiors

Control from above, by administrative superiors, is constantly criticised in Soviet sources as an ineffective weapon against abuses. The main complaints relate to weak or *pro forma* inspections by the higher authority, inadequate accounting procedures, poor inventories of materials and manufactured goods, personnel policies which allow people with criminal records to get jobs involving financial responsibility, and failure to act on reports which do expose breaches of the law. The resulting lack of control provides considerable leeway for losses of materials and goods, either through negligence or theft. The potential for such losses no doubt varies greatly between different sectors, depending upon the nature of the product and the production process. But the basic problems with ministerial control are described in a similar way for a variety of types of activity. Thus, a republican Ministry of Light Industry was told off for 'serious faults with the accounting of materials and finished production';[48] the USSR Ministry of Chemical Industry was carrying out 'only formal' checks on its subordinate associations and enterprises, in relation to protection of socialist property, mismanagement and 'violations of state discipline' (including 'widespread embezzlement and shortfalls of materials');[49] 'leading officials' in an All-Union Ministry of Machine-building had failed to punish certain factory managers in connection with substandard output and report-padding, and had failed to exact damages in such cases;[50] departmental control in the State Committee for Agricultural Machinery was superficial, leaving 'yawning gaps' in supervision and inspection work;[51] the heads of the USSR Ministry of Forestry and Timber and its subdivisions 'did not take all necessary measures to prevent and stop embezzlement, losses, mismanagement ... which have become widespread in the system', and 'accepted people for posts involving material responsibility who had earlier been convicted of embezzlement and other crimes of personal gain';[52] in trading and catering establishments, a commentator says, 'people sometimes get in who have been tried for embezzlement and punished, when everyone knows that it is strictly forbidden to accept them in positions that entail material responsibility';[53] in a case of theft from a wine factory (an elaborate affair that drew in transport workers and retail people as well as the factory management), a journalist asked in mock astonishment: 'How could it happen that the association ... employed [a man] as head of the wine store who had had two convictions?'[54]

Some of these problems must be ascribed to the sheer technical difficulty of keeping a check on the activities of vast bureaucratic structures. But there is also the evident – and readily understandable – reluctance on the part of the higher authorities to expose their subordinates. It reflects badly on the higher agency, and on its choice of employees, if it is seen to have permitted waste and embezzlement. But in some situations it is more than a question of tolerance or family support, since some forms of abuse are directly encouraged from above. The case of report-padding provides perhaps the clearest example. Two striking recent illustrations that appeared in the Soviet press give an idea of some of the pressures at work. The first, reported under the title 'The Plant that Wasn't There', revealed a line of deceit stretching to the Vice-Chairman of the USSR State Committee for the Supply of Production Equipment to Agriculture. The Vice-Chairman had approved a statement from a state commission certifying that an engine repair plant was ready to go into operation – it was an important plant, designed to make capital repairs on tractor engines for farms within a large area. The commission had certified that a complex of 51 structures had been completed. But only 14 of them were more or less ready, and 14 had not even been started.[55]

The second story described false reports about a project to develop new methods for increasing petroleum yields. This time the participants in the eyewash included a Deputy Minister of the Petroleum Industry:

When the control period was over and it came time to report on what the use of the new methods of acting on the [petroleum] reservoirs had produced, quite encouraging figures showed up in the reports. No, the oil workers did not claim that they had attained the plan indices. They merely noted, modestly, that they had barely fallen short. However, it was only on paper that things were going smoothly. An inspection showed that throughout the five-year plan the ministry had done virtually no serious work ... The indices given in the report turned out to have been simply invented![56]

These examples illustrate the strong tendency to complicity by higher officials when the plan and the reputation of the ministry is at stake. They are not everyday examples, because the reports traced the pretence to such a high level. But numerous similar reports appear. They may describe complicity on a less exalted level, but tell much the same tale.

Control from Outside: Financial Agencies and People's Control

Since internal controls cannot be relied on, there must be provision for outside checks, and there is indeed no shortage of outside agencies with a supervisory role. Since abuse of office very often involves false reporting, financial institutions – especially the inspectors of the Ministry of Finance and the State Bank – are given an important part to play: they are obliged to pass on any incriminating information to the procuracy or to the People's Control Committees.[57]

The financial agencies evidently do provide some counterweight to inadequate internal controls. In the view of one Soviet observer:

> Our practice shows that it is because of departmental inspections that large-scale thefts remain undisclosed, that shortcomings in the work of various organisations and enterprises are not overcome. As a rule, such facts are disclosed by the inspectorates of the Ministry of Finance or the People's Control organs.[58]

Since ministerial inspections tend to whitewash subordinate organisations, and since the financial inspectorates still have to rely on information provided by internal controllers, it has been suggested that the inspection service should be radically reorganised and set up wholly under the Ministry of Finance. Given the feebleness of the present system of inspection, says one observer, 'it would be amazing if anyone doubted the need to reorganise the inspection service'.[59] Limited experiments have been carried out in some republics along these lines (e.g. in Georgia and Estonia), with some internal inspection functions transferred to the Ministry of Finance, but this does not seem to have led to any significant overall changes.[60]

Together with the financial institutions, a major role has been assigned to the *People's Control* to ensure that the material resources of the state are used efficiently and that the managers of all Soviet organisations act in accordance with the law. The People's Control is a ramified network of monitoring agencies which are called upon, in the words of a recent law, to 'conduct systematic checkups on the implementation of Party directives, Soviet laws and government decisions, to resolutely oppose everything that harms the state's interests . . .'[61] This monitoring work is assisted by a vast number of volunteer inspectors who belong to People's Control groups within organisations,[62] and form part of an even larger army of citizen controllers attached to the party, the soviets, the trade unions and the media. Indeed one of the central purposes of the People's Control Committees is to 'promote the development in citizens of a sense of responsibility for the affairs of society as a whole'. Among other tasks, the committees are supposed to monitor plan fulfilment, to identify reserves in the economy and to strive for a more efficient use of resources, and to 'combat violations of state discipline', including 'all attempts to deceive the state, and to encroach on socialist property'.[63] In this connection, the committees have the right to inspect documents and conduct checkups, to warn officials about violations and get illegal decisions rescinded by the appropriate authorities. They also have certain punitive powers: they can impose reprimands, recover damages from officials and in some cases order that a person be dismissed. But if they find significant breaches of criminal law they are instructed to pass the relevant materials on to the procuracy.

The People's Control Committees and groups receive an enormous amount of attention in the Soviet press. An impressionistic view suggests that their bark is a good deal worse than their bite, and that it is unlikely that Soviet managers lose much sleep over them. However, they provide one source of information for other law enforcement agencies concerned with abuse of office, and are undoubtedly an important instrument of public involvement. The significance of that involvement, in a broader context, will emerge later.

4 THE LEGAL APPARATUSES

So far, I have considered agencies which are supposed to act as informants if they come across breaches of criminal law by people in official positions – they themselves have only limited rights to impose sanctions on offenders. The enforcement of the law on abuse of office will, then, depend vitally on the policy adopted by legal agents in a narrower sense, in particular the procuracy and the courts. By their action or inaction they will to a large extent determine the risks attached to breaches of criminal law. A few words on the formal position of the procuracy and the courts within the Soviet legal system will therefore be appropriate.

The procuracy, which is organised on the familiar Soviet hierarchical and territorial pattern, plays a key role within the structure of law enforcement as a whole in the USSR. As has been pointed out by several commentators, there is no close equivalent to the procuracy in Western legal systems. It is peculiar in combining two main functions. It is responsible, first, for 'supreme supervision' over legality in general. This is described in the latest legislation on the procuracy as supervision over 'the precise and uniform execution of the laws by all ministries, state committees and departments, enterprises, institutions and organisations, executive and administrative agencies of local soviets, collective farms and cooperative and other public organisations, officials and citizens ...'[64]

Procuratorial supervision includes the power to 'protest' the decisions of any other agency (except the party). Protests may be generated by 'signals' from other organs of control, from the press or from citizens' complaints, by periodic investigations or by selective monitoring of instructions issued by officials. Procurators can also recommend that officials be given administrative or disciplinary penalties where violations of law are discovered. Protests do not give the procuracy the power to demand that certain actions be taken or to prohibit others. But if an agency ignores a protest, the procuracy can transfer the matter to a higher procurator or appeal to a higher administrative level. The power of protest includes the power to appeal against court decisions, a process that occurs independently of appeal to a higher court by the litigants in a case.[65]

The second main function of the procuracy is to investigate and prosecute crimes. Criminal investigations may also be carried out by the police (under the Ministry of Internal Affairs), and by the KGB. One department in particular within the regular police, the Department for the Struggle against the Theft of Socialist Property (OBKhSS), has an important role in the investigation of embezzlement. But most offences involving abuse of office appear to be the responsibility of the investigative sections of the procuracy, and in general the regular police play second fiddle to the procuracy in criminal investigation.

In addition to investigation, the procuracy is also responsible for prosecution of criminal cases in court. Most such cases are heard first in district People's Courts, which are composed of one professional judge and two lay 'assessors'. (In theory all three carry equal weight in reaching a decision, but in practice, it seems, the lay assessors are usually wholly guided by the presiding judge.) Procurators and defence lawyers (*advokaty*) present evidence incriminating or exonerating the accused, while all participants can question witnesses. After a verdict has been reached, appeals can be made through a number of channels: (a) litigants can appeal to a higher court – unless it is a verdict of a republican Supreme Court or of the USSR Supreme Court; (b) procurators can protest a court decision, that is, appeal to a higher court against any verdict which is contrary to law – unless, again, it is a verdict of one of the Supreme Courts; (c) higher courts can review the decisions of lower courts by way of 'supervision'. A number of options are open to appellate courts: they can leave a lower-level decision intact, or modify it (but not increase the penalty), or annul it and remand the case for a new investigation or trial, or else abrogate the earlier decision entirely.[66]

A survey of published Soviet comment on the legal apparatuses quickly reveals two things. First, 'official', 'economic' and 'socialist property' crimes occupy a major part of the energies of those agencies, and are at present at the forefront of discussion about law and order in general. Abuse of office has for a long time been an important element in law enforcement efforts. But lately, in broad accordance with party policy, it has been getting more emphatic attention. A recent expression of party policy was a major Central Committee resolution of September 1979 on law and order. It singled out attacks on socialist property, especially in agriculture, transport and construction, as a key source of concern, and appealed to controllers and legal agencies to 'establish strict order everywhere in record-keeping and storage of valuables', and to 'resolutely eradicate mismanagement, waste, report-padding and hoodwinking'.[67]

Following this injunction the USSR Procuracy reminded local procurators that 'in many branches of the economy there is still great harm caused to the state by losses, waste, theft, mismanagement, report-padding, poor quality goods', and that they should adopt a more vigorous policy towards these problems.[68] Meanwhile the chairman of the Criminal Chamber of the USSR Supreme Court put abuse of office at the top of a list of tasks for the future, saying that it remained a 'very important task to increase the effectiveness of court practice in the struggle against embezzlement, waste, abuses of office, bribery, report-padding ...'[69]

Alongside such appeals, there has been an enduring pattern of criticism from central political and law enforcement authorities, suggesting that the state of affairs with the investigation of abuse of office is unsatisfactory, and that judicial policy is generally too lax. In the discussion that follows I shall be referring mainly to a number of recent resolutions (1980 and after) by the Plenum of the USSR Supreme Court. But the substance of the criticisms can be found in very similar form in other resolutions of the past fifteen to twenty years in relation to embezzlement, false reporting, bribery and other abuses of office.[70]

The procuracy, as we have seen, is involved both in supervision of law observance and in criminal investigation. In both capacities, local procurators have been criticised for not intervening enough, or for intervening too leniently in relation to abuse of office. In their supervisory role they have been asked to adopt a more demanding attitude towards administrators at provincial and republic level who are responsible for control of the organisations subordinate to them, and to ensure that material about abuses reaches the investigative agencies.[71] In the context of investigation itself, the main criticisms are these: (a) local procurators are too often unwilling to initiate criminal proceedings when they have the information to do so;[72] (b) the investigation of the circumstances of the crime is too often superficial, and investigators too willing to drop a case once an investigation has started, on the grounds of lack of evidence to proceed;[73] (c) investigations focus frequently on people in secondary positions, avoiding those in higher posts who have as much if not more responsibility for the offence;[74] (d) indictments are sometimes brought under inappropriate articles of the law, with the common effect of softening the impact of law enforcement.[75]

The typical criticisms of the courts are similar in tenor to those directed against the local procuracy. They can be summarised as follows:

(a) Penalties for abuses of office (in particular, false reporting, embezzlement and bribery) tend to be too light. Hence we find the complaint that 'some courts still underestimate the social danger of report-padding',[76] and in a similar phrase in another directive, that 'some courts underestimate the great social danger of embezzlement'.[77] Similarly, a Supreme Court judge criticises 'excessively low penalties' for bribery offences, often justified by reference to vaguely stated exceptional circumstances.[78]

In appropriate cases the courts are obliged to impose additional penalties, either in the form of confiscation of property, or in the form of an injunction that prohibits the offender from occupying a particular type of post (usually a post involving financial responsibility) for a specified period. This latter penalty, according to a recent survey, was 'rarely' applied to convicted report-padders, although grounds for this existed in 'most cases'.[79] Court sentences in embezzlement cases 'do not always follow the demands of the law' in relation to confiscation of property and exclusion from particular posts.[80] According to some information relating to 1978, confiscation was imposed on 27 per cent of convicted bribe-takers in the USSR as a whole, and on 14 per cent of those convicted of bribery in the RSFSR, while the question of excluding bribe-takers from specified positions was 'very rarely discussed'.[81] Along similar lines it is frequently complained that damages are often not paid in full or not paid at all.[82]

(b) The courts are too willing to adopt an inappropriate article of the law as a basis for conviction, thereby reducing the level of permissible penalties. For example, when report-padding is prompted by 'intentional illegal acquisition of bonuses and other payments', offenders should be charged with embezzlement as well, but this is not always done.[83] Also, courts sometimes mistakenly qualify embezzlement as 'abuse of power or official position'.[84]

(c) The courts, together with the investigative agencies, are criticised for tending to focus on secondary people who may bear less responsibility for the offence than people in higher positions. A Supreme Court directive thus states, in relation to report-padding:

> There are cases where sentences are imposed on the basis of insufficiently thorough investigation, and as a result secondary participants in the crime are made answerable or else people who were not at all responsible for the given actions, while those who are mainly responsible, including the organisers and instigators, and those who connive at violations of state discipline, remain unpunished.[85]

In similar vein, speaking of embezzlement, it has been said that 'The courts sometimes ignore the fact that there has been an unjustified refusal to bring a charge, or that a case has been dropped in relation to people participating in embezzlement, as a result of which many go unpunished.'[86]

(d) In appropriate cases the courts are expected to issue so-called Special Rulings, commenting on the causes of the crime, the behaviour of the individuals and agencies involved in a particular case, and pointing out action that should be taken to remedy defects that have been discovered by the court. They have been repeatedly criticised for failing to take advantage of this opportunity, or depriving such rulings of teeth by taking a purely formal approach to them.[87]

These sorts of criticisms have constantly recurred in the past twenty years or so, and testify to a solidly entrenched bias in investigative and court procedure, and in the way that certain types of offence are defined in practice.

In saying this, I am not suggesting that investigative and sentencing policy is always lenient in relation to the variety of offences that are included in my umbrella term 'abuse of office', let alone that the Soviet legal apparatuses in general can be faulted for their excessive liberalism. As I shall show later, there is no uniform pattern of leniency.[88] In some circumstances, the law relating to abuse of office is harshly enforced. Offenders will be immune from severe sanctions only under certain conditions. It will depend on the nature and seriousness of the offence in law, on the character, size, prominence and success of the organisation, on the political influence of the offender. Still, the fact remains that the local legal apparatuses are regularly criticised for their unwillingness to prosecute, and, if people are prosecuted, for dealing with them too leniently. The main explanation for this lies in the subordination of law enforcement to political considerations, and especially in the stance adopted by local party officials.

5 THE PARTY

The strong tendency towards indulgence on the part of Soviet legal agencies in relation to abuse of office is closely linked to the attitude of local party officials, who are at the centre of the local network of political control. It would be an exaggeration to say that the procuracy and the courts are mere puppets of the party apparatus. They are institutionally separate and there is no evidence of day-to-day interference by party officials. But it can be surmised that investigators, procurators and judges have a pretty clear idea, without such day-to-day interference, of the limits to politically feasible intervention in cases of violation of criminal law by managers and officials. There is a strong tendency for party organisations to protect the managers of organisations within their domain, a tendency which is likely to be broken only if there is very definite pressure from above to act. To the extent that this is so, legal intervention is likely to be very selective, and restricted to small-fry. In general it is likely that a lot of punches will be pulled.

One does not need to look very far to explain the reluctance of local party authorities to see criminal charges brought against people in responsible positions within their domain. In the first place, the party people know that certain forms of law-breaking are unavoidable if plans are to be met, and that some leeway must therefore be given to managers in this respect. The position and prospects of party officials depend heavily on the economic success of the enterprises within their domain, and success is measured in terms of plan fulfilment. One Soviet journalist, in the course of an interview with a party official, remarked on this in the following way: 'Sometimes a clearly unprincipled and dishonest worker is protected. Usually in such situations it is explained that "he knows his business, though", or "however, he has a firm hand, he knows how to knock out the plan".'[89]

Secondly, party officials will have a strong interest in maintaining a good image for the locality. This will affect, in particular, the attitude towards report-padding. As one observer put it: '... in the local party organs they easily submit to the hypnotic effect of figures: as the saying goes, if your accounts look alright, then you'll be honoured' (*azhur v otchete – ty v pochete*).[90]

A third important consideration is this. It must be remembered that all higher-level managers come within the party *nomenklatura*, the list of positions which are filled with the authorisation of the appropriate party organisation. Depending on their rank, managers have been supported and promoted by the district, city or provincial party apparatus, and in the case of very high-level positions by the republican or central organs. Any exposure of a prominent manager is therefore a reflection on the personnel policies of the party organisation. As one journalist wrote (it was an investigative article on abuses of office in Ashkhabad): 'If the city party committee officials expose a dishonest manager promoted by them, this means that to some extent they must accept their own lack of discrimination ... And this affects their "regimental honour".'[91] This tendency to protect people whom party officials have helped to promote is likely to be especially strong where managers are members of local party committees – which is often the case. In this event, party and managerial people may be friends or acquaintances, thereby reinforcing the already powerful reasons for inaction.

The local party apparatus is strongly inclined, then, to turn a blind eye to abuse of office. Its own image and reputation is at stake. But party officials may also be more directly involved in breaches of law. The possible encouragement of report-padding is one example that I have already mentioned. Another, apparently frequent form of direct involvement is the diversion of construction material and manpower to uses not provided for in the plan. One such case, reported in *Pravda*, involved a construction trust set up under the RSFSR Ministry of Procurements to build and repair storage units for grain. Despite a shortage of labour it became involved in various sideline activities – building rest-homes, a ski-run, a poultry factory, repairing a shop – all under the instructions of local party and government officials. The authors of a report on the affair had this to say:

Grain is everything: on it depend the strength and well-being of the people, the economic independence of the state ... People and resources were gathered together to build and repair granaries. But these resources ... are being pilfered as a result of bureaucratic interests ... Whose? The Saratov city committee of the party took the decision that the Saratov administration of the 'Roszagotov-spetsremstroi' trust should build the poultry factory, giving it a programme of 189,000 rubles. The Zheleznodorozhnyi district party committee and Kraznoyarsk district soviet executive committee compelled (that was how it was written in the instruction – to 'oblige') the head of the Krasnoyarsk repair-construction administration to rebuild the 65 metre ski jump ...

Of course, the poultry factories are needed, as well as ... good sporting facilities ... but in the last analysis the programme of work of 'Roszagotovspetsremstroi' is to build and repair elevators, grain driers. This is the plan, and that means a state law, and no one is permitted to manipulate it.

The head of the trust V. Pleshakov tried to explain the situation: 'But we cannot ignore the local powers [*vlasti*]. As you yourself understand, we are in their terrirory, and that means we are dependent on them.' He thereby ignored the fact that it is in the interests of the trust itself to indulge the local demands. Those who order country homes and rest houses know quite well that they are making use of the services of the construction people illegally, and are therefore always ready to 'show their gratitude'. If necessary they will sign any percentages [*protsentovki*] – and the management's plan is done. And the plan figures are the most important thing for the trust ...[92]

In addition to this type of direct involvement, there is also the possibility that party officials receive gifts from managers in some sectors in return for general political protection. Party secretaries may get special privileges from trade organisations, or 'tribute' in agricultural districts. This phenomenon has recently been much emphasised by Simis (1982), but on the face of it overplayed. This is not to deny that such tribute is sometimes given, but there are surely many good reasons why local party officials should want to protect 'their' people, without reference to a corrupt link of this kind.

It can be seen that a number of influences combine to encourage the party to take an indulgent attitude towards abuse of office, and to protect managers if the question arises of bringing criminal charges, or convicting offenders with the full force of the law. The local procurators and judges know this and act accordingly. This is not to say that the legal agencies never make 'mistakes', but broadly speaking it will not be difficult for them to guess which prosecutions are going to be unpopular with the local party secretary. Party officials have an important additional lever in this context. The great majority of those who are open to charges of abuse of office, especially at higher levels of responsibility, will be party members. There seems to be an informal rule that party members cannot be convicted in a Soviet court on a criminal charge unless they have first been expelled from the party. The *written* rule is that a party member who commits criminally punishable acts is 'expelled from the party and made answerable in accordance with the law'.[93] In Soviet law defendants are not assumed guilty before they have been convicted, so the expulsion should properly happen after any conviction, not before. But in practice the party member must be expelled before a successful criminal prosecution can be brought, and this expulsion requires the sanction of the local party committee. This gives the committee a very simple and effective weapon. It is possible, in principle, to imagine a zealous procurator trying to bring a criminal prosecution against the wishes of the local party. But such a procurator would quickly be made to look foolish if the expulsion were refused.

It is not surprising to find that these informal links between the party and legal agencies do not get much attention in published Soviet sources. It is true that in Soviet ideology the party acts as a supervisor of all other agencies. But there is a strict attachment in theory to the formal independence of the procuracy and the courts, which are responsible only to the law. Still, hints of the informal pressures have appeared on occasion in the Soviet press. I shall mention two examples. The first concerns an incident at a state farm in Vladimir province, where several hundred head of cattle were lost because, it appears, the farm was not provided with enough fodder. A prosecution was brought against some of the farm managers on grounds of criminal negligence (which 'cost the state 40,000 rubles'), and they were given conditional sentences. During the course of the trial the court also established criminal negligence on the part of local agricultural officials responsible for providing the feed. But the court in a special ruling 'asked' the province agricultural administration whether or not they should institute criminal proceedings. The report commented: '... the judge is a jurist ... [and] of course he knows that the "opinion" of the province administration in this case has no legal significance whatever ...'[94]

This is a form of rhetoric typical in Soviet journalism, which seems to point ironically to the opposite of what is actually being said. The judge knows perfectly well that the 'opinion' of local political officials counts for a lot, and cannot be lightly ignored.

The second case concerns the chairman of the local soviet of a town in Odessa province: together with two other officials he was charged with illegalities in the allocation of housing. A local resident, who wrote a letter to the press about it, commented:

> ... the leaders of the municipal executive committee had been engaging in bribery, they had committed serious crimes in full view. But their trial was rather strange: they were tried separately and far away, [two] in Odessa, [one] in Kotovsk. Why not here in our own town? ... rumours are going around the town that both the bribe-givers and the bribe-takers have the support of a 'strong hand' in the district and even higher in Odessa. That's why, people say, they were tried far from their own localities and why they were given minimal penalties.[95]

The effect of these pressures and constraints is to pull the teeth out of criminal law enforcement in relation to abuse of office. As a rule – with important qualifications to be discussed later – criminal proceedings will go ahead only as a last resort. Furthermore, when they do go ahead, there will be a tendency to soften the impact of such proceedings by focusing on less highly placed people, by accepting extenuating circumstances, and by avoiding extra penalties like confiscation of property.

Local political officials are here faced with a dual pressure. On the one hand, they cannot allow the law to be flouted with total impunity, and are under pressure from above to be seen to have taken at least some form of action. On the other hand, they are reluctant to bring themselves into bad repute by having 'their' managers exposed, especially if this is going to involve expulsion from the party and criminal prosecutions. These conflicting pressures can explain the great popularity of reprimands or strict reprimands through party channels as a substitute form of punishment. Party reprimands are not entirely empty gestures. For example, if a reprimand is still 'on the books', it could prevent a manager from finding a job elsewhere, should she want to leave. The procedure, according to a former manager in a radio plant, is that 'after a year you write a statement to the party organisation: please cancel my reprimand ... since it has served its educational function. And the reprimand is cancelled.' The same informant also observed:

I must tell you that I picked up many reprimands. I had four, true my work book was covered in rewards, but I had reprimands as well . . . In the factory [this] didn't do me any harm. But if I had got annoyed and had said that I didn't want to work at the factory any more, then it's unlikely that another factory would have taken me. Because I had a party reprimand on my card.[96]

If a reprimand seems too feeble a response, a manager can be dismissed on party initiative, and this also avoids the taint of criminal sanctions – the legal apparatus need not come into the picture. No doubt dismissal is a significant penalty in some circumstances. But the dominant impression one gets is that it is unlikely seriously to affect someone's career. A manager will typically step sideways, and then perhaps upwards again. This outcome, which causes some indignation in the Soviet press, is assisted by often allowing the guilty people to leave 'voluntarily'. According to a report on one region, this formula for discharging people, namely 'left at his own request', was 'very, very popular' in the case of managers who had been exposed in connection with abuses. The writer of the report gave the example of the director of a technical college who left 'voluntarily' in such a situation, and commented:

What happens to an executive removed, let us say, for abuse of office? Where did Aliev go? To an executive post. He became chief engineer of one of the departments of the North Ossetian industrial construction trust, and a little while later he went even higher: chief engineer of a republic association. It would be embarrassing to recommend someone if he had been dismissed for financial irregularities . . . others who have left voluntarily also as a rule have simply changed their addresses, while remaining in executive positions . . .
In the light of such facts, one can understand the psychology of people who, when they get into the orbit of executive positions, consider that they are in it for good. They may remove him, but he'll find another portfolio . . .[97]

6 LAW ENFORCEMENT: SOME VARIATIONS

We have seen that there is a strong tendency towards indulgence by the party and legal apparatuses in relation to abuse of office. But it does not follow that the authorities are consistently tolerant. Some offenders in some circumstances are vulnerable to prosecution and may indeed be harshly penalised. This too needs to be explained. Unfortunately general figures on prosecutions and court sentences for different types of offence are not published in the Soviet Union. But one can get some idea of the pattern by drawing on press and legal reports about abuses. I have taken three samples for this purpose: (a) a sample of 56 press reports dealing with offences that had been exposed as a result of whistleblowing. These were selected randomly from the national press, mostly from *Pravda*, in the period 1979–82;[98] (b) a sample of 68 press reports on a variety of 'economic', 'official' and 'socialist property' offences. This was not a random selection: most of these reports were taken from the *Current Digest of the Soviet Press* (covering the period 1975–81), where the choice of stories was clearly weighted towards cases in which there had been heavy penalties;[99] (c) 35 cases reported in the Bulletin of the USSR Supreme Court, dealing with reviews of decisions on abuse of office by lower-level courts (covering 1971–82).

To begin with, I shall focus on the 124 press reports. The following rough picture emerges from this material:

(1) As Table 2.1 shows, embezzlement and bribery are much more likely to be harshly penalised than other offences. To some extent this is to be expected simply by virtue of the wide range of penalties allowed for in law for different types of abuse. It is none the less striking that almost all the custodial sentences are for embezzlement and bribery and that the other offences consistently incurred relatively mild penalties, although custodial sentences are provided in law. One gets the impression of a great diversity of response. On the one hand there are the mildest reactions, suggesting that a wide range of practices have been effectively decriminalised. On the other hand, under certain circumstances, law enforcement in relation to abuse of office is extremely harsh. Long custodial sentences were handed out in some cases of embezzlement and bribery, and four trials ended up with the death sentence. The ultimate penalty was used in the following circumstances: (i) the director of an All-Union furniture supply organisation had received large-scale bribes from the representative of a Western firm; (ii) officials of an organisation trading in manufactured goods in a number of cities in Kazakhstan had engaged in embezzlement on an especially large scale; (iii) the chairman of a district local authority in Tbilisi, Georgia, had received large-scale bribes; (iv) managers in a local industry knitwear factory in Azerbaidzhan had embezzled very large sums through the sale of goods that had been illegally produced within the enterprise.[100]

TABLE 2.1   *Penalties for different types of abuse of office*[a]

Offences	None[b]	Reprimand[c]	Discharge or transfer	Corrective labour or fine	Expulsion from party	Suspended sentence	1–5 years	6–10 years	11–15 years	Death sentence	Total
Embezzlement[d]	2	4	7	1	3	1	2	8	14	2	44
Bribery	1	—	—	—	1	—	3	10	5	2	22
Report-padding and forgery	4	6	5	—	1	—	—	—	—	—	16
False reporting of wages	5	3	2	—	2	—	—	—	—	—	12
Deceit of customers	—	1	2	—	—	—	—	—	—	—	3
Private use of enterprise materials and time	1	1	2	—	2	—	—	—	—	—	6
Illegal allocation of enterprise housing, etc.	2	1	1	—	1	—	—	—	—	—	5
Other[e]	3	4	2	3	—	2	2	—	—	—	16

[a] For this table I have selected *one* clearly identified offence from each case, and *one* penalty (the most serious).
[b] No penalty had been given, so far as I could tell, at the time the report was written.
[c] Most of the reprimands were through party channels.
[d] In 11 cases, report-padding is mentioned as the mechanism of theft.
[e] Includes barter exchange between enterprises, quality offences, criminal negligence, drinking on the job, safety violations, pollution, poaching. (The custodial sentences were given for the last two offences.)

SOURCES   Soviet press reports, 1975–82.

(2) Some sectors are much more vulnerable to severe penalties than others. Table 2.2 shows that the tougher penalties are heavily concentrated in the sphere of trade and in services. These have been lumped together in the table, with services defined broadly to include education and health, transport, repairs and other services provided by local government authorities. Custodial sentences are very much less in evidence in industry and construction – though there was one capital sentence for a manager in local industry. In agriculture, to judge by the sample, the chances of serious sanctions are somewhat greater than in non-agricultural production, but still considerably less than in distribution and services.

(3) The great majority of reports seem to be about small or medium-sized organisations, and typically in peripheral areas, not in the major industrial centres. In sample (a) there are two reports each about Moscow and Sverdlovsk, and one each about Omsk, Kuibyshev and Odessa. With the exception of one industrial enterprise in Sverdlovsk, the organisations involved were within trade and services, and none of the offenders merited more than a discharge. In sample (b) there was a similar absence of reports about major industrial or construction enterprises in the main urban centres, with one exception; an exposé of false reporting in the Ministry of Petroleum Industry in Moscow. Other reports about abuse of office in the bigger cities (Moscow, Baku, Erevan, Tbilisi, Kharkov) were, again, concerned with abuses in distribution and services.

These variations in the pattern of law enforcement can be partly explained by objective differences: by the wide range of penalties allowed for in law, and the greater criminal potential of some types of organisation. The opportunities for theft and bribery are considerably greater in the trade network and in services than in production, greater in agriculture than in industry. It is also possible that small-scale organisations are more in evidence in the more crime-prone sectors, and that in the major urban centres managers and officials are more law abiding than on the periphery.

These things can tell part of the story, but not the whole of it. Just as the ability to evade law enforcement is to some extent a political matter, so also the loss of political protection will leave some managers relatively defenceless. The degree of political protection will depend on the size and prominence of the organisation (how big a fish is the director?), and on its success (how well is the director able to 'knock out the plan'?). It will depend too on the personal political and social skills of managers, and in particular their ability to establish good relationships with local party officials. If the enterprise is small or unprestigious, or has been systematically failing to fulfil targets, or if an individual has fallen out for whatever reason with the local powers-that-be, the enterprise or individual becomes more vulnerable to outside scrutiny and perhaps to legal intervention – especially if a campaign is started from above and there is a general tightening of law enforcement for a time.

TABLE 2.2 *Penalties for abuse of office, by sector*[a]

Penalty	Industry	Construction	Agriculture	Distribution and services	Total
None	4	1	2	10	17
Reprimand	8	4	2	6	20
Discharge or transfer	3	2	4	12	21
Corrective labour or fine	2	—	—	2	4
Expulsion from party	4	2	2	2	10
Suspended sentence	—	1	1	1	3
1–5 years	1	1	3	2	7
6–10 years	1	—	3	15	19
11–15 years	2	—	2	15	19
Death sentence	1	—	—	3	4

[a] This table is based on the same sample as Table 2.1. The same explanatory notes apply.

SOURCES Soviet press reports, 1975–82.

One informant, the former head of a large and successful construction firm in the Ukraine, gave a vivid illustration of the support that he could get by virtue of the size and importance of his organisation and his personal contacts (he was a member of the city party committee). He was describing a time when they got a visit from Kiev, from an inspector concerned with supervision of large cranes on building sites. At the time, some wall panels were due to arrive by train:

We received the panels in carriages, and we had to pay very large sums for demurrage. So we were very concerned that the carriages should not be left standing. The carriages came ... This inspector came from Kiev ... but we had only just managed to put the cranes in place, there were some violations. I was rung up from the section and they told me that someone had come from the crane inspection and was sealing the crane. That meant that the carriages would stand idle ... there would be very big fines. I arrived. He pointed out to me some not very serious violations ... I told him that in a day or two I would get the whole maintenance crew together ... he could stay here in V. [the city where the informant worked] ... He says to me, I don't want to hear another word about it. So you don't want to hear about it? I took the seal ... and tore it in front of him. The matter got to the [Ukraine] central committee. I immediately rang the obkom secretary, and told him what I had done. No doubt I was wrong, but I had no alternative ... he didn't know what to say to me. [But the obkom] defended me in Kiev ... the obkom secretary even rang Kiev himself. They arranged a meeting with [the inspector] to smooth things over. He was terribly indignant and he was right because it was a blatant violation ... I don't think that anybody could have allowed themselves such a thing at the level of V. or even Kiev ...[101]

This story gives a flavour of the personal relationships that are necessary to give a manager immunity (a fragile immunity even here), and the great importance of the party in this context. It would be hard without reference to such factors to explain fully the bias in the pattern of law enforcement towards relatively small and unprestigious organisations away from the major centres, and the general tendency to convict less prominent people. Of the 124 cases in the sample, there were only 5 in which managers in industry were at all heavily penalised. It is true that in one of these cases the death penalty was used: as we have seen, it was a case of illegal production and sale of consumer goods in local industry. According to the report, this had led to the theft of more than two million rubles over a three-year period. It seems that this form of abuse, when it is exposed, is usually dealt with very harshly indeed – no doubt because it represents a direct intrusion of private enterprise into state-managed production, and thus offers a more direct challenge to directive planning than any other kind of managerial offence.

Of the other four convicted industrial managers, three worked in light industry (textiles, sugar, beer) and one in a machine tool factory. This last case, which appears to involve a relatively prominent enterprise, is itself instructive. Eight people from the plant were prosecuted, in connection with report-padding to the tune of several million rubles, and the receipt of tens of thousands of illegal bonuses, which in Soviet law is technically theft. The report said that this was 'perhaps the first trial' in Kostroma province arising from report-padding. At the first trial the offenders 'got off with a light scare', and remained in their posts. The district and city party secretaries had argued that no mercenary motives were involved. But later, after a protest by the RSFSR Procuracy, the offenders were retried and given a variety of short custodial sentences.[102]

One gains the impression, then, that criminal sanctions are used very selectively and unevenly. This impression is reinforced by an examination of the third sample of reports. These are reviews by the USSR Supreme Court of lower-level judicial decisions on abuse of office. In many cases, people have been convicted and penalised by the lower courts with the full force of the law for minor offences, providing a stark contrast with the minimal response to serious violations of law in other organisations and settings. For example, in two separate cases people in very modest positions had received sentences of eight years in the lower courts for taking bribes totalling 70 and 100 rubles, and in another case a minor official was given ten years for taking a bribe of 90 rubles.[103] Meanwhile, in a contrasting case, two offenders who had received bribes of 2000 and 1500 rubles over a four-year period, were given only suspended sentences.[104]

A brigade leader, charged with embezzlement of 670 rubles through false reporting of wages, was given ten years by a lower court.[105] The managers of a municipal services establishment were similarly charged with embezzlement by means of report-padding, gaining 760 rubles each in illegal bonuses (the total *pripiska* was 3300 rubles). According to the lower court they had brought 'serious damage to state or social organisations' and received terms of between six and fifteen years.[106] In a third embezzlement case, the managers of a textile factory were given terms of between two and six years for false reporting involving the receipt of a total of 2800-ruble bonuses, averaging 60 rubles each.[107] Meanwhile, in one of the cases in sample (b), the director of a state farm who had participated in the theft of 330 000 rubles was only expelled from the party and discharged,[108] and a similar fate befell the director of a local industry factory who was exposed for report-padding to the tune of 380 000 rubles.[109]

It seems, then, that although the great majority of people exposed in connection with false reporting get off with a reprimand or a discharge, or even less (see Table 2.1), in a few instances the procuracy and courts have decided to prosecute and convict with great severity. In almost all the abuse of office cases reviewed by the USSR Supreme Court, the penalties were reduced or the case was sent for retrial. But the reports are revealing about the biases of legal intervention lower down. They typically criticise the lower courts for an inadequate examination of the case, and the tenor of much of the comment strongly suggests that criminal charges were brought not because serious offences were committed, but because people had fallen out of favour with their superiors or with local political officials. Since breaches of law are endemic in Soviet managerial and administrative practice, managers and officials are very vulnerable under these circumstances. There is a popular Russian saying: 'Take any person, and you can find a crime' (*Byl by chelovek, a delo naidetsya*). It reflects very clearly the dangers surrounding abuse of office in an environment where the criminal law has such a wide-ranging potential presence.

Those dangers are greater for less prominent, successful and influential people. This has not given anyone unconditional immunity from outside scrutiny and sanctions. Some highly placed officials have been caught in law and order campaigns, even in the 1960s and 1970s, a period when the position of the whole managerial and political apparatus became greatly stabilised. In the Khrushchev period in the early 1960s, there was a major campaign against certain kinds of economic crime. The managers involved were not prominent figures, but several local party and law enforcement officers, up to the provincial level, were involved as protectors. The campaign focused on the private production and sale of consumer goods, which has proliferated in some areas (especially, it seems, in the Ukraine, Central Asia and Transcaucasia) in small firms that had been set up under the jurisdiction of departments of local industry. It was at this time that the death penalty was introduced for particularly serious cases of embezzlement of socialist property, and it was applied to a number of such 'entrepreneurs' who had made large sums of money by economising on materials and selling the illegal part of their production through the official trade network.[110]

Since the early 1960s no campaign of this severity has been waged against private 'left' production, but the practice did not disappear and in the intervening years a number of major trials have been held, with charges of large-scale embezzlement and bribery, and heavy penalties. In one case in Azerbaidzhan, which is included in my sample (b), two republic procuracy officials, together with one manager, were sentenced to death for bribe-taking, embezzlement and other offences in connection with the illegal production of knitwear goods.[111] This shows that if the political will is strong enough, or the offences have become sufficiently blatant, the law can still take its course even against highly placed officials.

In the Brezhnev period, the biggest campaign was the one conducted in Georgia, starting in 1972, in an attempt to root out pervasive corruption that had engulfed large parts of the political and law enforcement apparatus, including the republican party leadership. Similar efforts have been directed at the other Transcaucasian republics, Armenia and Azerbaidzhan, although they have not gained the same notoriety in the West. In all these cases, particular cultural and economic conditions encouraged the emergence of a number of islands of protected illegality. These have been eroded to some extent by the campaigns of the past ten years, but recurrent reports suggest that the forces of protection are still very strong.[112]

7 CONCLUSION

I have tried in this chapter to describe the conditions under which some typical breaches of law by Soviet managers and officials arise, to draw a picture of law enforcement, and to link this picture with a broader set of political relationships. A wide gulf has opened up between officially stated legal norms and moral values on the one hand, and managerial practice on the other. The reasons could not be fully explored here. But we have seen that they are tied up with the ever-continuing struggle for the plan, with systematic attempts to keep up appearances, and with a variety of efforts to take advantage of the powers and resources of the job for personal gain.

The tension between law and illegality is reflected in a general tendency to indulgence by the legal apparatuses, which in turn is closely related to the informal protection offered by local party officials to the people they have helped to promote, and on whom they rely. But the protection is conditional. It depends on the prominence and success of the organisation, and the ability of its managers to establish good political connections.

Even if there is political protection, this does not mean that the law can be flouted with complete impunity. There are legal agencies with a job to do and institutional interests to protect, and there is recurrent pressure from higher up in the party hierarchy to see that justice is done and that people who break the law are called to account. But the general thrust of central injunctions is constantly blunted by networks of political support. The pattern of law enforcement suggests that there are definite limits to the ability or the willingness of the central party authorities to see that law enforcement takes its course. Thus the same centralised edifice which seems to require elaborate legal norms as a condition of its operation also constantly inhibits the attempt to make practice conform to law. These observations can be much reinforced by looking at what happens to citizens' complaints about management illegality. The account in this chapter has served as a necessary starting point for an understanding of the political relationships in which such complaints become immersed. But a study of those complaints will also help to clarify the political conditions that encourage and inhibit abuse of office.

3 Whistleblowing: Some Cases

1 INTRODUCTION

One of the ways in which the Soviet rulers try to keep abuse of office in check is by appealing to individual citizens to act as watchdogs of the norms written into Soviet law, to 'blow the whistle' on illegal practices if they encounter them. The party leaders, as would-be guardians of the general interest, encourage the citizens to act with total honesty and offer to protect them against possible retaliation by management and local officialdom if the whistle is blown. This channel of action is in fact frequently used by Soviet citizens, either in the pursuit of personal grievances, or in the more disinterested attempt to prevent the use of public office for private ends. The aim of this chapter and of Chapter 4 is to illustrate and analyse the origins and outcome of this type of initiative from below. By doing so, one can throw further light on the issues that emerged from the discussion in the previous chapter. By tracing the course of a complaint about abuse of office, and the problems that Soviet citizens encounter in trying to make a complaint stick, one can get a very concrete picture of the extent and limits of protected illegality, and of the relationship between central and local political power. At the same time, something can be learnt about the role of citizens' complaints in the law enforcement process and in the Soviet political system as a whole.

In this chapter I shall present a number of narratives about whistle-blowing, taken from the Soviet press, in order to provide a background for a later investigation of this type of complaint. But before doing so, it will be appropriate to put whistleblowing in context by discussing some general features of the Soviet petitioning process.

It should be stressed that in examining the responses of the Soviet public to abuse of office, I shall be looking at only one manifestation of opinion 'from below' in the USSR. The Soviet Union has a long-established and very widely used set of procedures for individual petitioning. The Soviet political authorities and media receive a vast number of letters and personal visits on a great variety of matters. Whistleblowing is just one type of submission among many others. Systematic information on the quantity and character of petitioning is not available in Soviet published sources. But some observations can be made which will give an idea of the procedures and the extent to which they are used.

Current procedures are set out in a Supreme Soviet decree of March 1980, which modified an earlier law of 1968 in the light of provisions in the 1977 Constitution. The 1980 regulations say that

All state and social organs must provide the citizens of the USSR with the necessary conditions for the realisation of their rights, proclaimed by the Constitution of the USSR and by Soviet laws, to make proposals in written and oral form to state and social organs about the improvement of their activity, to criticise shortcomings in their work, to make statements to them, to complain about the actions of officials of state and social organs.[1]

The officials of all these bodies are obliged to accept and carefully examine such statements and complaints and to give well-argued decisions. If requests are refused, the reasons are to be indicated. Answers are to be given normally within one month of the submission, and if dissatisfied, citizens can appeal to a higher authority. Agencies are instructed to 'systematically analyse and summarise proposals, statements and complaints, together with the criticisms contained in them, in order to discover and eliminate in good time the causes giving rise to the violation of the rights and interests of citizens, in order to study public opinion, improve the work of state and social organs, enterprises, establishments ...'[2]

It is further stated that 'in the event of violation of the established procedure ... and also the victimisation of citizens in connection with the submission of proposals, statements and complaints, or in connection with the criticism contained in them, the guilty officials will incur responsibility in accordance with the law'. Where such violations cause 'significant harm to state or social interests or to the rights and legally protected interests of citizens', officials incur criminal responsibility under the appropriate legislation on official crimes. However, citizens who make submissions for slanderous purposes also incur responsibility in accordance with the law.[3]

The decree makes it clear that the officials of all agencies must accept complaints about other officials in relation to whom they have some authority or responsibility. Thus, in appropriate cases one may appeal to administrative superiors, to the executive committees and deputies of the soviets, to the procuracy and the courts, to the People's Control and to social organisations. 'Social organisations' include the party and the trade unions, although neither is specifically mentioned in the legislation. In addition, complaints may be received by agencies through the press, television and radio, and statements in connection with such complaints may be made in the media. In this case, the relevant officials must respond within the time limits laid down in the decree.

These are the main provisions. To what extent are such channels of information and protest used? This cannot be judged with any precision, but the number of petitioners is clearly vast, and has been increasing over recent years. White (1983) provides some figures on submissions to the Central Committee of the party which gives an indication of the scale and the trend. The Central Committee figures show a general trend upwards, with 'bulges' in Party Congress years (1971 and 1976) and in 1977, when the draft Constitution was under extensive public discussion.

TABLE 3.1 *Letters to the CPSU Central Committee*

1971	482 100	1976	693 260
1972	352 500	1977	657 360
1973	368 680	1978	558 740
1974	375 060	1979	570 880
1975	429 960	1980	671 600

SOURCE *Spravochnik partiinogo rabotnika*, vyp. 21 (Moscow 1981) pp. 503–4; White (1983) p. 47.

During the period between the 25th and 26th Party Congresses, according to a Central Committee statement, the Central Committee received nearly 3 million letters and nearly 100 000 visitors. Meanwhile local party organs received 15 million written and oral submissions.[4] Citizens also appealed in great numbers to the trade unions: during the period of the 10th Five-year Plan (1975–80) the central offices of the trade unions, including the All-Union Council, received 2¼ million written and oral submissions.[5] One may safely assume that the soviets and legal agencies also have big postbags and 'surgeries' to attend to, while vast numbers of letters are sent to the press as well. White (1983) quotes a Soviet estimate that all Soviet national newspapers together receive 60 million to 70 million letters a year. The biggest circulation national dailies – *Pravda, Izvestiya, Trud* – get about half a million letters annually, and these figures have been steadily growing in the recent period:

TABLE 3.2   *Letters to soviet newspapers, 1952–81*

Year	Pravda	Izvestiya	Trud
1952	n.a.	37 301	n.a.
1955	250 000[a]	46 974	n.a.
1960	299 000[b]	211 000	209 160
1965	300 000[c]	500 000	338 500
1970	382 000[d]	493 000	373 800
1975	456 000[e]	467 858	548 174
1981	514 000	520 000[f]	415 417

[a] Largest annual total, 1955–7
[b] Average for 1958–9
[c] 1967
[d] 1971
[e] 1974
[f] 1977

Sources   Various Soviet publications. See White (1983) p. 52.

The agencies that receive submissions are instructed to review their postbags and visits periodically, to provide summaries (*svodki*), and to send these to the appropriate agencies. For example, lower-level party apparatuses prepare summaries for party committees and for other bodies in the area, and send them up through the party hierarchy for information. Analogous procedures are followed by the soviets, the trade unions, courts, People's Control Committees and the press. It is reported that seven to ten 'thematic reviews' are sent by *Pravda* every month to party, state and other bodies.[6]

It would be interesting to know what everybody is writing about, but the summaries are not publicly available. Not all the letters are complaints – for example, some are hymns of praise to the party and the nation – but it is fair to assume that a very large proportion of the submissions are connected in one way or another with attempts to get something done about problems or perceived injustices.[7] Much of the letter-writing has to do with comments about the supply of consumer goods and services – an issue of constant and pervasive concern. Housing problems also figure largely, together with complaints about conditions of work. There are numerous suggestions for improvements in this or that organisation, there are appeals for support in getting technical innovations accepted, comments about the state of public order, about waste of resources and about labour discipline, and a host of other matters. Whistleblowing, that is complaints specifically directed at abuse of office, is a fraction – I do not know what fraction – of the total.[8]

Official encouragement of citizens' letters and complaints, and the whole idea of criticism from below, has a long history in the Soviet Union. 'Criticism and self-criticism' became a major party slogan at the end of the 1920s, with the onslaught on private agriculture, the rapid expansion of state industry and a general extension in the arena of political management. During the Stalin years official support for critical initiatives from below acquired at times a very sharp edge, when a variety of anxieties and discontents were mobilised as part of efforts to activate the whole state machinery. The process took on an especially acute form during the struggles within the political apparatus of 1936–8, when a violent campaign was launched by the central leadership (or by part of it) against local officialdom – a campaign that was apparently able to capitalise on widespread hostility to the arbitrary practices of local bosses and 'little Stalins'.[9]

Something akin to this process, though without the accompaniment of violence, happened again during the Khrushchev period. Party slogans in the late 1950s and early 1960s laid great emphasis on participation from below, connected in part with Khrushchev's own efforts to shake up the political apparatus. But it was during the Brezhnev period that citizens' 'proposals, statements and complaints' began to receive solid support from the party – though whether the process became any more effective is another question. A Central Committee resolution on the issue was passed in 1967,[10] followed soon after by a USSR Supreme Soviet decree in 1968.[11] The Central Committee returned to it again in 1976,[12] and in 1977 the new Constitution included two articles (49 and 58) establishing the right to submit proposals and to criticise the actions of officials.[13] These rights already existed in law, but had been absent from the 1936 Constitution. In 1978, a Letters Department was set up under the Central Committee.[14] In 1980, in the decree that I outlined earlier, the 1968 law was revised in the light of the Constitution, and a USSR Supreme

Court directive reminded the courts that officials were criminally liable in certain circumstances if they failed to respond to proposals and complaints, or if they took reprisals against citizens in connection with criticism.[15] In April 1981 there was another Central Committee decision, stressing the responsibility of party organisations to take all submissions seriously and not to give a purely formal response to them.[16]

After Brezhnev's death in November 1982, exhortations on this matter did not diminish. If anything they were stepped up as part of the overall campaign on law and order, which enlisted a great deal of critical comment from below about the state of discipline and legality in the country. In addition to all this, considerable attention was given in the press to critical letters and commentaries upon them. I do not know how the coverage during recent years compares with the 1960s and early 1970s, but it seems evident from the tone of official pronouncements and of press material that a definite public worry has built up over the issue. In the next chapter I shall return to this point, comment on party propaganda in greater detail, and offer some possible explanations for recent official pronouncements about the petitioners.

The practice of petitioning and lodging complaints is a key part of the political mechanism in the Soviet Union and in other societies of the Soviet type.[17] First, submissions from citizens are an important source of information about a variety of social problems which are seen to require political and administrative intervention. If individuals send signals about abuses ('signals' is a common Soviet expression), this helps law enforcement. The law enforcement agencies would be less effective than they are, if they relied only on the initiative of the ministries, procuracies, financial agencies, People's Control and party organisations. Criticism from below about breaches of law assists the state to mobilise the initiatives and concerns of individual citizens in the overall process of political management.

Second, the complaints procedure gives Soviet citizens an opportunity to respond to what they see as injustices, either in the pursuit of personal grievances or simply in the attempt to uphold officially espoused laws and moral values. It provides an important form of political legitimation because it makes it possible at least in principle to set up a concrete identity between the concerns of the individual and the state.

Both these elements are reflected in the standard official statements. For example, a Central Committee resolution put it this way:

The Soviet people in their letters addressed to party, soviet and economic organs raise questions that have great political and economic significance, they introduce suggestions about the improvement of the work of industrial enterprises, transport, agriculture etc. ... Statements and complaints also indicate short-comings in the work of party, soviet, economic and social organisations, point out cases of negligent attitudes to social property, violations of law and of the rights of Soviet citizens. The letters of working people are one of the important forms of strengthening and widening the links between the party and the people, the participation of the people in the administration of state affairs, a means of expression of public opinion ... [18]

This can be compared with the USSR Supreme Soviet decree of 1980 on 'Procedures for examining citizens' proposals, statements and complaints', which has the following preamble:

The citizens' right to appeal to government and social organisations with proposals, statements and complaints is an important means of defending the interests of the individual and of strengthening the ties of the state apparatus with the population; it is a significant source of information which is essential in deciding current and long-term questions of state, economic and social–cultural construction. As one of the forms of participation by the working people in administration, citizens' appeals allow the people to strengthen their control over the activity of state and social organs ... [19]

These formulations are not purely rhetorical. They seem to express a definite reality, since the constant and widespread use of the petitioning procedures actually creates the wished-for identity between the individual and the state, even if the procedures work badly. It is therefore not surprising to find Soviet political leaders welcoming the stream of submissions. However, this state of affairs can be welcomed only up to a certain point and in a certain sense. In the first place, there must be some level at which the flow of complaints becomes dangerous – if the stream becomes a flood, that reflects a high level of public dissatisfaction. It is dangerous also if petitioning threatens to become a collective act. Petitioning in the Soviet sense is a means of political expression of a special and limited kind. Essentially, it relies on the expectation that one arm of the state apparatus will come to the defence of the individual citizen by acting upon another arm of that apparatus, in the name of the rules. The citizen is trying to ensure that the rules are implemented, not to change them, and is engaging in an individual not a collective initiative. It may be collective in the sense that several people from a single organisation together, for example, sign a letter of complaint about illegal practices. But if a petition is collective in the sense that it crosses institutional boundaries, then it becomes a political act of quite a different kind that is seen to challenge the legitimacy of the state itself.

The possibility of collective action is, then, one danger to guard against. The second problem is that the procedure must *work*. It is true that it need not work very well, but it must work in a certain proportion of cases if it is to keep its 'unifying' function. If complaints are systematically ignored at the local level, if local officials are systematically protected by higher ones, this cannot have a good effect. Petitioners may then abandon their efforts in disgust and resign themselves to thoroughgoing cynicism. Alternatively, and this is no doubt worse from the point of view of the political leadership, they may turn into real troublemakers, determined to ensure that the laws are not flouted with impunity, whatever the cost.

As one might expect from the discussion in Chapter 2, to make a complaint about abuse of office stick is very difficult. The individual citizen is pitted against a set of powerful local interests and must gain the support of agencies whose relationship to those local interests is at least ambiguous and at most solidly protective. None the less, complaints of this kind are by no means uncommon. Despite the immense difficulties, it is clear that very many people are sufficiently troubled, sufficiently encouraged by the occasional successful petition, or sufficiently ignorant about the difficulties to pursue their claims through the established channels.

A good idea of the character and effects of whistleblowing can be gained by a review of the Soviet national press, which I have largely relied on for my account. Before examining the results of that study, I shall present some examples of the kind of narrative on which the analysis is based. This will have the advantage of giving readers some idea of how the Soviet press handles such complaints, and some basis for judging whether or not the analysis is convincing.

The stories that I have chosen and translated have been selected because they seemed to me vivid, and because they deal with frequently recurring themes. I shall offer some brief comments on each narrative, but shall reserve a more detailed discussion of the causes and consequences of whistleblowing until Chapter 4.

2 SOME CASES

Case 1

V. Danilov (*Pravda* correspondent), Sverdlovsk province, 'A refutation of a refutation', *Pravda*, 3 January 1979, p. 3.

V. Klyushnikov, an electrician at the smelting shop of the Urals precision alloys factory, wrote to *Pravda*:

'There are many people in our enterprise who need housing, but the ones who get flats are usually those who have no justification for it, mainly the managers and their relations. A lot of us ask why it happens that way.'

The editors passed on this complaint and asked the Berezovskii party committee to provide an answer to the question. The first secretary of the city committee, A. Kuzminykh, replied: 'in connection with starting up the experimental shop, the USSR Ministry of Heavy Industry sent us some specialists. According to the agreement we were obliged to allocate comfortable housing for them. The distribution of flats was discussed at a meeting of the factory trade union committee and was endorsed by the executive committee of the city soviet.' In a word, everything was in order, there had been no violations.

The reply was dated 31 October 1977. But already on 1 December, that is only a month later, a resolution from the buro of the city party committee appeared which said: 'at the factory there have indeed been violations of the rules on registering citizens who need housing and on the allocation of housing. Working people do not get to see the lists.' The buro decided to give reprimands to the factory director N. Vyatkin, his deputy G. Gulyaev, and former chairman of the trade union committee V. Sergeev, and to give a warning to S. Maslov, secretary of the party organisation.

As we see, one document refutes another.

Complaints about disorder in the distribution of housing at the Urals precision alloys factory began a long time ago. However, the enterprise management, the trade union and party committees, the city party committee either failed to notice these complaints or else did not take them seriously: there will always be dissatisfied people, they might say, you can't please everyone.

As is now known, the substance of V. Klyushnikov's letter also failed to arouse concern among the officials of the city committee and in the factory management, although both developed the liveliest interest in the person of the author: who was he and why did he decide to write? The main focus of attention was on this question. And then measures were taken. Not measures to get rid of the shortcomings that had been pointed out in the complaint, but measures to eliminate the person who had pointed them out.

To begin with, the electrician was given two reprimands for things that he had not done. Then they set up an exam to test his knowledge of the safety regulations. And, of course, they failed him. The director N. Vyatkin dismissed V. Klyushnikov from his duties as electrician, and the cadres department offered him the choice of a number of worse-paid jobs, including yard-keeper and cleaner. They hoped, no doubt, that this insubordinate person would surrender and give in his notice. But he did not give in his notice. They decided to mobilise 'public opinion'. They organised a meeting of a group of workers, who appealed to the shop-head to 'defend them against the demagogic talk' of Klyushnikov. But that did not have any effect either. Nobody took this dispatch seriously, since it was obviously engineered. The comrades in the shop did however make a serious request: to stop victimising this worker. They wrote about this to the party organs in particular. Thanks to their signal and intervention by officials of the Sverdlovsk province party committee, V. Klyushnikov was reinstated in his previous position.

The vexed leaders of the factory administration, in the thick of the battle they had started, did not notice that they had themselves shown the absurdity of the accusations against the electrician, that they had refuted their own conclusions. Someone who, in the opinion of the administration, was only capable of carrying out the duties of a yard-keeper, who did not know the safety rules, was suddenly offered the position of – foreman. The calculation was a simple one: having got a promotion maybe he would keep quiet. Klyushnikov refused to take the post offered.

Meanwhile a commission of the province party committee arrived in the town of Berezovskii. After a long time, the complaints that had come from the Urals precision alloys factory were investigated by a commission from the province committee of the metallurgical industry trade union. The most flagrant breaches of the rules on the allocation of housing were discovered. Without sufficient grounds extra housing space was given to the head of the department of material–technical supply A. Bykov, to the son of the deputy director G. Gulyaev, the daughter of the director N. Vyatkin, the daughter of the chief engineer I. Gorlach and some others. It became known that this issue was to be discussed by the province party committee. It was then that a meeting of the city party committee was urgently called, which at last admitted the mistakes that had long been obvious, at least a month before.

I was having a discussion with A. Kuzminykh. He did not say a word about violation of rules on allocation of housing, nor about reprisals for criticism, nor about his own blunder. He talked only about V. Klyushnikov: about his quarrelsomeness and his tendency to criticise.

In fairness one should say that the city committee and the management studied the biography of this rank and file electrician as if it was the life story of a renowned general, with the difference only that what interested them was not the details of his military feats, but any facts, features and particulars that might in the slightest way compromise him.

What did they discover? Klyushnikov's character is indeed not like honey: he is a troubled person, he can be sharp, he likes to say what he thinks, without respect of persons. That is why he several times came into conflict with the managers of the enterprise where he used to work.

All this is so. But in the first place, nobody showed that when he got into a conflict he was wrong. And secondly, can the personality of a worker, even a quarrelsome one, justify violating the rules on housing allocation, can it justify abuse of office?

In the opinion of the enterprise management and the city party committee, V. Klyushnikov is casting aspersions on the collective.

'At a recent trade union conference', said A. Kuzminykh, 'speakers were asking indignantly: "For how long, on account of Klyushnikov, are various commissions going to come and impede our work?"'

Well, it is quite possible that one of the speakers spoke in just that way (I was not able to clarify this, because for some reason on the day of my visit the record of the conference was not to be found). But that is not the important thing: if there had been a normal situation at the factory, there would have been no commissions. There is nothing for commissions to do if measures are taken in good time to eliminate shortcomings, and if just criticism is not brushed aside.

Let us summarise. The Berezovskii city party committee did not want to give a serious response to a letter, to investigate thoroughly the facts that it referred to. The province party committee had to intervene. Hence the result, this long drawn out story, which has still not come to a close.

When will it? And what will be the outcome? At one time the

province party committee correctly pointed out the disorder in the allocation of housing at the Urals precision alloys factory. But unfortunately there has been no judgement on the attitude of the city committee and of its first secretary. And this may convince other managers that to send purely formal replies to newspaper editors is perfectly acceptable, that one can turn a blind eye to unsightly behaviour, that one need not wash any dirty linen in public until the higher organs have intervened and corrected the situation. It is convenient for them ...

Comments

The story illustrates many of the recurring problems described in Soviet press reports about complaints arising from abuse of office. The following points may be noted about this case:

(1) The complaint arose out of a perceived injustice. The management was breaking the rules in order to dispense material privileges to the members of a personal circle, not to people with a prior claim. Such complaints about the allocation of housing are common.

(2) The management tried to silence the critic by one means or another – by finding a pretext to discipline him, by mobilising public opinion, and at one point by promoting him. The enterprise trade union was part of the management circle and did nothing to protect the complainant from management reprisals.

(3) The complaint reached the local party organisation (the city party committee), which defended the management and tried to ignore the complaint, even when it had been sent on by *Pravda*. The province party committee was then called on to intervene. The result was a province trade union investigation and some action by the city party committee, which led to the reinstatement of the critic in his previous job.

(4) Although the complainant got some redress, the implication is that the offenders got away with their breach of the rules. The higher authorities had intervened, but the story had 'still not come to a close'. The forces which sustained illicit management privilege (including local party protection) are still alive and well. No one within the management circle lost their jobs or their housing.

(5) It is difficult to say why this particular enterprise and local

political authority were singled out for criticism in the press. It is possible that the number of complaints about housing had reached an unacceptable level, or that the enterprise and local authority were vulnerable to criticism for quite different reasons.

(6) The style of reporting is heavily ironic and morally charged: the actors represent the forces of good and evil. There is ambiguity, but it lies in the outcome of the struggle rather than in the characterisation of the protagonists. The story cannot therefore convey the complexity of action and motivation that lie behind the conflict. But it is detailed enough to give one a hint of such motives, and more than a hint about the political relationships in which such a complaint becomes embedded.

Case 2

I. Novikov (*Pravda* correspondent), Grodno (Belorussia), 'About bonuses', *Pravda*, 12 October 1979, p. 2.

Some people like to explain what happened by reference to the saying: 'it was the devil's work'. He was to blame, let him answer for it ... When you examine the matter thoroughly, you become convinced that an evil spirit was indeed abroad, but not at all the one that people talk about.

When the province paper reported that the Grodno house-building combine, after the results of the first quarter of this year, had won the challenge Red Banner of the USSR Ministry of Industrial Construction and the branch trade union central committee, and was also rewarded with bonuses, few people had doubts about it. The collective has a good reputation. For example, the house-builders were one of the first to adopt the brigade contract. They did not stand aside either from the Rostov initiative: 'Let's work without laggards.'

In a word, the honours they received appeared to be deserved. All the more discordant, then, was the sound of a statement made by L. Gavrilova, an economist at the house-building combine: 'We were not working too badly, perhaps, but we did not deserve the bonus. We achieved it with the help of ... report-padding.'

Gavrilova discovered report-padding even before the materials about the results of the competition were sent off. The figures on output and profit were overstated. For example, it was reported that all the work on one unit, to the tune of 236 000 rubles, was carried out by the combine itself, when more than 100 000 rubles was the responsibility of a subcontracted organisation. The wages fund was over-spent, but to conceal this 15 000 rubles was taken from the bank, ostensibly for workers' leave.

What was this, an 'initiative' on the part of a member of the planning department? Alas, an investigation (it was carried out by two commissions from Minsk), and the behaviour of the combine executives themselves, showed very clearly that the report-padding was done with their knowledge. Moreover, they made considerable efforts to remove this unexpected obstacle on the road to false fame. The chairman of the trade union committee G. Gvozdev, to whom the economist first trustingly turned for support, did not think to examine the documents and accounts, but hastened to warn the director A. Kubasov about Gavrilova's 'intrigues'. The director issued an instruction: 'Don't let the self-appointed inspector anywhere near the documents!'

L. Gavrilova turned out to be a strong character. She went to the party secretary, V. Mishin. Here, at least, she expected support. But the secretary cut her short: 'Don't interfere in things that don't concern you!'

The head of the planning department V. Gerasimov – he was Gavrilova's immediate superior – was only waiting for the moment to take revenge on his obdurate colleague. Of course, he forbade her to make use of any materials, even those that she needed simply in order to carry out her normal duties. Petty fault-finding began, and it became common practice for people to raise their voices against Gavrilova. They even blamed her for obstruction in connection with tasks that she could not carry out because she had been forbidden access to the necessary documents. Everything went ahead! While the economist was getting a 'thrashing', the combine's application for an all-Union bonus went around the authorities. And then it was announced that the collective had been given 18 040 rubles as a reward for their good performance.

Of course this was happy news, nobody was indifferent to it. The house-builders are proud of their enterprise and accepted this high evaluation as if it were deserved. This is a natural reaction to a reward in any collective: people get enthusiastic, they want to work even better ... Well, and if the reward is undeserved? What then? A person's behaviour in such a situation is very revealing. This is a kind of touchstone, which proves one's moral qualities.

It must be said that many employees of the combine with whom I have had a chance to speak, reacted to this exposure by L. Gavrilova as befits honest people. Their view was this: if report-padding had indeed taken place, then this should be declared openly, those responsible should get their deserts and the bonus should be refused.

'Let them say that in order to win first place we would have to do some more hard work. Would we refuse?' said M. Tereshko, a brigade leader, to the *Pravda* correspondent. 'Dishonestly earned money burns your pockets.'

He was supported by his fellow brigade leader, carpenter E. Nazarov: 'We are not money grubbers, that's not the way to win competitions.'

One can be sure that if they knew the real situation, other workers and specialists of the shops would take the same view. But that's just the trouble, that they try hard to conceal the truth of what has happened from the collective. When people do hear rumours, they attempt to influence them against Gavrilova, depicting her as a trouble-making and quarrelsome person.

Gerasimov, the department head, tries especially hard. After all, he knows Gavrilova's weaknesses better than other people. For example, she is quick-tempered. Why not use that for one's own ends? The head attempts in every way to provoke her to conflict, and then says with a gesture: 'You see, it's impossible to work with her ...' That is how a matter of principle concerning methods of management got reduced to a question of personal relations between the head of the planning department and the economist.

Failing to get support on the spot, Gavrilova appealed to Minpromstroi BSSR (Belorussia) to which the enterprise is subordinated. What did the ministry officials do? It was clear that they were very worried ... about their regimental honour. How is this, they ask themselves in Minsk, we put them forward for a bonus and now we get this disgraceful situation ... an unpleasant business. Can't we smooth things over a bit? Although two commissions sent by the ministry had confirmed the facts exposed by Gavrilova, still they did not want to admit the errors. And so the draft directive prepared several months ago lay in the ministry without being signed. The directive proposed a strict reprimand for the head of the combine, the discharge of the head of the planning department, and a fine of one month's salary for the chief accountant.

The directive lay there, meanwhile they had time to give Gavrilova a reprimand and then a strict reprimand. The eye-washers were triumphant. What, they said, had she achieved? They hoped that the economist would not tolerate the situation, that she would leave 'voluntarily'.

Gavrilova did not leave. She decided to turn to the local *Pravda* office, and it was only when the paper got interested that the minister I. Mozolyako finally signed the directive.

It was just at this time that I was able to visit the Grodno combine, to talk to people. The visit aroused strong feelings, because even after the order had been signed, few people knew about it. The acting director V. Glukhov was secretly keeping it in his desk, not wanting to publicise it.

It would be relevant to add that a sample check showed that in previous years there were also machinations with bonuses at the house-building combine. For some employees it seemed to have already become a habit to 'dress things up', to 'knock out' illegal rewards. It is not difficult to see that in such a situation people who like their rubles, even if gained by dishonest means, will prefer to stay on the surface of things. A kind of shift in psychology occurs, one's principles and sense of responsibility get blunted. Some people think that to tell the truth about machinations is to 'wash your dirty linen in public', to disgrace the collective. In short, everything is turned upside down.

'I don't see anything special in what has happened', said V. Yarmak, an employee in the department of labour and wages, 'after all, they do it in other construction organizations!'

'And what if someone had taken some money out of your pocket? What would you call such a person?'

'Well, that is quite another matter!' she protested. 'Still, if you want to know my official view, you're welcome: I condemn report-padding. But after all we are not at a meeting, from a human point of view you can understand ...'

It appears then that there are two assessments of unseemly behaviour: one 'official', for the sake of form, and the other 'human', which is more advantageous for oneself. This latter assessment is sometimes used by people in responsible positions. You mention to them the dishonesty of trying to make a good showing with the help of 'chemistry', and not by organising things in a model way, and you get the feeling that you are not being heard. Whence this deafness, when it is a question of state money? What is it that has corroded a demanding attitude to oneself and to others? Some officials, one notices, start to play around with words, they try to find a softer, more streamlined term for a misdemeanour.

For example, I rang the chief engineer of the combine V. Glukhov and he declared that in his opinion there had been no report-padding but only 'distortions in the accounts, brought about by various circumstances'. Thus there was no serious blame, again it was the devil at work . . .

But what is a 'distortion' in the accounts? The very same report-padding! Yet how difficult it is for the managers of the combine, who are used to violating state discipline with impunity, to accept their responsibility! How difficult to draw the correct conclusions from what has happened and not present black as white.

And the attempt to snatch unearned honours and bonuses, and to tolerate self-seekers and money grubbers – that is also a form of self-seeking which erodes a healthy atmosphere in a collective. It interferes with the process of educating people in a feeling that they are really masters of their enterprise, a feeling of great responsibility for the general cause, for their own actions. This is a dangerous phenomenon and those honest workers of the combine who demand decisive measures against violators, and active measures to improve the situation in the enterprise, are right.

Comments

(1) The whistleblower in this case was a financial specialist. It can be assumed that a complaint about false reporting, which is a common theme in press reports on whistleblowing, could normally be made only by someone on the inside who has access to the figures.

(2) The management response, as in all the stories in this chapter, was very hostile, though in the present case it appears that attempts to put pressure on the critic have failed, and that she kept her job.

(3) The account stresses the reluctance of the ministry officials to act when their own reputation is at stake.

(4) An image of the eccentricity of the whistleblower and of the normality of the phenomenon (after all they do it in other construction organisations . . .) is allowed to emerge, as well as the clear distinction that is drawn by the offenders between 'stealing' from the state and from a private individual.

(5) The penalties, when they come, are very mild.

Case 3

A letter from G. Zinkevich (Engineer–Economist), Belotserkov district, Kiev Province, 'Who to keep in step with?', *Pravda*, 26 October 1981, p. 3.

For a long time I have been a regular *Pravda* reader, but I am writing to you now, dear editors, for the first time. I earnestly ask you: what should I do next, how can I go on?

First of all a few personal words about myself. I have a higher education, I have two children, I am a party member, I have worked for 25 years – and for 11 I was chief economist at the Kalinin state farm. I was a member of the People's Control group, a propagandist, a deputy to the village soviet, a delegate at party and trade union conferences.

Now directly about the matter which has persuaded me to write to the paper – and about the farm where I worked. Once it was an advanced farm, it made 1½ million rubles profit during the Ninth Five-year Plan. But then the profit turned into a deficit, and the Tenth Five-year Plan ended with big losses. They say that this was to do with various 'objective' reasons. But I considered then and still consider that it was due to poor management, an irresponsible attitude by the managers to their work, a lack of the necessary educational work with people.

I could not accept this. I exposed shortcomings at meetings of the buro of economic analysis, and named the people responsible. The director of the state farm N. Gruzinskii, who took over a successful farm and then started spoiling things, did not like this. And later, when I informed the People's Control organs about some disgraceful matters, other managers were displeased too.

They quickly organised an attack on me. First they took me off the housing list on the quiet, and I lost my place in the queue for flats, and then all of a sudden I was dismissed. I was obliged to appeal to the republic People's Control Committee. I was reinstated. Then the director approached the matter differently: he closed the planning department, and transferred all its work to me alone, ordered the secretary not to type material on planning questions, prevented the accounting department from giving me material for analysis, prohibited my attending meetings with workers on the farm. For two years I was not given the leave due to me, and if eventually I got it, it was through the procuracy. More than once I and my children were evicted from our 17 square metres room in a hostel which was temporarily allocated to us while waiting for permanent housing. The humanity of our laws each time enabled me and my family to return. Then my rent was increased to 11 rubles 32 kopeks per bed.

Let me add to this that N. Gruzinskii himself lived for four years in a many-roomed government flat with all comforts, while a private home was being built for him, and during all this time he didn't pay a single kopek in rent, which amounted to nearly 1700 rubles, not a kopek for the use of electricity, which the chief accountant wrote off as a farm expense. Now Gruzinskii lives in his two-storey brick house with a brick barn, a cellar and a fence, built by casual workers [*shabashniki*] who had been hired to put up production units.

The director built himself an expensive house. But I am not writing this out of envy. It is painful to think that the summer camp for livestock that he started building was never put into use and is now broken up. The disinfectant bath, the annex to the farm hostel, etc. are also unfinished, and bricks, concrete, asphalt, lime, timber for building them were written off. And all this was above the norms and without proper accounting, overstating the losses.

Superintendent V. Gorbenko and his wife Z. Gorbenko, a norm-setter, drew up false work rosters for the *shabashniki*, which the director then authorised and the chief accountant V. Parniko signed. Gruzinskii hired a home help, whom Gorbenko put down on the roster as a building worker. On Gruzinskii's instructions the farm took on 'dead souls' who did no work but received money.

The deputy chief accountant M. Shatskaya paid out a large sum of money for a clearly phoney work roster, and when I made a fuss about it because if we went on like that the whole farm would be robbed, she was allowed to give in her own notice. O. Gruzinskaya, the director's wife, an inspector in the cadres department, forged Shatskaya's workbook, giving her an uninterrupted work record when in fact there had been several interruptions. The head of the pig farm M. Dovgo was short of 262 centners of meat on 1 January 1978. Gruzinskii and his wife drew up a voluntary discharge. Tons of meat were falsely written off, as if the meat had spoilt. Farm horses were sold off to some scoundrels ...

In sum, the list of the most various abuses could be extended. I informed the district party committee and the republic Ministry of Food about them. My letters were sent back to the same place where these things had occurred, and there they 'drew conclusions', 'took measures' – they evicted my children from the hostel, and generally covered me with dirt. They even expelled me from the party. As they say, I was 'put under expulsion'.

I appealed to the province party committee. Thanks to the head of the agricultural department A. Kikot', instructor M. Gashchenko and other comrades, who took an honest attitude to this matter, my party card was returned to me. The province soviet of people's deputies restored me to my place in the housing queue.

After this my submission to the investigative organs concerning the squandering of socialist property, about which I had earlier told the district party committee, was confirmed. The farm director Gruzinskii was removed from his post, and criminal charges were brought against the culprits.

The general director of the Belotserkov production agricultural canning association, to which our farm is subordinated, appointed a new director, M. Mandzyuk. But he had evidently already adopted the appropriate attitude, because he immediately began looking for various 'blemishes' in my work, and wrote a number of statements about me to the association. After that one directive after another descended on me ... And now I have been dismissed again.

Yes, I would like to tell you about another matter. It was established that the former director Gruzinskii and his friends overpaid the *shabashniki* by 25 709 rubles, which brought the farm a significant loss. True, the Belotserkov procuracy issued a resolution pardoning them under the amnesty. The resolution was sent to the district party committee, so that those communists guilty of criminal acts would be penalised through party channels. From there it was sent to the farm, to the primary party organisation. And what happened? At the party meeting not a word was said against the former director and his friends.

The meeting restricted itself to a discussion about Gruzinskii and his circle. The district party committee changed this decision because of its lack of principle. But this was later. On that day I again got into trouble. The new party secretary V. Genailo (related by blood to the 'circle'), who was sent to us from outside, declared that he was going to expel me from the party and kick me out of my job; he abused me personally although I am old enough to be his mother. The director V. Mandzyuk supported him, and threw all the village gossip at me.

What for? I cannot understand what motivated the party secretary who had worked on the farm and in his party position for 21 days. I cannot understand what motivated the director. Sometimes he made demands on me that were apparently correct, but then himself turned out to be dishonest. After his appointment to the post of director V. Mandzyuk illegally received 500 rubles travelling expenses and returned them to the till only after a year, following inspection.

They say that I am an unsociable person, that I am nervous, that I can lose control and be rude. I admit that it happens. And afterwards, if I feel that I was wrong, I apologise. I have been criticised and penalised through party channels for this. But not once has anyone asked why it happens. With 25 years of service and 11 years working at the farm, I still have not obtained normal housing conditions and am still living with my children in the hostel. Meanwhile, V. Usmanov, someone who came to the farm from goodness knows where, a lover of spirits and a former party secretary, was given a five-room detached house for a family of two. Gorbenko also got a similar detached house. Neither of them now work at the farm but they have retained their homes. The new party secretary V. Genailo has also been allocated a six-room cottage. And these people say to me: be polite ...

Chief accountant V. Parnikoza, in spite of her financial 'tricks', stayed on as chief accountant at the farm, but now with a personal supplement to her salary, and now she lectures me: I suffered all these misfortunes because I 'didn't keep in step'. Gruzinskaya is still working in her post, also with a raise. Her husband, the former director of the farm, was appointed by general director Pavlov as head of the transport shop of the association. And they want me to smile at them?

They certainly 'keep in step'. But I do not want to and cannot do that. True, I once gave in and did them a favour. I helped the director to issue an illegal instruction transferring some farm machine operators who were working on the harvest to another grade, giving them somewhat higher wages. But I don't commend myself for this. My father, an invalid of the Great Patriotic War, taught me another way. My older sister, whose work in the years of post-war ruin was rewarded with a Gold Star and two Orders of Lenin, also taught me another way.

No, I am not able to engage in deceitful methods of planning, which my former managers constantly demanded of me. I cannot lie – draw up a plan understating the weight of cattle and pigs, and artificially understating the production of milk, meat and vegetables. This path of deceiving the government has been chosen by our association and by some other farms in the district. Last year we had millions of rubles losses ...

Five years ago I passed a course of higher education in Odessa with distinction. Two years ago I passed a reassessment at the farm with distinction. And now it appears, I am a good-for-nothing specialist, a poor worker ...

From the Editors
When G. Zinkevich's letter was already at the printers, she wrote to us again: 'On my request, instructor M. Gashchenko from the agricultural department of Kiev province party committee again paid a visit. As a result I was fixed up with a similar post in another farm.

But what concerns me is this: why don't we struggle enough with those who behave illegally, who abuse their positions, pursue only their own interests? People tell me in such cases that our state is massive – that you can't keep an eye on everyone. I disagree with this point of view.'

As we see, a person who insists on our principles comes into sharp conflict with her colleagues. What is their position? What is the position of the party organisation, the district party committee? This is what needs to be seriously discussed, and needs to be evaluated in a principled way. It is a question of the duty of a party member in the struggle against shortcomings.

'Who to keep in step with', *Pravda*, 28 December 1981, p. 3.
The editors have received a reply from V. Tsybul'sko, first secretary of the Kiev province party committee, to G. Zinkevich's letter published in *Pravda* on 26 October under the headline 'Who to keep in step with?' He told us that the statement had been discussed by the buro of the province party committee. It was noted that the facts described in it had indeed occurred, in particular those connected with the violation of party principles in the selection and education of cadres, violation of financial discipline and labour law, mismanagement, report-padding and abuses, and also the lowering of economic indicators in the Kalinin state farm under the Belotserkovsk fruit and vegetable processing plant.

The provincial party committee has closely studied the situation in the district, the style and methods of work of the Belotserkovsk district party committee and district executive committee. The party organisation, the party committee of the state farm and its former secretaries, V. Gorbenko and V. Ginailo, indeed failed to give the necessary political assessment of violations and abuses. They often covered up and protected the culprits, helped to create a family circle, themselves violated the norms of party life and permitted reprisals for criticism.

The general director of Belotserkovsk fruit and vegetable processing plant, Yu. Pavlov, and his former deputies, did not ensure the necessary level of control of their subordinate enterprises. They were unscrupulous in assessing the unsatisfactory state of affairs with the fulfilment of plans and socialist tasks, the cases of mismanagement and abuses on the part of certain executives and specialists, violations of labour law, and the transfer of managers who had discredited themselves from one post to another.

The district soviet executive committee, and personally its chairman E. Shevchuk, did not always carry out real control over the activities of agricultural enterprises in the district, did not ensure a strict observance of soviet laws, an active struggle with the squandering of socialist property. The chairman of the district executive committee and his deputies flagrantly broke the established rules for registering and allocating housing, permitted red tape, bureaucratism, a soulless attitude to people, and sent incorrect information to the higher organs about letters and submissions by citizens concerning violations in the allocation of housing.

The buro of the Belotserkovsk city party committee and its first secretary, V. Lapada, knew about all these shortcomings. But instead of responding to them in a timely and principled way, and putting a decisive end to the abuses and incorrect behaviour of some managers, they checked the signals superficially and restricted themselves to half measures.

After the paper's statement, there was a meeting of the primary party organisation, where communists gave on the whole a correct, principled response to the negative phenomena that had occurred.

As a result of a resolution of the Belotserkovsk district party committee, the former directors of Kalinin state farm Gruzinskii and Mandzyuk have been expelled from the party, together with former chief accountant Parnikoz, chairman of the state farm workers' committee Shevchenko, and district procurator Pavlovskii. The general director of the Belotserkovsk fruit and vegetable plant has been given a strict reprimand to be entered in his work record; other people who allowed violations have been strictly punished.

The buro of the province party committee, taking this into account, drew up a resolution pointing out serious shortcomings in the style of work of the Belotserkovsk district party committee, in the selection, allocation and education of cadres, pointing out its incorrect approach to flagrant breaches of party and state discipline. The first secretary of the district party committee V. Lapada was strictly reprimanded for these shortcomings. The chairman of the district executive committee E. Shevchuk was given a strict reprimand to be entered in his work record. He has been discharged from his post. The province procurator, party member V. Bogachev, was criticised for exercising inadequate control over criminal proceedings against people who had permitted abuses.

The buro of the province party committee noted that I. Lysenko, chairman of the executive committee of Kiev province soviet, and his deputy A. Shulga, did not adequately supervise the work of Belotserkovsk district executive committee, did not make enough demands on its chairman and deputies, did not take the necessary personal action to eliminate the shortcomings that had been described in the letter. The buro noted the statement by A. Shulga that the province executive committee is taking concrete measures to help Kalinin state farm and the association to improve their economic performance.

It was also noted that secretary of the province party committee N. Tkachenko tolerated the superficial approach to the response to violations by executives of the farm and association, did not make sufficient demands on province and district party committee officials to take steps after investigating the letters.

The province and Belotserkovsk executive committees have been instructed to resolve the problem of housing for G. Zinkevich's family in the near future. At the same time certain shortcomings in her own behaviour were noted. On her request she has been given a job as chief economist at 'Rossiya' collective farm, where she is at present working.

The province party committee buro obliged the city and district committees of the party to strengthen their struggle with violations of party and state discipline.

The editors also received a reply from the deputy procurator of the Ukraine SSR, S. Skopenko. He informs us that the material in 'Who to keep in step with?', which raises questions about abuses by officials of Kalinin state farm and about the fact that criminal proceedings against the former director of the farm N. Gruzinskii and others were dropped, has been checked by an on-the-spot visit by an official of the Ukraine SSR procuracy. The facts set out in G. Zinkevich's letter were confirmed.

As a result of the complaint by G. Zinkevich, and on the basis of an investigation and an inspection of financial–economic activity at Kalinin state farm, Belotserkovsk district procuracy brought criminal charges under article 165 of the Ukraine Criminal Code (abuse of official position) and carried out an investigation. It was established that as a result of violations of existing norms and rates, together with other abuses by the farm managers, the farm suffered a loss of 30 000 rubles.

After establishing the guilt of the managers, investigator I. Baliichuk twice unjustifiably dropped the criminal proceedings. At present the decision to drop the case has been reversed by the Kiev province procuracy and an additional investigation has been ordered.

The matters raised by G. Zinkevich have been discussed at a meeting of the collegium of Kiev province procuracy. The Belotserkovsk district procuracy investigator and district procurator V. Pavlovskii have been strictly reprimanded for allowing red-tape, an incomplete investigation, and dropping a criminal case without justification. This has been brought to the attention of S. Bondarenko, head of the investigation department of the province procuracy, in the clearest terms.

The letter 'Who to keep in step with?', and the course of investigation of this criminal case, have also been discussed by the Ukraine SSR procuracy.

Comments

(1) Complaints to the press about abuse of office are usually reviewed by journalists. But on occasion, as in this case, a letter is published in full, and the critic is allowed to speak for herself.

(2) The writer has a solid record as a rank and file political activist. Complaints about abuse of office often come from such people, who perhaps find it difficult to cope with the conflict between their role as guardians of law and morality, and the demands made on them by 'real life'.

(3) As in case 2, the story concerns financial irregularities, and the uncooperative employee was someone with inside financial knowledge. But more was involved here than padding the accounts in order to get 'undeserved bonuses'. There was also embezzlement of meat, illegal use of building materials for private construction, forgery of documents and phoney work rosters.

(4) The account gives a vivid impression of the tension between indulgence from the district and province authorities (party, government and procuracy) and pressure from higher up to ensure that something is seen to be done. In this case the higher party authorities (either in Kiev or in Moscow) evidently took a grave view of the matter. The ramifications were serious enough to allow the exposure of an extensive network of protection, and some relatively stiff penalties (expulsion from the party) were handed out. The first secretary of the province party committee was put in the position of publicly criticising the province committee itself, as well as the lower levels. The emphasis in the report on the complicity of the legal apparatus is also a sure sign of the seriousness of the response that the affair eventually produces.

Case 4

V. Ermolaev (*Pravda* correspondent), Stavropol province, 'Although the facts were established', *Pravda*, 2 October 1979, p. 2.

A letter came to the Irkutsk city party committee. R. Bogaichuk, warehouse head at the fruit and vegetable trade agency, said that an atmosphere of complete indulgence and impunity had developed in the collective. Department head T. Nakonechnikova, for example, was abusing her position, was rude to subordinates, and the director V. Borchevskii was conniving at it.

The letter was sent on to the Kirov district party committee. The party committee instructed an activist, Ya. Lisitsyn, a participant in the Great Patriotic War and a former people's judge, to investigate the signal. This principled and competent person uncovered the same shortcomings in the trade organization that had been mentioned in the letter, together with many others. Produce is badly stored, losses from spoilage are great. There have often been cases of embezzlement and the offenders are not always made answerable.

On the basis of the materials of the investigation the first secretary of the Kirov district party committee told the city party committee:

'The facts have been established. The primary party organisation will discuss them.'

And so a meeting of the party buro of the trade organisation was called. The tone of the meeting was immediately set by the director:

'There is no need to discuss the results of the investigation in the collective. This meeting will be enough. I'll say it straight: we won't hold anything against Taisa Stepanova.'

Other members of the buro supported him, lavishing compliments on the department head. If a stranger were to appear, he would surely think that this was some sort of celebration in honour of Nakonechnikova in connection with some special services, or that it was a jubilee. The discussion did not in any way consider the serious misdemeanours.

There was someone there from outside. And not just anybody, but a representative of the city party committee, G. Samoilenko. One might have thought that she would turn the discussion in the necessary direction, would remind them what the meeting was about, would say that people had earlier complained, and with justice, about T. Nakonechnikova. But it happened otherwise. In her speech, Samoilenko, a city party committee instructor, gave the party buro members the following advice:

'You should penalise Bogaichuk for "scribbling". Things are going quite well here, one feels a sense of solidarity.'

How can one explain an official of the city party committee adopting such a position? Maybe Samoilenko, after thoroughly examining the situation, did not agree with the results of the investigation carried out by the district party committee? She had explained her conclusions to the city party committee and was now acting on its behalf? No, nothing of the kind. The essence of the matter was different. Samoilenko is a friend of Nakonechnikova, and since she valued her long-standing personal relationship above all else, spoke in her defence. Thus unscrupulousness got the upper hand.

Only a statement by party buro member N. Panezhina differed from the chorus of enthusiastic praise addressed to Nakonechnikova. She did not agree with the incorrect appraisal of the department head and said:

'Everyone, Taisa Stepanova, knows about your rudeness. You dress people down and insult them.'

The participants in the discussion appeared not to hear these words. They were not to be found later in the typed minutes of the meeting, although N. Panezhina was taking notes and had written down the important points of her own statement.

The buro resolved: to restrict itself to a discussion of the results of the investigation of the letter, and to take its author before the comrade's court – for bringing unfounded accusations against the managers of the organisation.

And this is the most amazing thing: Yu. Barkhatov, secretary of the district party committee, approved the substance of this unscrupulous resolution, setting it out in his reply to the city committee. Having first admitted that the facts had been established, he suddenly agreed with a quite different opinion. Why? Yurii Mikhailovich sighs:

'The complaints from the trade organisation usually mention that the management is protected by officials of the city party committee. This is how it happened in the present case.'

Serious shortcomings were uncovered when the letter was checked, but after the 'discussion' at the party buro meeting, the shortcomings were not eradicated, the guilty people did not suffer even the slightest anxiety. But life became unpleasant for the author of the letter. They started to take reprisals against R. Bogaichuk immediately, as soon as she had appealed to the city party committee. Before that she had no bad marks against her name – on the contrary, she had been rewarded for her conscientious work. And now all of a sudden the director issued three reprimands in nine days!

Reprisals against the warehouse head were organised in the comrade's court as well. G. Shcherbatyuk, chairperson of the court, refused to chair the hearing, pleading that she was too busy. But the hearing was held none the less, and in order to please the director it was decided that the warehouse head should be dismissed and the materials passed on to the investigative organs. The accusations were so obviously unobjective that the management did not even attempt to carry out the 'sentence'. Bogaichuk had got a fright – and that was enough. It would teach her not to criticise the management again!

She turned to *Pravda*. The editors sent her letter to the Irkutsk city party committee to be checked. But there was no check on the substance of the matter. In the city committee and in the trade agency they again reproached R. Bogaichuk for 'scribbling'. The reply to the editors ran: 'Certain events took place and appropriate measures were taken at the time.'

But were they appropriate? For example, criminal proceedings were started against a number of employees for large-scale embezzlement. They were dropped in connection with the amnesty. The guilty ones were fined, except for T. Nakonechnikova. She was not disciplined through party channels, and there was no demand for her to pay damages.

'So, she's writing!' was the first angry reaction of the management to the intractable warehouse head. Now it was decided to get rid of her once and for all. By any means. During the severe frosts her radiators were switched off. The message was: it's time to leave. She held firm. Then the warehouse was closed down, under the pretext that it was going to be demolished, and her job was cut.

The 'plaintiff' was transferred to the accounting department, where the pay was less. Soon a procuracy commission decided: R. Bogaichuk had been cut unfairly and must be reinstated; there were no grounds for bringing her before a comrade's court, giving her a reprimand. But the director ignored the findings of the commission.

Another letter came to the paper, from Ya. Lisitsyn, who was outraged by this gross suppression of criticism. This time the editors asked the Irkutsk province committee to examine the long drawn out affair. Their investigation uncovered an extremely unsightly picture in the trade organisation. Losses by that time had reached half a million rubles. Spirits were being drunk on the premises with managers taking part. They were entertaining themselves with funds allocated to the winners of competitions. They permitted 'distortions' in the allocation of bonuses. The critical remarks of the working people were ignored. Many employees say indignantly: T. Nakonechnikova, while scoffing at her subordinates, engaged in real blackmail. For example, she takes produce from shops, but if a naive shop head should mutter something about payment, he will hear abuse or an ironic: 'You'll manage!'

After the check on Ya. Lisitsyn's letter, P. Mosyagin, the secretary of the province party committee, told the editors: 'The Kirov district committee has been instructed to examine the abnormal state of affairs in the trade agency, the cases of incorrect behaviour on the part of certain managers.'

Yet the months passed and the district committee remained silent. Ya. Lisitsyn again writes to the editors. In Irkutsk they look for the materials relating to the investigation of the communist's letter, and all of a sudden the materials can't be found: there was no record of them in the district, nor in the city, nor in the province party committee. What happened was this.

On the day when the buro of the party committee met to analyse the situation in the trade agency, a frightened T. Nakonechnikova came to the secretary of the city committee I. Osadchii: 'They want to punish me and to consider dismissing me!' And so Yu. Barkhatov was advised to postpone the discussion ...

Let us suppose that the city party secretary doubted the correctness of the district committee's proposed resolution. Then there should have been a further investigation of the facts, perhaps at a meeting of the city party committee. But the documents were simply removed and hidden in a safe. I. Osadchii did not allow the district committee to carry out the decision of the province party committee – to assess the behaviour of the managers of the trade organisation from a party standpoint.

There should have been a rigorous appraisal of the attitude taken by Samoilenko, who shamelessly protected her friend. The instructor's unscrupulous behaviour of course called for a tough discussion within the walls of the city party committee about the duty of party officials.

The Kirov district party committee did, very belatedly, examine the results of the checks. But the state of affairs in the trade organisation was not thoroughly analysed. There was no question of considering T. Nakonechnikova's dismissal. She was given a strict reprimand to be entered in her work record 'for shortcomings in her work and for rudeness'. There was no mention of abuses. V. Borshchevskii and other ardent defenders of the department head were not even reprimanded.

Two and a half months later a closed party meeting was held at the trade organisation. On the advice of the director, communists were simply informed about the district committee's resolution, and there was no discussion. They took note of it and then, it's true, forgot to listen to the management's report on measures to eliminate shortcomings pointed out by the district committee.

'There have been no significant changes here', according to the deputy director V. Balkanov. Taisa Stepanova goes on insulting her subordinates. She shows a great interest in warehouses and depots, where she gets people to run around for her. Meanwhile she neglects her own department – retail trade. The number of complaints from customers has now doubled.

This state of affairs is also causing concern to the new secretary of the party buro G. Shcherbatyuk. The director rarely consults her, the role of the party organisation has been undermined. Of course, Galina Nikolaevna is herself partly to blame, since she has not shown the necessary firmness and consistency. But the district party committee has not helped her either.

Many good employees are leaving the collective. Especially those who did not accept the shortcomings, who were uncomplimentary about the managers when the complaints were being investigated. The accountant N. Panezhina was also driven to leave – a member of the party buro and a non-staff inspector of the city People's Control Committee. She often criticised the disorganisation, tried to put a stop to abuses which occurred with Nakonechnikova's participation ...

So that was how things turned out: communists exposed serious shortcomings in the trade organisation, but no significant measures were taken to improve the position. First instructor G. Samoilenko behaved unscrupulously out of 'friendship', then the city party committee secretary turned out to be an ally of V. Borshchevskii and T. Nakonechnikova.

The attitude taken by certain officials of this party committee causes special concern. Sometimes they not only fail to help the district committee to improve work with cadres, but also hinder it. The fruit and vegetable trade agency is not the only example. For instance, there were complaints about the head of the trade department of the city executive committee I. Torgovnikova. Using her position she helped her relations and 'important people' to acquire cars. The city committee informed the province committee: they had recommended that I. Torgovnikova should be discharged. But she was allowed to leave 'voluntarily', and was immediately appointed director of the Levoberezhnyi trade organisation.

G. Samoilenko, 'friend' of the fruit and vegetable trade agency, is also doing alright. Recently she was appointed deputy head of personnel for the province trade administration. One must hope that the appropriate organs will finally deliver the necessary judgement on this ugly affair, and on those that protect employees who have compromised themselves.

Comments

(1) There is not much detail about the offences. But it seems that they were serious, since there is a mention of criminal proceedings in connection with large-scale embezzlement.

(2) The story again highlights the pressure on party committees (and on procuracy officials) to be seen to be doing something, but also shows how the control was blunted by relationships of protection. The effect was that criminal proceedings were dropped, that some lower-

level people were penalised (very mildly), and that the higher-level offenders got off scot free. One of the main protectors in the city party committee was even transferred to a sensitive position in trade.

Case 5

Yu. Mukimov (*Pravda* correspondent), Tashkent, 'It's not a question of obstinacy', *Pravda*, 26 September 1979, p. 3.

F. Efimovskii, a worker at the Tashkent excavator plant, sent *Pravda* a long confessional letter. It starts with the story of how, five years ago, he gave in his notice 'voluntarily'. What induced him to come to such an extreme decision?

The main motive was the almost complete absence of the necessary safety conditions in the workplace. He spoke about this many times to the foreman – it didn't help. He wrote a memorandum to the safety engineer – that didn't produce any reaction either.

Efimovskii's announcement met with a hostile reception from the plant management. Efimovskii was summoned to the director's office. There already waiting for him were the party secretary, the trade union chairman and the shop-head. The conversation started with a threat:

'So, you've decided to quit? OK, we'll let you go, but not voluntarily, we'll dismiss you for absenteeism.'

'But I've had no absences!' said the amazed Efimovskii.

'If you haven't had any yet, you soon will!' replied the shop-head Yu. Pelishenko.

Quickly they got together a false document about Efimovskii's absences and similar fake minutes of a supposed meeting of the shop trade union committee that had 'demanded' the dismissal of the 'absentee'. True, later an investigation easily showed that this was a sham. Yet nothing happened to the people guilty of the forgery.

After a time it was suggested to Efimovskii that he should transfer to the foundry. They said: 'The pay is better there. In the foundry you'll be first in the queue for a flat.' Efimovskii agreed, although he did not want to move from his old workplace. He understood: he wasn't wanted. Soon his family of three were indeed allocated housing. But not a flat as was promised, but a room in a hostel. Yet it was clear to everyone: if they had wanted to they could have arranged proper housing for a skilled worker. It should be noted too that

Efimovskii's wife, Galina Ivanovna Kibireva, also worked at the factory, she was a young specialist.

I must point out that this young worker is not just concerned about his own needs. Most of all he is worried by the unhealthy climate in the collective, about the fact that the factory year after year is among the laggers, that the norms and principles of labour law are being broken.

Back in 1973 a decision was taken to close down the foundry, where the conditions of work did not meet technical and health standards. After the decision was taken, the ventilation system was dismantled. But a certain time passed and another directive followed: to carry out a reconstruction of the shop without halting production. To this day no one has considered restoring the ventilation. The shop has been operating for six years now without it.

'It is hard working in the foundry', says the head of the enterprise dispensary N.A. Kovalevskaya, 'in the street it is 40 degrees, inside the building the temperature is even higher. Sometimes you can't go past the shop with open eyes – you'll get dust and soot in them. And nearby there are houses, a nursery, an orthopaedic clinic.'

Of course, the foundry workers understand that you cannot carry out a reconstruction in two seconds. But it's been six years and the matter has not been resolved. The plant management blame the situation on the sluggishness of the builders, the latter in turn have complaints about the management. And things do not move.

The difficult conditions of work are further complicated by serious shortcomings in the organisation of labour. Here is an extract from Efimovskii's letter to *Pravda*: 'Every day on the notice board at the main entrance they put up the latest information. They always tell us about the same thing – about troubles in setting up production and turning out products, about systematic failure to carry out delivery plans. It happens that they send a report to the ministry about plan fulfilment, when down in the plant we are "making up fulfilment". We have to work on rest days. For the same reason it sometimes happens that for the first ten days we are working on account for the previous month.'

The young worker has more than once already raised the question of disorganisation in production. With what results? There have been many checks, which confirmed everything that Efimovskii wrote about. But nothing was actually done to get rid of the shortcomings. And now, someone is already spreading rumours about Efimovskii as a 'collector of gossip', a 'scribbler, casting aspersions on the collective'. As if in passing, they have started saying about him: 'Doesn't Efimovskii understand whose hands he's playing into? Isn't it time to silence him?' He began getting penalties one after another.

But he wasn't 'silenced'. As an honest worker he couldn't remain indifferent to mismanagement. At the same time he sometimes got excessively angry, allowed himself to get quick-tempered, but this was understandable.

There is a lot of idle time in the shop, but so-called 'idle time sheets' do not get filled out. Because of low labour discipline, two shifts have become standard, an idle shift being compensated by working on rest days. No distinctions are made between the quality of work by brigades in different shifts, poor work gets thrown into the common pot and it turns out that people who produced the best results suffer a considerable economic loss.

It had become commonplace to reduce the rates without preparing the machines. For example, they used to pay a ruble for doing a part. Now they pay 60 kopeks – the other 40 are paid as bonuses. As a result the whole notion of bonuses is eroded. Only administrative personnel get bonuses for overfulfilment, what's more these are often illegal because, as already pointed out, the reports about plan fulfilment are fictitious. The thirteenth pay packet has become almost symbolic.

Under these conditions it is clear that the moral climate of the collective cannot be healthy. And not the least reason for that is the confusion that reigns in the payment of wages: for some there is over-payment, undeserved bonuses, others on the contrary are underpaid.

The enterprise is not carrying out its house-building programme. It cannot boast one rest-base, not one dispensary, nor a decent pioneer camp.

A year ago the Kuibyshev district party committee in the city of Tashkent, replying to a signal by workers to the editors of *Pravda*, stated that 'there were indeed shortcomings in the management of the Tashkent excavator factory. Conclusions were also drawn.' The secretary of the party committee M. Kulagin and chairman of the trade union committee M. Makarov have been discharged from their positions. The director B. Ramzi was also discharged and pensioned off. But there has not been a clear and principled discussion in the plant, with the participation of the collective, about the whole state of affairs.

A new management has come to the enterprise, with young and energetic people. One might have expected that they would definitely learn from the sad lessons of the past. But these expectations were not met.

It should be said that it is not only Viktor Efimovskii who is concerned about the situation at the excavator plant. The editors have received a similar letter signed by a large group of workers. So it is not at all a question of the 'scribbler' Efimovskii, as the managers of the enterprise still try to make out. Although they themselves admit that it is just these letters that help to expose shortcomings. We must understand once and for all: the workers, Efimovskii included, write critical letters not out of 'obstinacy', but because they are convinced that the enterprise can and must work better. One cannot brush aside such complaints, or dispose of them with half-hearted resolutions.

The Kuibyshev district and Tashkent city party committees ought thoroughly to investigate the situation that has developed here, to expose the causes of mismanagement in a principled way, to help the collective find confidence in its strength and succeed.

Comments

(1) This report stresses breaches of labour law. Most of the cases in this chapter involve such breaches, because of illegal attempts to get rid of employees. But here the emphasis is on the conditions of work – poor safety and illegal overtime. The story makes some effort to indicate the connection between these practices and the pressures of the plan.

(2) The report points to an apparently chaotic state of affairs in the payment of wages and bonuses and in particular, to the way in which false reporting in relation to wages is seen as necessary to maintain a certain minimum level of earnings.

(3) The plant had evidently been performing very badly for some time, which might explain why it came in for criticism. But the account mentions that a collective protest had been sent in by a number of workers – perhaps about the housing and poor facilities – which could also have encouraged the exposé.

Case 6

V. Kazakhov (Our special correspondent), Komsomolsk, 'Someone else's misfortune', *Sotsialisticheskaya Industriya*, 14 June 1979, p. 3.

Nine years ago V. Nizhnichenko, the head of 'Kremenchugrudstroi' trust, issued his first directive dismissing A. Kirichenko from his position as head of the department for production–technical acquisitions. In the directive it said 'because of staff cuts'. The second paragraph instructed the head of the cadres department 'to nominate a candidate for the post of head of the acquisitions department within two days'.

What lay behind these thin-looking 'staff cuts'? There was, undoubtedly, an earnest desire to dismiss A. Kirichenko. But such a desire can arise, for example, because of personal hostility to one's subordinate and for a number of other irrelevant reasons. That is why laws exist, gathered together in the Labour Code, which all people in responsible positions are obliged to follow. Did V. Nizhnichenko have legally justified objections to his subordinate engineer? If he had, they should have been stated in his directive, then he would not have had to resort to lies, the weapons of injustice.

The Kremenchug procurator naturally brought a protest against the directive. Then the director, 'after considering the procurator's protest', issued a second order dismissing A. Kirichenko, this time on grounds of 'unsuitability for the post'. And again the director misfired: the republic ministry and province procuracy said that this move was illegimate too. A. Kirichenko was given a job on the same level – he became head of a work planning group.

Finally, in February 1976 the director delivered his third blow to A. Kirichenko: he was removed from his post as head of the work planning group and was offered a job as senior engineer. He considered this demotion unwarranted and refused to take on the new duties. He got two reprimands for this and was dismissed.

I shall not weary the reader with a recital of all the ways in which the trust still tries to create the impression that A. Kirichenko's dismissal was lawful. An instruction from the 'Krivbasstroi' combine, to which the trust is subordinated, states quite unambiguously: 'The order dismissing A. Kirichenko was issued without sufficient legal grounds ... The dismissal order is to be withdrawn; a post is to be found for A. Kirichenko with the agreement of both sides.'

The epilogue: the head of the trust recently earned an honourable rest; they quickly found him other work to do in the town – easier and to his taste. Things were worse for Kirichenko: so far (after three years!) the present head of the trust, A. Petrenkov, has still not carried out the instruction to find Kirichenko a job 'with the agreement of both sides'.

That is the story.

And so, all the orders dismissing A. Kirichenko from the trust, issued between 1970 and 1976, were reversed at higher levels, they were all shown to be invalid and in contravention of the labour laws. How did it happen that the person who was found guilty and punished during all these years was the one who defended the law? After all, the conflict did not take place behind closed doors. There were people nearby, who had a right to sort things out and to put out the fire in time. Yes, there were, and A. Kirichenko knocked on these doors more than once. 'I sent off 349 letters to various organisations with a request for help', the engineer told the editors. 'But I received about 200 *pro forma* replies from unscrupulous officials, documents that wilfully distorted the labour laws, and also repeated all the gossip and lies.'

That was the point. The head of the trust was *allowed* to scorn the labour laws. And he was allowed to not because of a conscious collective defence of injustice (I am far from suggesting this), but for reasons of another kind.

The case of A. Kirichenko became for many people in Komsomolsk a test of one of the most important human qualities – the ability to be really attentive towards a person. Everyone knows what this quality means: to be attentive means to be incapable of ignoring someone else's misfortune, it means you are always ready to help. This is why you demonstrate real sensitivity when another person needs your help, not when you need something from someone else ... We all understand this quite well in principle. But suppose that life presents us with a situation when not words but deeds are demanded. How shall we prove our moral worth in practice?

The party organisation and trade union committee of the trust immediately took the administration's word, as if this was quite self-evident. Why? Did V. Nizhnichenko's conclusions seem to them convincing? Yes, they seemed convincing because accepting them was easy, it was simpler (besides if they supported the director, that would not threaten any unpleasantness in their jobs). And the arguments in defence of A. Kirichenko seemed unwanted because they demanded concrete and courageous actions. And that would mean using one's strength and energies ... Hence the response: everything which vindicated A. Kirichenko in his conflict with the director was ignored; only the arguments in favour of the director (even if the evidence had to be really dragged in by the ears) were taken into account.

Here is an example. A. Kirichenko explains the origins of his conflict with the head in the following way (it is set down in the record of one of the court hearings). When working as head of the acquisitions department, he once refused to sign a document writing off a wagon load of timber. He carelessly asked out loud: and what happened to 60 cubic metres of timber? In reply to this the trust head decided after a few days to cut the post of head of the acquisitions department.

Was anyone in the trust interested in this affair? Did anyone try to check it? And was it so difficult to do this in time, before they hastened to destroy the documents in the department? They simply closed their ears to the affair with the wagon load of timber. Similarly, the many submissions that A. Kirichenko made to the trade union committee and personally to the party secretary of the trust, N. Mandzyuk, were ignored.

Yet when there was no need for speed, the representatives of the social organisations were enviably efficient. The head asked for trade union sanction to dismiss A. Kirichenko – the union committee in just a few seconds (not one member of the committee had a chance to speak!), and in the absence of the person who was to be dismissed, unanimously raised their hands in agreement. In a little while this organisation would take an even bolder decision: to refuse to examine any of A. Kirichenko's submissions.

'Yes, we acted without principle, we could have been more sensitive', V. Dzyabenko, former trade union chairman, now admits. Yet the union committee, under its present chairman S. Solodnikov, to this day has not examined some of the engineer's complaints.

Of course, in order to justify this attitude, a screen was needed that would calm the conscience a little and at least give the impression that justice had been done. A. Kirichenko was declared a malicious troublemaker, with whom it was quite impossible to work because of his difficult character.

A. Kirichenko is no doubt indeed a difficult person, perhaps somewhat pedantic, and unnecessarily sharp with people. I say 'no doubt', because I saw him after many years of conflict with the trust, when he was without work, had suffered travails with tens of different agencies and courts. In these circumstances even an angelic character would turn sour. But even if we allow that he was never very pleasant in his relationships with people, why should he be judged for something other than that for which he deserves judgement? Why invent imaginary sins for him?

How did those who had positions independent of the trust behave?

A. Kirichenko complained to the city committee of People's Control. And what happened? There they composed a document: 'Taking into account that comrade A.M. Kirichenko has compromised himself in the trust collective with his unworthy behaviour, it is undesirable for him to remain in the collective any longer.' As if the engineer was asking them to help him decide whether it was desirable for him to remain in the trust collective. He was asking them to defend him against the illegal actions of the management, and instead got a regular telling off.

A. Kirichenko got a *pro forma* answer from the secretary of the city party committee A. Kovinko, and A. Verbin, chairman of the city executive committee, did not begin to go into the matter. Several times there were court hearings in connection with the engineer's claims – and here several mistakes were noted by the higher judicial organs.

Why did these mistakes occur?

They came from the same source – from a lack of attentiveness, from indifference to another person's misfortune. Hence the familiar disguise:

'Kirichenko? He's that sort of person, that sort of person ... He's quarrelsome, a troublemaker. He writes ...'

Everyone remembered the fact that Kirichenko *writes*. But nobody considered the main question: does he write the *truth* or not? For some reason no one was interested in the fact that 'that sort of person' had not once been disciplined during his years of work with the trust; the work planning group which he headed fulfilled and overfulfilled its production plans, his specialists won prizes in socialist competitions. I have in front of me a reference, given out to Kirichenko by an attestation commission: the head of the group is described as a literate engineer, a good organiser, socially active.

Now, when I had to show several officials in Komsomolsk documents defending A. Kirichenko, these people threw up their arms and were amazed: so that's how it was, and we didn't know ... But why didn't they know? After all the engineer knocked on their doors. But ... attentiveness always demands concrete *actions*, general phrases are useless; if a person is drowning, then you have to throw yourself in the river. But it's cold in the river, and your clothes suffer, and there isn't time – you're busy with everyday matters. And you start thinking: what sort of person is it who's drowning anyway? ...

Of course, we are all in favour of being caring and sensitive to one another. And whoever is uncaring gets only a critical reaction from us.

Because indifference to a person is always harmful. But there are different kinds of harm. It is one thing when a private person A. is insensitive to another person B. It is quite another when an official who is obliged to defend someone is uncaring. In this case, consideration and sensitivity to others is not just desirable but a duty. And every case of indifference on their part to another's misfortune is a blot on their record. The Philistines, reflecting in their own way on justice in life, have repeated through the ages: those are right who have the most rights. We must not, whether wilfully or not, play into their hands. After all this leaves its traces. To demonstrate this, I shall give a final example.

I asked many people about Anatolii Matveevich: what sort of person is he, how did he work, what sort of relations did he have with others? I was told about his difficult character, but people also noted that he was a knowledgeable engineer, an erudite person, a teetotaller, a good chess player. But I would like to emphasise one detail. The rank and file employees of the trust spoke to me about Kirichenko very unwillingly, warily, often glancing at the door. One of the employees in the work planning group, a former subordinate of A. Kirichenko, refused altogether to meet a correspondent. Why?

It's difficult to say. Maybe he just did not find the time, but maybe because he had drawn his own conclusions from the story of the quarrel between the director of the trust and one of his employees.

Comments

(1) In this story the original problem (the dispute over the disappearing timber) paled in the subsequent struggle over the engineer's rights in labour law. The breaches of labour legislation assumed quite striking proportions. In a period of six years all the attempts to get rid of the recalcitrant employee were reversed higher up, but the management evidently had little to fear as a result, and the hapless critic was apparently left without work for three years.

(2) The account mentions 349 letters. One can imagine the enormous amount of time and energy that this represents – he appealed in vain to 'tens of agencies and courts'. To pursue a case like this when you are pitted against the whole establishment (the People's Control and the courts did not help either) is to become a professional petitioner. The search for justice becomes a life commitment.

Case 7

V. Cherkassov (*Pravda* correspondent), Dnepropetrovsk, 'Sticky fingers', *Pravda*, 18 October 1981, p. 3.

As soon as N. Ustinova had completed her course at the Dnepropetrovsk medical institute, problems arose in her work. After being appointed as head of the in-patient division of the twentieth city hospital, she began the job one month late without good reason, and of course promptly received an administrative penalty. As we see, from the outset it turned out that a person's dream of becoming a doctor and their attitude to the patient are different things. Patients and colleagues alike gradually came to notice this distinction. When taking on patients for hospital treatment, N. Ustinova was for some reason especially interested in their material and social position, which greatly puzzled both the patients and her subordinates.

Later the reason for this great interest on her part, which had nothing to do with her duties, became clear. The new divisional head was engaging in graft [*pobory*]; when she accepted people for hospital treatment she took into account what she could take and from whom. To begin with she was content with things in kind – chickens, fresh fish, brandy, French scent, deficit fabrics. Gradually her appetite grew and she began going on pleasure trips with patients to the woods, to the riverside – with fish soup and shashlyk. Feasts were arranged during working hours.

Naturally, behaviour so unnatural for a person in a responsible position, or simply for an educated person, was punished through administrative channels. After this the jolly trips to the woods stopped, but only for a time. And gradually rumours went around the village of Frunze, which is on the outskirts of Dnepropetrovsk and in the area covered by the twentieth city hospital: the head of the in-patient division takes bribes. The residents became convinced: if you need in-patient treatment, then pay up. Otherwise, 'there are no vacancies'. A person who had once taken the Soviet doctor's oath had become a medical entrepreneur, she was robbing her patients without shame, not even disdaining to take valuable rubles.

The residents tolerated the extortion [*likhoimstvo*] for a long time. But finally they lodged a complaint with the province party committee of the Ukrainian Communist Party, with the Amur–Nizhnedneprovsk district party committee, and also with the Soviet organs. A joint commission of the province and district health departments and the district party committee was set up to check the signals.

The commission uncovered abuses of office and the Amur–Nizhnedneprovsk district procuracy started criminal proceedings. In the course of the investigation it was confirmed that there had been cases of extortion [*likhoimstvo*], so that the courts should have had the last word in this disgraceful story.

Unfortunately, for more than two years the courts did not say this last word. Meanwhile N. Ustinova was transferred from the far outskirts to work at the first city hospital in central Dnepropetrovsk. All this proved possible because of the light-minded and unconscientious attitude of a number of officials.

It started when Ustinova, during the investigation, ran off from the Amur–Nizhnedneprovsk district procuracy to the province psychiatric hospital. Here her brother S. Lubinets installed her in the department of nervous diseases with a unique diagnosis: 'A situational [*situatsionny*] neurosis, arising from a criminal investigation.'

Her attendance at the hospital did not however prevent Ustinova from writing more than ten complaints to higher party and Soviet agencies, in which she really poured dirt on everyone who had participated in investigating her abuses. Including officials of the Amur–Nizhnedneprovsk district party committee. Since she was quite unoccupied, and free to move about the hospital, Ustinova looked for 'useful' people.

Among these useful people was an official in the province procuracy, V. Dyakonov. He gave a personal directive, what's more in written form, to the Babushkin district procuracy in Dnepropetrovsk (to which the case had been transferred), noting that no evidence of bribery [*vzyatki*] had been found in Ustinova's actions, but only of graft [*pobory*].

The new investigator, P. Pavlovskii, immediately understood what his superiors wanted of him and ... dropped criminal proceedings on the grounds that there was no evidence of criminal activity: Ustinova's action was classed as an official misdemeanour [*dolzhnostnoi prostupok*], as graft [*pobory*] and not as a crime, not as bribery [*vzyatochnichestvo*]. His action was supported as well by the Babushkin district procurator I. Mezentsev. I. Mezentsev set out his position officially in a letter to the head of Nizhnedneprovsk district health department, N. Shtefan. After carefully listing which inpatients of the twentieth city hospital had given Ustinova 25 or 75 rubles, who had brought her fish or bottles of scent (all this was confirmed by the investigation), I. Mezentsev came to a surprising conclusion:

> The people listed (these were mostly pensioners *V.Ch.*) gave Ustinova money and fish products not so that she would perform some particular actions as head of the division, but in the hope that they would receive a more attentive attitude during their treatment. Neither in her capacity as head nor in her capacity as doctor did Ustinova perform any actions improving or worsening their position. According to article 168 (part 2) of the Ukrainian Code of Criminal Procedure, the agent of the crime can only be someone in an official position, which doctors are not. Hence, Ustinova cannot be held criminally responsible. For receiving money and fish and other products she can be held responsible on other counts ...

Exactly what other counts, I. Mezentsev did not explain. But so far not a hair on the head of this acquisitive person had been touched. Furthermore, for some time she had begun to look like the victim of a slander. Surprisingly, this amazing impression of her was given by journalists of the *Vechernyi Dnepr*. N. Ustinova approached L. Gamolskii, a correspondent on that paper. He twice wrote articles in its pages defending Ustinova. He made out that what had happened was a reprisal against her by the head of the district health department, communist N. Shtefan, supposedly out of personal hostility. He represented a dishonest person as a fighter for criticism and justice. He wrote these things without even meeting the investigator in charge of the case.

The Dnepropetrovsk city party committee buro, after representations from a party commission under Amur–Nizhnedneprovsk district party committee, examined both the statements in its newspaper, and concluded that they were groundless, incorrect and harmful. But N. Shtefan waited for an apology from the paper in vain. It did not come.

Then he wrote to *Pravda*, defending his honour and dignity as an official and a citizen. The case was dealt with by the province procuracy. It conclusively established that Ustinova had taken more than 700 rubles from her patients, not counting things in kind.

Recently there was a province court case. At its first sitting, under the chairmanship of P. Rumyantsev, the court decided to send the case back for a new investigation. This decision was not convincingly argued. It did not explain what it was that needed further clarification, nor who should carry out the investigation. The judge Rumyantsev and the court secretary recorded many important points in the hearing incorrectly, especially the evidence of witnesses. This was done so crudely that procurator L. Strazhnikov was obliged to send objections to the province court and to set out a correct picture of the court hearing. And the province procurator M. Oberemok brought a protest against the decision to the Ukraine Supreme Court.

The protest was accepted by the highest court in the republic. A new court was appointed under the chairmanship of V.I. Popruga. This court brought the long drawn out case to an end, sentencing the bribe-taker to eight years' imprisonment. For five years after serving her sentence she has no right to engage in medical practice.

Thus, justice triumphed. But the court and the procuracy quarelled for two years about how to classify Ustinova's actions: was it graft or bribery, did she accept gifts in her official capacity or in the capacity of rank-and-file doctor? But to patients it is not important under which 'article' they are being robbed, although from the judicial point of view this establishes the measure of punishment. As we have seen, the court finally took a decision which took into account a person's moral decline and the social danger of her actions. A free medical service is one of the victories of our revolution. And no one has the right to touch it with sticky fingers.

Comments

(1) This is an exposé of the apparently widespread practice of giving something extra to health service employees, in the hope of getting favourable treatment. The account differs from the others in this chapter in that the complaints mentioned were lodged by clients and not by members of the organisation. For understandable reasons, whistleblowing in such situations is not common, since both the giver and the taker are involved in an illicit exchange. However, these complaints were evidently not the immediate reason for the *Pravda* report, but rather the letter from the district health official.

(2) The ins and outs of the case, the personal and bureaucratic wrangles that lie behind it, are impossible to unravel from the narrative. But it is clear that it was the authorities at the district level (the party, the procuracy and perhaps the health department) that wanted to expose the doctor. But she was able to gain support from

some city and provincial officials and to impede this initiative. (Despite the prosecution brought by the province procuracy, she had sufficient support at the province level to put a brake on things.) However, party intervention at a higher level and an appeal to the republic Supreme Court finally decided the issue against her.

(3) The case shows how legal definitions can be manipulated by the procuracy and the courts. In Soviet law you cannot commit an 'official crime' (i.e. bribery) unless you hold an office – hence the search for an alternative description of the offence by the doctor's supporters.

(4) The sentence was a very heavy one. Compare, for example, the almost complete lack of sanctions in case 4, when large-scale embezzlement was said to have been involved. Despite the strenuous and heavy-handed efforts of the journalist, he is not able to show that this doctor was actually guilty of any heinous offence. The gifts and amounts of money involved were quite modest.

Case 8

V. Kravtsov, RSFSR Procurator, 'According to the norms of morality and law', *Pravda*, 27 January 1979, p. 3.

V. Shevchenko, a teacher at the Rostov road construction technical school, was removed from his post. Serious accusations were brought against him, that he had slandered the administrators of the school at meetings and in letters addressed to the party and Soviet organs, that he had tried to discredit honest people, and had misrepresented the state of educational work.

A situation of sharp conflict had developed at the school. Not much was needed: it was only a question of carrying out a comprehensive check and establishing who was right – the teacher or the administrators. And indeed a whole variety of inspectors came from near and far. But the trouble was that from the very beginning they adopted a one-sided and prejudiced attitude to their duties. Willy-nilly every inspector came under the influence of the rumours that were passing from mouth to mouth: Shevchenko is a slanderer.

If one reads the materials of the criminal case that was brought against the people who had denounced Shevchenko, one is amazed at the inattentiveness of the officials who were instructed to inquire into the substance of the issues that were disturbing the school collective. They pushed aside the important matters, the essence of the problem.

For some reason the inspectors focused all their attention on the person of Shevchenko. Who was he, why was he writing all the time, why didn't he stop doing the rounds of the 'authorities'?

Such a distortion, or to speak more correctly a lack of principle, led to false conclusions. The voice of truth was silenced, albeit temporarily. Someone who was not afraid to remain in the minority, to spoil relations with one or two people, someone who had given an example of principled behaviour, was left without support. And his enemies gloated.

The RSFSR Ministry of Road Construction also played an undesirable role in this affair. Brigades twice went out to Rostov-on-Don, led by E. Denisov, deputy head of the department administering education. In his briefcase he had several statements by comrade Shevchenko, in which there was a clear and concise description of the crimes committed by Pastushenko, the head of the school cadres department, and a description of the ugly behaviour of some other employees. But E. Denisov did not approach the matter responsibly enough. Everything that he found in the course of the investigation he explained as 'clerical violations'. The ministry official did not even find time to meet comrade Shevchenko and talk to him. Nor can one ignore the following fact. In the ministry directive, issued in connection with the events that had occurred in the technical school, there was no honest assessment of the behaviour of their representative. They simply pointed out to Denisov that there had been an 'insufficiently deep (?!) analysis in the visits to the technical school in 1977–1978'.

By order of the RSFSR Procuracy a careful investigation of all the circumstances that comrade Shevchenko had mentioned was carried out. It was confirmed that Pastushenko extorted bribes from students, engaged in forgery and falsification of documents. Criminal charges were brought against him and he was sentenced to a five-year term. Some other employees of the technical school were also strictly disciplined. The school administration has been strengthened. Comrade Shevchenko has been reinstated. The court case in Rostov drew the attention of public opinion and gained a wide response.

The finale was as it should have been. The suppression of criticism, as Leonid Ilyich Brezhnev indicated, is a 'violation of the norms of communist morality and of the Fundamental Law of the USSR. This is an evil which must not remain unpunished. We value highly the people's initiative, and nobody will be allowed to destroy this source of our strength!'

In giving full scope to the activity of the Soviet people in the social–political sphere, in production and as citizens, our democracy unites them, directing their efforts towards the common goal. For every working person to know the legal rules, and to be able to apply them in the interests of the nation, is an important feature of the political and judicial culture of socialist society. The Soviet way of life is incompatible with a state of affairs in which people try to counterpose themselves to the collective, in which they act like the Philistine: as long as I'm alright, it's no business of mine.

We have broad possibilities for citizens to express their views on the most diverse questions concerning the work of state, social and economic organs. Let us remember: more than 140 million people took part in the discussion of the draft constitution of the USSR. Their suggestions and comments were closely studied, and taken into account in drawing up the final text of the Fundamental Law.

The party constantly holds at the centre of its attention the problem of developing criticism and making it effective. Everyone who raises a voice against abuses, against attempts to gloss over shortcomings and to turn aside from just criticism must be certain that in any such case the situation will definitely be corrected and the offenders will get their deserts.

In the localities we still have officials who react to criticism as if someone had stepped on their pet corn, and after that they begin to judge everything in the light of their wounded pride ...

Comments

(1) Like case 7, this deals with bribery, although there is no ambiguity about how the actions involved are to be defined in law.

(2) Unlike the other cases, this account is written by a top official, not a staff reporter. This gives added political weight to the statement that it is important to support those who 'raise a voice against abuses'. The statement makes explicit what is present in the other accounts only as a background assumption: the political importance of establishing a link between the concerned citizen and the central controllers by supporting, when the need arises, a critical initiative from below.

4 Whistleblowers, Managers and the State

The cases described in the previous chapter give some idea of the problems that critics are likely to encounter if they blow the whistle. In the discussion that follows I shall explore these problems further and shall try to answer a number of questions that arise from an examination of such material. First, who are the whistleblowers, what practices are they complaining about, and why do they decide to lodge complaints about abuse of office? Second, how do managements typically react to such behaviour, and what resources do they have within the organisation to tackle their critics? Third, how do the agencies of appeal, especially the party organs and the press, respond to this sort of initiative? In addressing these questions one can throw more light on the tension between law and illegality, on the sources of protection, and on the relationship between central and local political power. At the same time, some conclusions can be drawn about the significance of the complaints procedure within the law enforcement process, and within a wider political context. I shall be relying throughout the chapter on a sample of 70 stories of the kind translated in Chapter 3. They were all taken from the national press, mainly from *Pravda*, in the years 1979–83. These stories have been supplemented by other press material, and by discussions with people who have participated in such dramas in one way or another.

1 THE WHISTLEBLOWERS

Who are the whistleblowers, and what are their main concerns? It is clear from the sample that people prepared to take action of this kind can be found in a wide variety of occupations and types of organisation. Their motives for blowing the whistle are also evidently varied. But certain patterns emerge from a study of the press stories, and are worth commenting on.

Occupations

From the 70 stories, I have selected 66 where the source of the complaint is clearly specified. In 25 of these (38 per cent) the complaint came from people in managerial or technical positions in the organisation: for example, engineers, accountants, economists, shop-heads, foremen. It is perhaps not surprising that a high proportion of complaints should originate from members of the administration in the broad sense. Many complaints concern violations which will be known about in detail only by people on the inside. Also, members of the administration are more likely to be asked to participate in illegal activities, creating possible conflicts with their officially defined duties.

Another 15 of the stories (23 per cent) describe criticism from activists: mainly active party members and rank and file People's Control volunteers, who may be in either manual or non-manual jobs. They too, it should be remembered, have been officially assigned the function of controlling and preventing abuses, and generally upholding proper standards, and could be faced with a similar dilemma to the one that might confront members of the administration.

A further 13 stories (20 per cent) were inspired by complaints from individual manual workers, and 12 (18 per cent) by a collective appeal from several people within a single organisation. In the remaining case the story describes the protest of an aggrieved consumer. Consumers and clients (for example, people on local authority housing lists) frequently take up their pens in an effort to see that justice is done. But such protests are unlikely to have the ramified consequences of criticism from within the organisation itself. It is no doubt for this reason that they appear rarely as the subject of investigative reporting.

Types of Organisation

A wide variety of organisations can be found in the total sample of 70 cases. They break down as follows: 29 cases (41 per cent) belong to the services sector defined in a broad way – including transport (11 cases), education (5), housing supply (4), trade (3), and other services (6). Some 19 stories (27 per cent) are about industrial organisations – for example, engineering, metal and electrical enterprises, and food manufacture. Twelve cases (17 per cent) are concerned with construction, 9 (13 per cent) with agriculture. A final case deals with a complaint about a police officer.

Detailed information on the size of the organisations is not usually provided in the press accounts. But it seems that they usually relate to small or medium-sized enterprises. I shall comment later on the significance of this.

Types of Complaint

The examples in Chapter 3 gave an idea of some of the more frequently recurring complaints about abuse of office publicised in the Soviet press. In the sample, 80 offences were given a clear mention. Report-padding was mentioned 16 times, and false reporting in connection with wages 12 times – together with 5 other complaints about wages and bonuses. Embezzlement was referred to on 11 occasions, and hinted at in 4 others. (If a manager is said to be illegally writing off materials, this is a strong hint.) In 9 cases, managers were accused of illegally using the resources of the organisation for personal ends (for example, using the enterprise work time and materials for private building). In 6 stories the enterprise management was said to be using its administrative control over goods and services in illicit ways in order to favour certain employees, especially through its control over the allocation of housing. Bribery was mentioned only 4 times. If complaints about bribery are relatively few, this is not surprising. It is a transaction in which both bribe-giver and bribe-taker are breaking the law, and it is relatively easy to conceal from outsiders.

A variety of other offences cropped up: barter exchange and the illegal use of enterprise funds for entertaining visiting officials; under-the-counter sale of goods in wholesale and retail trade; forgery of documents; violation of safety regulations; quality violations; drinking on the job; plagiarism (in the writings of an academic). In addition there were many complaints about unfair dismissal and other disciplinary measures against employees, which were a very frequent outcome of attempts to expose breaches of law. This list does not give a complete picture. Sometimes the account does not tell the reader exactly what the offence was, referring only to 'violations', 'abuses' or 'misdemeanours'. But it gives a fair idea of the range of complaints that get a hearing in the Soviet press.

Motives

Since the bending and breaking of law is endemic in Soviet managerial practice, and since many people within and outside the organisation can be said to gain from it, there are great pressures acting against whistleblowing. Why then does it happen? It is difficult to pin this down from the press, but the following range of possible motives seems to me plausible, bearing in mind that more than one motive could play a part in any particular case:

(a) the people who blow the whistle are simply too conscientious to go along with the law-breaking that they encounter (this may lead to dilemmas, especially where the person is in a job that involves special financial responsibility, since part of the job is to prevent abuses);

(b) the risks have become too great (for example, because of the scale of embezzlement, or because the enterprise is too blatantly covering up for failure by means of false reports), and the complainants want to dissociate themselves from the activity;

(c) employees are angry about the unjust distribution of various rewards, which are concentrated in the hands of a management clique;

(d) the managers of an organisation have made themselves unpopular with an employee for some reason, and trying to expose abuses is one way of getting one's own back.

No doubt those who are engaged in a wholly disinterested pursuit of justice and legality are a small proportion of the people who register protests about abuse of office – though they may be well represented in the stories publicised in the press. A former Soviet journalist, with experience of the complaints procedure, suggested that about 10 per cent of complaints to the press were motivated by a general 'search for justice', as opposed to some direct personal concern:

90% of [complaints to the press] are of a personal kind ... They didn't give me a flat, a bonus, I was dismissed from my job, they gave me a reprimand without justification, transferred me to lower paid work, work conditions are poor, there is no ventilation ...

10% of complaints come from so-called truth-seekers [*pravda lyubtsy*], who are indeed fighting for justice. Something really is wrong: there is embezzlement, everyone is suffering from poor conditions of work, the distribution of flats is unjust, the pay is low ... this kind of thing. But there are very few of these ... Most people begin to write when they have been personally grabbed by the throat ...[1]

A distinction of this kind is necessary, but is also problematic. No doubt it is true that people will generally be moved to lodge a complaint only when they have been personally affected by the abuses they find unacceptable. But this does not necessarily mean that their concerns remain purely individual. Personal difficulties can be closely linked to, or can develop into, a wider social concern. In some cases it looks clear: the petitioner has nothing to gain personally from a successful outcome to the complaint, or else, in the opposite case, is exclusively interested in getting personal satisfaction and not at all in illegality as such. But the motivation is surely often more complex than that.

Individual concerns are perhaps most apparent in the case of complaints about the illegal distribution of material reward – category (c) above – though even in these situations there is room for ambiguity. Here are a few examples:

(1) Several employees in a timber organisation complained that the Department of Worker Supply was selling deficit goods to favoured employees straight from the warehouse, so that they did not reach general distribution. It became 'a department of self-supply for the employees of the department, and for people useful to them'.[2]

(2) The head of a Worker Supply Department in the railway network was removed because, among other things, he had been selling carpets and cars on the side to favoured people in the organisation. Earlier he had been warned in connection with 'gross violations of laws concerning the allocation of flats', which were intended for distribution to 'advanced workers' within the organisation.[3]

(3) A provincial party organisation had a post bag that included letters about the unjust allocation of housing at a ship repair factory: the housing was distributed 'not according to people's place in the queue, as is required, but, so to speak, by rank'.[4]

(4) A group of drivers working in road transport services wrote criticising their director for favouritism: 'B. [the director] has adopted the rule of keeping spare parts for cars in his own office and giving them out only to those whom he favours. Drivers that he doesn't favour are compelled to find spare parts anywhere and by any means.'[5]

(5) An elderly member of a collective farm complained that she had been unfairly treated in the provision of feed for her cow, while others who were on better terms with the management got all they needed. When the province party paper intervened, she was promised the feed, but then the transport for it was delayed: 'Others get it straight away',

she said, 'but with me they keep on delaying. It's all a question of personal relations.'[6]

(6) A brigade leader on a building site protested in the following terms: 'I think that flats are being incorrectly allocated by the [construction] trust ... Some people don't move in the queue at all but on the contrary get pushed back, while others get their new housing by jumping it ...'[7]

(7) A worker in a Mobile Mechanised Column criticised his boss at a party meeting for his extravagant life-style. Only recently he had lived in a four-room house but decided that he needed something still bigger, and built, at the expense of the organisation, 'a huge detached home with a garage and a bath-house'. Meanwhile there was a long queue of workers waiting for housing and 'in the workshops there aren't even the smallest washstands, or even tables for the workers to sit down when they are eating'.[8]

(8) A dispute between a People's Control group activist and a manager on the renowned BAM construction project finally aroused the support of the district People's Control. The chairman wrote:

> There are real enthusiasts on our great construction project, but together with these you can find people who are looking only for personal profit ... The country has a lot of concern for the people working for BAM, and we get many goods that are in great demand. But the administration has not resisted the temptation to enrich themselves at the expense of the community. For example, leather jackets and other deficit goods went first to the head [of the column] and his wife, to other managers, to the chairman of the trade union committee. The People's Control demanded that this disgrace should cease, to establish a clear and fair arrangement ...[9]

(9) The following complaint was inspired by a court case involving 'large-scale machinations' with the sale of bread (as a result of which the bread in the shops was substandard):

> My sons, who know the value of money, cannot accept the fact that some of their peers, not having earned a ruble, squander hundreds, drive around in their own cars. Our town is not very large, many of us know each other well, we know who works where and how much they earn. And if someone is living beyond their means, this is immediately obvious.[10]

In all these cases there is a reaction against illegal material privilege. It is possible that such protests are inspired only by the fact that somebody has failed to get a cut of the cake, and not by 'injustice' or illegality in itself. But this is only one form of whistleblowing. Many other complaints, especially about embezzlement and false reporting, cannot be plausibly explained in this way. As already suggested, some may arise out of a fear of exposure. But one should not underestimate the importance simply of a sense of social duty. Even if we accept the comments of the journalist quoted above, suggesting that only a small minority of complainants could be described as 'seekers of truth', still this 'search for truth' is a significant social phenomenon.

The terms 'seekers of truth' or 'seekers of justice' are approximate translations of the Russian *pravdalyubtsy* and *pravdaiskateli*. The full flavour of these words cannot be easily conveyed in English. What is involved includes a concern for law and legality, but it is broader than that. There is a reaction against informal privilege, against deceit, against a lack of responsibility, and generally a high level of 'social consciousness'. The point is this. There are still many Soviet citizens – perhaps they are a dwindling number – who take seriously the official injunctions to act honestly, to abide by the law, to take responsibility for one's actions and to make others answerable for their actions too. Such motives, I believe, prompted some of the complainants who appeared in the stories in Chapter 3. They also seem to underlie statements of the following kind. The first is about false reporting:

> I want to ask why ... the heads of a number of production collectives see nothing reprehensible in the fact that they constantly, from month to month, deceive both their collective and the higher organisations? ... As a participant in the People's Control I often come across situations where the plan has not been fulfilled, but it's 'stretched out' with the help of various sorts of loopholes, in a deceitful way, anything to make it look like 100.1% – the necessary figure to get the bonuses. It's time to put an end to these lies.[11]

The second is about embezzlement and bribery:

> It is hard to understand why people who have illegally enriched themselves often live conspicuously beyond their means and flaunt their ill-gotten wealth instead of trying to conceal it ... The evidence is everywhere: a fancy house suddenly gets built with

unheard of speed in a dacha settlement where there are not even supposed to be any vacant lots. Someone holds a huge and lavish wedding with 200 guests that no two honest families restricted to legal earnings could ever afford. Women show up at the theatre laden with diamonds and wearing sable stoles ...

It is time for society to teach bribe-takers, extortionists and swindlers to fear exposure by the people around them ... A great deal depends on us. When a hooligan offends a passer-by on the street, we don't hesitate to call the police. What prevents us, then, from reporting a crook who insults everyone around him by brazenly living beyond his means on money stolen from other people and the state?[12]

The language of these protests is the language of official Soviet public discourse, a language that still adheres to an ethic of thorough-going personal responsibility. It is true that Soviet ideology also owes a lot to a highly deterministic form of Marxism. But official norms and injunctions are saturated with a humanist rhetoric. The citizens of the Soviet state are constantly reminded of their personal responsi-bility for the outcome of collective practices. In the official discourse, 'objective reasons' for abuses will not wash. You cannot always be blaming 'the system', when after all it is concrete individuals who comprise it and who alone can make it work.

The peculiar thing, then, about the 'seekers of justice' is that they have taken such an ethic of responsibility to heart. They cannot accept that people are rewarded for work that is not done (for what else is the purpose of report-padding)? Nor can they accept that the distribution of benefits in society should be determined by informal social net-works, by rank and 'good connections', and not by a real contribution to society. They want a rational system of allocation in which people will get a 'fair day's wage for a fair day's work'. Of course all these formulations are problematic (what is a contribution, what is fair?), but this is the flavour of many of the more disinterested complaints.

Because of these attitudes, such citizens stand outside the main current, outside the networks of patronage and reciprocal favours that pervade Soviet organisational life. Often they are loners, with a dogged and eccentric attachment to the formal rules. The press reports tell us that one whistleblower is 'quarrelsome' and 'likes to say what he thinks'; another is an 'obdurate colleague'; a third is an 'unsociable person'; a fourth is a teetotaller and 'perhaps somewhat pedantic'; a fifth is 'not afraid to remain in the minority, to spoil relations with one or two people'; a sixth hasn't yet 'learnt the rules of the game'.[13] In responding in the way they do, the 'seekers after truth' act in full accordance with official Soviet ideals. But they also turn themselves into outsiders.

The fact that the truth-seekers take the official humanist ethic seriously is no doubt one reason why complaints about abuses get so much coverage in the Soviet press. They are easily transformed into morality plays, in which the protagonists represent the forces of good and evil, while both sides bear full responsibility for the part they play in the drama. The real-life dramas of the whistleblowers are indeed similar to some fictional ones. *The Bonus*, a successful film based on a play by Alexander Gelman,[14] provides one example. The hero is Potapov, a brigade leader on a construction site who, along with the rest of his brigade, refuses to accept his bonus. It is not deserved, he says, since the work that it represents was not in fact carried out. This starting point provides a platform for many critical observations about disorganisation and lack of responsibility on the site, all of which emerge at a party meeting that is called to discuss Potapov's extraordinary gesture. It transpires that Potapov has an ally in the administration. She has provided him with some figures, and on the basis of the figures he is able to present a case that the plan for the site was genuinely fulfillable if only certain avoidable errors had not been made. Towards the end of the action, the director reveals that the whole project was threatened from the start because certain essential preliminary work could not be carried out. Potapov then asks the director why he agreed in that case to take on the project at all, to which the latter has no ultimately convincing answer, except to say that it would have been futile in the end to refuse it: it would have been a totally quixotic gesture.

The story itself is implausible enough. But the moral point it makes is a powerful one, and is very similar to the point that is made through the real-life accounts of the whistleblowers. The buck has to stop somewhere, and if individuals would take it on themselves to intervene, to refuse to participate in certain actions, serious improvements could be made.

2 THE MANAGEMENT RESPONSE

What response is a whistleblower likely to get from the management of the organisation where he or she works? It is clear from almost every story that there is little love lost between the management and their critics. By raising a fuss, and above all by trying to take the complaint outside the organisation, they will quickly be seen as troublemakers, as 'scribblers' (*pisaki*) and 'nit-picking critics' (*kritikany*) who are out to slander the management, to tarnish the name of the whole collective, and in general to make life harder for everyone. This happens far too often to be put down to the eccentric vindictiveness of a few unusually venal managers – although that is how the matter is often presented in the press. The press accounts make little attempt to put the ensuing conflicts into a context in which the reactions of managers could be made intelligible. However, one can use these accounts, together with the analysis in Chapter 2, to construct such a context.

The management reaction as described in the press conveys both a strong sense of self-justification, and a sense that the whistleblowers' efforts might prove embarrassing. Both these dimensions can be understood from the account given in Chapter 2. Many offences, as we saw, help to create the conditions under which targets can be met, or appear to be met, while others may have come to be regarded as 'normal', if clearly illegal, ways of supplementing one's income. Rule-breaking is normal: it is the critics who are behaving abnormally by expecting a rigid adherence to law. At the same time, the response of management to the whistleblowers betrays a definite nervousness. Breaches of law are not unconditionally tolerated. Immunity from outside intervention by law enforcement agencies will depend on keeping abuses within certain bounds (law enforcement agents cannot be seen to be condoning blatant criminality), on the prominence and success of the organisation, and generally on the ability of the management to secure the personal support of superiors and of local political officials. Where these conditions cease to obtain and the support begins to weaken, for whatever reason, the illegalities that are part of everyday practice may begin to be noticed. It is this which gives the whistleblowers a chance. The party authorities remember the importance of the ritually intoned principle of 'criticism from below', and the voice of the critics may be heard. In the light of this un-doubted vulnerability which attends breaches of law, it is not surprising that managers are anxious to silence their critics.

The chances of success for a critic will depend, then, on the amount of support that the management can get from the various law enforcement agents, and especially from the party apparatus. The chances will depend also, though, on the influence that the management wields within the organisation itself. I shall dwell on this aspect first, and in the next section go on to discuss the role of outside agencies in relation to whistleblowing.

In the effort to disarm a critic the management has a number of weapons which will weigh quite heavily against the whistleblower from the outset. These sources of defence are based on (a) support from the workforce, (b) support from the party secretary, (c) the possibility of penalising the critics through the use of sanctions that are formally permitted in labour law, (d) the possibility of getting back at whistleblowers through counter-accusations of malpractice. I shall consider these in turn.

The Workforce

It seems that the 'letter-writers' are often isolated within the organisation. First, the director is likely to have the support of other managerial and administrative personnel. Even if they were secretly to agree with a critic, they are dependent on the director's patronage, and many may have received the benefits of illegal practices. In particular, people do not want to lose their bonuses. In one story, the head of a department in a wine plant was able to use this to discredit someone who had sent a signal from inside. The department head protested at an open factory party meeting that 'every engineering-and-technical worker has lost 180–200 rubles in bonuses because V.M. [a shop head] has informed the higher organs about report-padding'.[15]

The support will often extend further than the higher echelons of the organisation, especially when it is a question of illegal wage payments and other indulgences towards the workers by management. It is not surprising to find a certain respect for a manager who can treat the workforce to additional rewards, and a definite lack of sympathy for whistleblowers if their efforts are concerned with this kind of abuse. In one case, a mechanic in a transport enterprise was trying to stop drivers fiddling with speedometers and making private use of their vehicles. He threatened to make life uncomfortable for everyone. One of the department heads then complained that 'S. [the mechanic] is concerned neither with the plan nor with people: he has started up a squabble and has set himself against the collective.' At a general meeting of drivers, the mechanic was singled out for attack, and just to rub the point in, the wall-newspaper contained a poem that included the words: 'Just forget about the speedometers, we've been turning them and we'll go on turning them!'[16] An inspector with the city People's Control, then commented that 'Present-day suppressors of criticism ... will find even democratic-looking ways of taking revenge on those who get in their way.'[17]

In another of the stories in the sample, a shop manager and foremen in an engineering plant had, according to the report, 'generously "endowed" people who were useful to them: they added them to work rosters, artificially increasing their earnings ...' In this way the shop-head 'acquired the reputation as something of a benefactor'.[18] A similar state of affairs was described at a mink farm. An economist by the name of Sheina had been complaining about financial irregularities, and wage-padding in particular:

> Sheina according to her official duties was obliged to put a stop to any breaches of financial discipline. Here are just a few examples. The director's chauffeur, E. Savvateev, was registered also as a welder and a sanitary worker. According to his monthly work norm he is supposed to 172 hours; in fact it came to more than 400 hours. Stoker V. Klichuk contrived to 'work' ... 587 hours! All this was done with the blessing of V. Kolchin (the director). For what purpose? The motive was simple: look, he says, what a good boss I am, I'm not mean. So you, lads, don't let me down, do your bit![19]

The profits of management illegality are not, then, necessarily monopolised by management itself, though this is sometimes the case. In protesting against violations, the law-abiding critics may be upsetting a mutual set of interests which affect a large number of people in the organisation.

The Party Secretary

The management will typically be supported by the secretary of the enterprise party organisation. It is not unknown for party secretaries to quarrel with directors.[20] But they are very unlikely to support a whistleblower. In many of the press exposés, the party secretary appears alongside the director as a 'co-conspirator', and if some sort of penalties are eventually meted out, it is common to find the party secretary receiving them together with the director. This is under-standable, since the director and party secretary are jointly responsible for the performance of the enterprise, and have a joint interest in silencing critics who threaten to upset the delicate balance of informal tolerance towards illegal practices.

In addition to this, the director has some power of patronage over the party secretary's regular job, if the organisation is not big enough to make the party position full time. This was hinted at in one case where the party secretary, together with the trade union chairman, had been automatically supporting the director of a construction enterprise against an internal critic. This was the easiest course to take, according to the report, because supporting the director did not threaten any unpleasantness with their jobs.[21] The deputy party secretary at a collective farm made a similar point in the following comment:

> In party meetings, yes, we are equal. But as soon as the meeting has finished, the ladder of positions again comes to life and a com-munist who has criticised an executive immediately takes the role of subordinate and maybe even a supplicant. Either he needs hay for his cow, or a horse for working over his personal plot ...[22]

All these considerations put party organisers in a very weak position to defend a whistleblower. There are three cases in the sample where party secretaries threw in their lot with critics within the organisation. But none provides a convincing counter-example. In one of these cases, the factory director had already come under criticism from local officials, and a large part of the rest of the collective had turned against him as well.[23] In a second, the party secretary of a sanitary-epidemiological station had supported doctors who were refusing to sign documents giving the go-ahead for some factory buildings, because they did not meet health requirements. As a result she was blackballed at the next party election, evidently with the support of the district party committee. Someone else was put forward who 'always supported the head doctor'.[24] The same thing happened in the third case, where the party secretary of an agricultural research institute had criticised the administration, leading to an investigation by a local party commission. He failed to gain reelection the next time round, and the general opinion was that this was 'in reprisal for insubordination'.[25]

Penalties

The position of an internal critic is further threatened by the fact that it is possible for the administration to use some of the provisions in labour legislation to counter attack. On paper, Soviet labour law offers tight protection against arbitrary disciplinary measures against employees, and in particular against dismissal. But in practice it is not very difficult for a manager to get rid of a recalcitrant employee if certain formalities of procedure are followed. This is an important issue which affects the fate of many a whistleblower, and I shall devote a separate discussion to it in Chapter 5. For the present I shall simply note that a management has the authority to impose disciplinary measures on a number of grounds laid down in the Labour Code. The measures include transfer to a lower-paid job, loss of bonus, reprimand, dismissal. The permitted grounds for such penalties include systematic neglect of one's work duties, and absence without good cause. In addition it is legitimate to discharge an employee in the event of staff cuts imposed by a higher authority, or if it is decided that an employee is by qualification 'unsuitable for the post'. (Technical personnel may be asked to undergo a periodical certification process, and if they fail can be discharged.)

These penalties and non-disciplinary measures can be imposed only with good cause, and good cause does not include personal antipathy to one's subordinates. But ways can be found round this. For example, it does not seem to be difficult to find a pretext for imposing reprimands, which in turn can serve as grounds for eventual dismissal. Out of 66 cases, there were 26 in which the whistleblowers were dismissed at some stage during the conflict (although some of them were reinstated), while 13 received some other form of penalty. Four left 'voluntarily'. So far as could be told from the reports, 23 did not suffer any special unpleasantness. I shall return to these figures and discuss them in more detail in Chapter 5.

Counter-accusations of Malpractice

It is possible, finally, for management to counter-attack by casting aspersions on the integrity of their critics. Two employees (one in the quality control department, the other a shop-head), who were protesting about the high level of spoilage, got the following response from the director:

They [the complainants] are blackmailers! They tried to insure themselves by writing letters to various organisations so that they could say that they were being dismissed because they had criticised, and not because their work was unsatisfactory.[26]

Whispering campaigns may be set in motion, and meetings called at which the whistleblowers will be criticised,[27] and collective letters denouncing them may be sent to local law enforcement agencies.[28] Rather more drastically, a manager may try to get a criminal charge of slander brought against a critic in order to turn the whole thing round.[29] Finally, management may try to tarnish critics with the same brush that they are attempting to use against management. This occurred, for example, with a farm worker who was complaining about the illegal release of livestock.[30] It happened also to a deputy chief accountant who had sent a signal about report-padding in a construction institute. She was dismissed for 'flagrant violation of her official responsibilities' in connection with false reporting.[31]

From this discussion it should be clear that the balance of forces is weighted heavily against the whistleblowers, at least if we restrict ourselves to an examination of the internal relationships within the organisation. But the outcome of a conflict that arises out of the situations that I have described will of course depend further on how agencies outside the organisation respond to the attempt to expose illegal activity.

3 THE AGENCIES OF APPEAL: THE LOCAL PARTY APPARATUS

Executives and officials who break the law are immune from exposure and sanction to the extent that they can get protection or indulgence from the agencies that are responsible for preventing and penalising abuse of office. By the same token, executives and officials are immune to the efforts of the whistleblowers to the extent that the latter fail to get the support of those agencies in the pursuit of their complaints. What chances does a critic have of making a complaint stick, and what is the significance of criticism from below in the overall process of law enforcement?

Two propositions are I think indisputable. On the one hand, a certain proportion of investigations into abuse of office by party, legal and other agencies are the result of the initial 'signalling' and letter-writing of individual citizens. Law enforcement would be less effective than it is if the rulers relied on the initiative of the controlling agencies alone. On the other hand, it is also clear that for a critic 'from below' to get support from the agencies of the state is, to put it mildly, an uphill struggle, and in the vast majority of cases probably without avail.

The most unpromising path of all is to appeal to one's superiors within the administrative hierarchy. The press stories suggest that one will usually be faced with a brick wall of indifference, since the higher-level officials will generally share the definition of the situation held by the management lower down. They will be anxious to protect the reputation of their subordinates within the hierarchy, and thus indirectly their own reputation.[32] Thus, if people at a higher level do act against their subordinates within the hierarchy, this will almost certainly be as a result of pressure to do so from outside, from agencies that have been assigned a watchdog function. But critics who turn to such agencies at the local level are very likely, again, to be faced with indifference or outright resistance to their efforts. This in turn means that there is a constant pressure of complaints upwards in the attempt to get some kind of action taken, and often in the attempt to defend oneself in the face of reprisals from management for having tried to take the issue 'outside' in the first place.

To illustrate this point, and to explore the effects of such upward pressure, I shall focus on the role of the party organisations in relation to complaints. The party plays a key role in selecting executive personnel in the organisations within its domain, and in establishing the climate of law enforcement within a given territory. The authority of the party apparatus is also reflected in the frequency with which citizens appeal to it for assistance in trying to get action taken against abuses. For these reasons such a focus seems to me to be appropriate. But one should bear in mind that in the course of any particular dispute arising out of criticism from below, the critics may appeal to many other agencies as well. This emerged clearly from the accounts in Chapter 3.

In nearly all the cases in the sample where the party is involved, the local party at district or city level appears very reluctant to act on complaints arising out of the type of situation that I have described. As one journalist wrote, with the ritual understatement characteristic of much press criticism: 'Sometimes, party committees close their eyes to cases of evident suppression of criticism.'[33]

The reasons for this have already emerged in earlier discussion.

Local party secretaries know that certain forms of illegality are unavoidable if targets are to be met; they have a shared interest with management in keeping up appearances; they are prepared, under certain conditions, to tolerate more venal offences; they do not want, if they can help it, to expose 'their' people whom they have supported and assisted in their careers. Thus, when complaints from employees at an electronics factory about staffing abuses and other violations reached the city committee, the latter were only interested, so we are told, in the fact that it had the reputation as the most successful enterprise in the town:

> He [the director] acquired the solid reputation of a manager who was able to 'make' the plan. And as is well known, it is often not just the success of the enterprise that is judged by the plan. A little honour also falls to the city ... so how could one not support such a director?[34]

When complaints were made to the city committee about the director of a transport services enterprise, some of the committee officials defended him in these terms: '[Although] the autocolumn is a small enterprise, it is fulfilling its plan.'[35] When a wholesale trade organisation was criticised from below, the district party official said of the director: 'He is a good manager, and he has promised to correct the faults in his character.'[36]

For reasons which are by now familiar, complaints about false reporting from zealous accountants, and from other people responsible for honest reporting, are not likely to impress party officials. In one story some doctors were refusing to sign a document giving the go ahead for new factory buildings: they did not meet health requirements. But the head doctor of the province sanitary–epidemiological station explained to them that she had no room for manoeuvre: 'It is difficult for me to stand out against the provincial leadership [*rukovodstvo*].' She made it clear what the 'leadership' meant: if she refused to sign she was 'sure to get a reprimand through party channels'.[37] In similar vein an employee working for an agricultural repairs service, who had tried to send signals about report-padding to the local party, explained: 'In the district committee they don't respond very much to such signals. They want the district to look prettier, they don't want to wash their dirty linen in public.'[38]

Even if local party officials have no direct interest in illegal practices in connection with meeting targets or keeping up appearances, they are still likely to want to keep matters quiet in order to preserve the general reputation of their domain. When a state farm manager wrote in critical terms to the republican party newspaper about 'our omissions and shortcomings', he was later expelled from the party on the stated grounds of 'indiscipline' and 'abuse of office'. The district committee supported the decision. The journalist explained it in these terms: 'Why did they do it? ... The logic was simple: today Z. [the whistleblower] would "wash the dirty linen of the farm in public", tomorrow, perhaps, he would start criticising the district organisations ...'[39]

The typical response of the local party will be a *formal* reply to the petitioner, usually to the effect that 'such and such facts have not been established'. Such a reply is known in Russian as an *otpiska*, that is, a reply for form alone, which meets the requirement that a submission or complaint should receive a response, but gives no indication of what if anything has been done, and no indication of the reasons why a complaint is rejected as groundless. One can imagine that many hundreds of such 'responses' to the letters of Soviet citizens are written by party committees and other agencies every day.

Since the lower party agencies, which are responsible for following up submissions from citizens, are reluctant to act, there is a strong pressure of submission upwards: '... many people at first appeal to the district organs. But ... it sometimes happens like this: time passes and nothing has been done. The people are obliged to "write higher" ...'[40]

'Writing higher' may mean to the province or republic or national party committee, or to the party press, which is an important arm of the party apparatus, and a much used agency of appeal. Once an appeal has gone higher, there is some chance that pressure will now be applied on lower organs to get something done: to send in a party commission, to carry out an investigation and send in a report confirming or rejecting the allegations made by the whistleblowers. In that event, lower officialdom must satisfy their superiors that some action has been taken. For example, the provincial party committee will request an investigation by the city or district committee, or the republic central committee will request that action be taken by the province committee. In exceptional circumstances the Central Committee in Moscow (usually through the Committee of Party Control) will intervene directly and produce its own report. But typically, responding to a complaint means asking for a report from further down about the truth of the allegations and a statement about what measures have been carried out. The normal outcome of such an exchange is a form of action which satisfies superiors that something has been done, without jeopardising the mutual support between higher and lower levels of the party hierarchy. This has already been illustrated in several of the stories in Chapter 3. But let us provide a further example to clarify the point.

The case concerns Maksimenko, one of the managers of a construction trust, who had quarrelled with Esterlein, the head of the trust, in connection with a variety of financial irregularities, and had been dismissed. He appealed for support to the provincial party committee, giving a description of the offences in question. The account continues:

> At the provincial committee, after receiving this letter, they instructed the Karaganda city committee of the Kazakhstan Communist Party to investigate the conflict. A commission was set up headed by a city committee department head, U.S. Dospaev. The commission could easily have discovered the facts indicated in the letter, but did not even attempt to check them. Meanwhile the statement by one member of the commission, the head of the legal department of the 'Karagandaugol' association V. Shtykov, that B. Maksimenko had been incorrectly dismissed, was ignored by the city committee. B. Maksimenko did not agree with the conclusions of the commission and appealed for help personally to the first secretary of the provincial committee V.K. Akulintsev. Another commission was appointed, which finally decided that Maksimenko had been illegally dismissed.
>
> The provincial committee recommended that the Kirov district committee of the party, the 'Karagandaugol' association, and the party committee of the 'Karagandauglestroi' trust should examine the question of Maksimenko's dismissal. Esterlein was obliged to sign a directive reinstating Maksimenko in his previous post.
>
> We are now approaching a question that it has long been necessary to ask. Who gave the right to an executive to treat so unceremoniously people who had come out with justified criticism? The answer must be sought above all in the position of the Karaganda city party committee . . . [41]

This account, like many accounts of whistleblowing, suggests that the relationship between higher and lower party officials is a symbiotic one. There is generally no desire or will at higher levels to come to the active defence of a critic against the collective wishes of management and local party interests at a lower level. But there is also a tension in the relationship which arises from the constant pressure being exerted downwards through the party hierarchy to keep breaches of law within certain bounds. Illegal practices cannot be allowed to continue with complete impunity, and something must be seen to be done. Just what is done will depend on the degree of political pressure (during a law and order campaign it will be greater), on the state of play in the relations between higher and lower party officials, and on the clout that a manager is able to wield in the face of criticism. What the whistleblower does is to *publicise* breaches of law and make it difficult for the higher authority to ignore the submission completely. But to make a complaint stick it will usually be necessary to go very high, and even then the power of local officialdom to blunt the effect of political pressure from the central party authorities remains considerable. These points will become clearer in the next two sections.

4 THE TIDE OF COMPLAINTS: THE RESPONSE OF THE PARTY LEADERSHIP

We have seen that at each level the tendency of the party authorities is to respond with only formal gestures to citizens' complaints about abuse of office. This in turn tends to exert a constant upward pressure of requests for action towards the centre. This is true of all kinds of submissions and requests, not just those connected with abuse of office. The problem is not a new one. Ever since a highly centralised Soviet political machine was established in the 1930s, it has relied for its functioning on relationships of patronage which have always helped to create a 'loss of control' by the centre, a tendency for sanctions to lose their bite in the process of implementation, leading to recurrent criticisms of 'localism'. For just the same reasons, there have been recurrent criticisms over the failure of local officials to respond with due attentiveness to citizens' appeals. But in recent years there seems to have been a growing concern at the centre about the volume of complaints and the manner in which they are handled, if concern can be measured by the number of resolutions and injunctions that give verbal and legal support to the cause of the petitioner in general and the whistleblower in particular.

In an earlier discussion I mentioned some of the indications of this increased official emphasis on the importance of citizens' submissions, especially from the late 1970s onwards: the 1977 Constitution, party resolutions, a new Letters Department in the Central Committee, a Supreme Soviet decree and a resolution of the Supreme Court.[42] In addition there have been a number of *Pravda* editorials that have repeatedly stressed the importance of a sensitive response by officials to the citizens.[43] The main points that emerge from these injunctions can be summarised as follows:

(1) There is a restatement of the importance of the nation's letter-writers and petitioners as assistants in the management of the whole social edifice, as constructive critics from below:

> The letters and suggestions of working people help the party organisations to establish a better orientation, to evaluate more objectively the work of party, soviet, economic and social organisations, to see shortcomings more clearly and develop methods for overcoming them, to work out correct political decisions . . .[44]

(2) There is in particular a strong emphasis on the importance of signals about breaches of law: the letter-writers do not just assist in social control, they are keepers of the nation's conscience. 'In many letters', says a *Pravda* editorial, 'questions are raised about strengthening the struggle against the squandering of resources and against attacks on socialist property, against violations of discipline.'[45] This can be compared with a more recent Politburo statement, after a Politburo discussion of letters to the Central Committee and the Supreme Soviet:

> In many letters facts are described which show that in a number of places the required struggle is still not being carried out against people who permit mismanagement, eyewash, report-padding, the uneconomic and wasteful use of material resources. Signals are also sent about the need to strengthen the struggle against violators of public order, and against theft of socialist property.[46]

(3) Party and other agencies have been reminded that they have a duty to respond to submissions and complaints in good time and to give a full explanation for their action or inaction. In particular, '[The] need for a timely and businesslike response to letters justifiably calling attention to irregularities . . . has been raised to the level of an immutable party and state requirement.'[47] But agencies which

are supposed to deal with submissions come in for heavy criticism, as in this injunction from the Central Committee:

> ... the Central Committee notes that in some central government, economic and social organs, in some local party, soviet and other organisations there are serious shortcomings in the examination of written and oral submissions by citizens. There have been cases in which a soulless and bureaucratic attitude has been taken towards lawful requests and justified statements, the failure to carry out promises previously given. This compels citizens to appeal to higher organisations and establishments, to make long journeys in the attempt to get their requests satisfied.[48]

A later editorial explains further that 'Sometimes letters received by party committees get merely a formal reply, instead of help and advice people get an answer written for form only ... [this] causes dissatisfaction, creates idle talk and conjecture.'[49]

(4) Special attention has been paid to the importance of responding to allegations of 'suppression of criticism'. One *Pravda* editorial had this to say:

> Sometimes attention is paid not to the substance of the criticism, but to the personality of those who offered it. The main energies are directed not towards removing shortcomings, but finding fault with the critics, seeking ways of putting their comments in doubt. And already they say about such people that they are 'washing dirty linen in public'.[50]

This was followed up by another injunction: '[party committees] must put a decisive end to attempts at suppression of criticism, attempts to take reprisals against the authors of letters ...'[51]

(5) All agencies and officials responsible for dealing with submissions are being urged to develop a more sensitive attitude, and more effective forms of dialogue with the public. The main new initiative in this context has been to encourage so-called 'open letter' days to increase the publicity given to the handling of submissions. In the same spirit, officials have been urged to make on-the-spot visits to consider personal requests at places of work or residence,[52] and editors have been enjoined to publish letters more often.[53]

(6) The procuracy and the courts have been reminded of their role in

enforcing the law on the handling of submissions and complaints. The USSR Procurator's Office has stressed the importance of procuratorial supervision in this area, and has protested that local procurators 'do not always display adherence to principle or achieve the elimination, in actuality, of violations that have been disclosed, and they do not always raise the question of the accountability of officials who are guilty of such violations'.[54] Meanwhile a resolution of the USSR Supreme Court has reminded the courts that under certain circumstances the 'suppression of criticism' and the failure to respond in the appropriate manner to complaints is a criminal offence. If in the course of their work the courts discover breaches of law in the handling of complaints, or evidence of victimisation for criticism, they should issue a Special Ruling informing the appropriate authorities or social organisations, and if necessary initiate criminal proceedings. The basic condition for the presence of criminal responsibility is that the actions of officials have caused 'significant harm to state or social interests or to the rights and legally protected interests of citizens'. Three articles of the RSFSR Criminal Code are mentioned in this connection: article 170 (abuse of power or official position); article 172 (negligence in the fulfilment of official duties); article 138 (violation of labour law). In relation to article 170 the resolution says:

> Reprisals against citizens in connection with their proposals, statements or complaints, either because of the criticism contained in them or in connection with citizens' activity in implementing People's Control, should be qualified under article 170, if the reprisals are carried out by an official with intentional infringement of the rights and legally protected interests of citizens (undermining the dignity of the person, removing an individual from the housing list, depriving the individual of the right to use plots of land, etc.), and if they cause significant harm or bring about serious consequences ...[55]

The resolution adds that where reprisals take the form of illegal dismissal, failure to carry out a court decision on reinstatement or any other 'intentional significant violation of labour law' (illegal transfer to other work, deprivation of bonuses, etc.) the offender will incur responsibility under article 138. I shall return to this point later.

These are the main things that have been emphasised in the recent propaganda efforts on citizens' submissions and complaints. How is

all this to be explained? It is difficult to offer more than some speculative suggestions in answer to this question. One sort of answer – it
would fit in with the way the issue is often presented by Soviet
commentators – might stress the special importance of public
participation at the present stage of development of the Soviet system.
The propaganda support for the letter-writers is one part of the
attempt to involve citizens in public administration and law enforcement. It is one expression of a higher stage in the advance of Soviet
democracy, which increasingly draws the public into the management
of society and also protects individual citizens from arbitrary attacks
on their rights. This formulation is drawn from the rhetoric of party
propaganda itself. I suggested earlier that the official rhetoric was not
all froth – though some of it is. The support for the petitioners reflects
a real link between the state authorities and the individual. Even if the
state rarely lives up to its image of protector, through its ideological
support for the petitioner it helps to create the looked-for unity
between the individual and the state.

The party rhetoric is not then purely rhetorical. But it is not much
good as an explanation for a particular campaign. One possibility is
that the sheer volume of submissions has now reached an unacceptable level. They have been increasing over the years, and because of
obstruction at lower levels of political authority, it may be that the
volume of complaints has simply caused a serious overload at the
centre. Setting up a Department of Letters in the Central Committee
could be seen as a response to such a development. If so, then one is
immediately faced with the ambiguity of the party response. The
letter-writers are welcome as an expression of 'the indestructible unity
of the party and the people' (that was the expression in a recent
Politburo statement).[56] But letters to the centre are also a constant
reminder of the dissatisfaction of millions of people, a reminder of
intractable social problems, and a result of the failure of political
authorities at lower levels to give an adequate response to individual
grievances. That failure leads to 'idle talk and conjecture'.[57]

Thus the campaign can be seen as an attempt to reduce the weight of
complaints on the centre – it is a response to real popular pressure,
expressed in an accumulation of individual grievances. But the letters
also help to give a 'democratic' image to political intervention which
occurs independently of the stream of complaints itself. In the past
few years law and order questions – 'white-collar' and 'blue-collar'
crime and crimes of violence – have become major political issues.
Official injunctions in support of the petitioners not only help to

improve the flow of information about law and order problems, but also give the campaign a popular image. This seems clear with the policy initiated under Andropov very soon after Brezhnev's death. It mobilised a great deal of criticism from below in the attempt to improve law enforcement and discipline, and to give the policy popular backing.

Finally there may be wider political issues at stake. It is possible that party policy on the letters is related to the continuing efforts to take the teeth out of political dissent. Serious frustration over an ordinary, non-political complaint – let's say, about an unfair dismissal – can lead an individual finally towards an 'oppositional' view of Soviet reality. If there is no justice, if officials are allowed to ride roughshod over the laws and get away with ignoring a completely justified complaint of this kind, what sort of system is it that permits this to happen? The defence of the petitioner turns out to be a charade. Sentiments like this seem to have inspired the formation of a Free Trade Union Association in 1977, to which some 200 people attached themselves. The signatories were all people who had started off with ordinary complaints. They had quarrelled with management at their places of work in connection with abuses, and had lost their jobs as a result. But they had failed to get any satisfaction from local or central agencies. According to one of their documents:

> Wherever we turn – to the Procurator's Office of the USSR, the Supreme Court of the USSR, the Council of Ministers of the USSR, the Presidium of the Supreme Soviet of the USSR, the All-Union Central Council of Trade Unions and the Central Committee of the CPSU – *everywhere* we are refused even a hearing and our complaints are sent to the very organs against which we are lodging complaints. Or we are fobbed off with formal rejections.
>
> The only reason is that we are decent, principled people who have come out against bribery, swindling, theft of socialist property, concealment of industrial accidents and other abuses by managers at the enterprises where we used to work ...[58]

The people who joined the association had been reduced to a state of extreme frustration after years of struggle as individual petitioners, which had got them nowhere, and had often led to long periods of unemployment. Between them they must have written thousands of letters and knocked on hundreds of doors. What evidently happened was that a few individuals encountered each other in a variety of central offices in Moscow in the course of attempts to see officials, told each other their stories, and in desperation hit upon the idea of joint action. They decided to set up an autonomous association to put their case to the Soviet authorities and to make it public to the Western media. In doing so they ensured that the KGB would come down on them very quickly. They had broken the cardinal rule of Soviet petitioning, namely that you act alone, or together with other people from the same organisation. You do not cross institutional boundaries because you thereby create a direct challenge to the legitimacy of the state. That, at any rate, is how the matter is seen by the Soviet rulers. But such an event must none the less have acted as a sharp reminder of the deficiencies in the petitioning mechanism. If a series of ordinary complaints could boil over into an oppositional gesture of this kind, it surely testified to the importance of improving the image of the complaints procedure.

Internal political problems must also have appeared in a new light after the events in Poland in 1980–1, and perhaps gave an additional boost to the official Soviet rhetoric on complaints. The setting up of Solidarity and the ensuing struggles between the new trade union and the party leadership, exposed an enormous political gulf between the authorities and the mass of the population, and revealed a strong popular reaction against official illegality and privilege. Some lessons could be learned from that as well.

These are some of the possible reasons for the greater publicity given to letter-writing and to 'suppression of criticism' in recent years. It is quite another matter how effective such publicity is likely to be, or whether any significant sanctions are likely to be taken in connection with the handling of complaints. In the light of the analysis so far, it would be surprising if the campaign were to make a big impact. Local officials are too solidly entrenched, and higher-level officials too reluctant to support the petitioners against the local powers.

A few stories, it is true, have recently appeared in which officials have been penalised over their response to complaints. In one of these cases, after an investigation by a province party commission, a manager was found to have ignored 80 letters of 2 to 3 years' standing – mostly requests and complaints in connection with housing. He was expelled from the party because of violations in the allocation of housing and a 'soulless attitude to letters'.[59] In another case the head of a local authority housing office was given a suspended sentence because he had ignored a number of serious protests about urgently needed housing repairs, which had led to repeated submissions to the city and central organs (the temperature in some flats had fallen to minus 6 degrees during winter, walls were covered in fungus, and floors had fallen through).[60]

Such penalties seem to have been rare, and it would be fanciful to expect the publicity campaign to be accompanied by any significant sanctions against those who fail to respond promptly to the petitioners, or against those who 'suppress criticism'. In the course of preparing an article, a journalist asked two provincial party committees how many party members had been penalised in the past two years in connection with 'suppression of criticism'. The answer was 'one' in the first province and 'none' in the other. The author's description of the main problem would be difficult to dispute:

> A mass of evidence shows that suppression of criticism happens as a rule where there is connivance and where people can act with impunity. How much do we struggle against this evil? To put it mildly, we struggle against it very feebly. We appeal to people to encourage criticism, we wallow in nice-sounding phrases and then adopt a liberal attitude to those who organise reprisals against the seekers of truth [*pravdalyubov*].[61]

5 PETITIONING AND THE PRESS

We have seen that whistleblowers face very great difficulties, and that the course of a complaint about abuse of office hinges on the extent of political protection, and on the relationship between central and local political power. The whistleblowers are able to benefit from the conditional nature of protected illegality, and to take advantage of a certain tension between higher and lower levels of political authority in the arena of law enforcement. But the symbiotic character of that relationship also means that a whistleblower will have a very tough time if she wants to make a complaint stick. The extent and limits of central political power, and the way this impinges on complaints about abuse of office, can be further clarified by looking at the role of the press in the petitioning process.

The press, especially the national party press, provides a key element in the complaints procedure. First, the press has considerable authority as an arm of the party apparatus, and can exert pressure on other agencies to get things done.[62] Second, it can give broad publicity to certain selected responses and criticisms from below. This gives the press a vital part to play in preserving the link between the state and the concerns of the individual. The press typically appears in the role of protector of rank and file citizens if they are treated arbitrarily by managers and local officials. It is customary for newspapers to devote a definite proportion of space every week to the publication of critical letters and commentaries on letters received,[63] and stories about whistleblowing make a frequent appearance. A former journalist with a major national daily described the importance of critical letters as follows:

> ... they [critical letters] are as it were the voice of the people. This is something akin to democracy, one is saying that here is a person who has made use of their rights, has come out against the director – the director has broken the law, but the law will be enforced ... any material that shows that justice was done raises the authority of the paper ...[64]

This statement is certainly faithful to the general tone of Soviet investigative reporting, which in the great majority of cases comes out as a defender of the aggrieved citizen and employee. Yet the form and content of Soviet press coverage of complaints also testifies to the power of local officialdom, and shows that the central authorities are generally unable or unwilling to push the matter very hard. This can be brought out by considering the criteria of selection, the opposition that editors may face if they overstep certain limits, and the general question of the effectiveness of press criticism.

The Problem of Selection

Given the enormous number of letters that Soviet newspapers receive every day, it is evidently a very big job to sort them out and to decide what to do with them. Letters that are published or commented upon, or investigated by the paper itself, are a tiny proportion of the total amount received. What are the procedures and the means of selection? A former journalist with a major republic party newspaper, who also did work for other papers, described the process:

> Every paper has a complaints or letters department. All the letters received by the editors go to this department ... which sorts them out by section. Suppose, for example, that a complaint comes about a dismissal at a factory. As a rule, this would belong to the industry department, so the letter would be transferred there ... The head

of the department would then give the letter to one of his colleagues ... I, for example, was concerned with engineering ... Let
us suppose that a complaint comes about the director of an engineering factory. This letter will almost automatically reach me ...[65]

Decisions about how to respond to complaints may be taken by
rank and file journalists, by heads of newspaper departments, or by
chief editors, depending on the size and prominence of the organisation in question, and the authority and experience of the journalist.
In some cases a reply will be sent to the writer saying that 'unfortunately our paper does not deal with such matters'. In others, the
complaint will be sent on to an appropriate agency or organisation
with a request that the matter be looked into and, if necessary, action
taken. In the case of complaints about abuse of office, judging by the
sample I have taken, this is very often the district or city party
organisation. The paper may also in certain cases send one of its
central or local correspondents to investigate the complaint on the
spot and to see if there is a newsworthy story in it. The most vivid and
informative accounts are indeed those written by special correspondents, especially those who are based in the local area and are
familiar with local conditions and people.

According to the journalist I have just quoted, the criteria used in
selecting critical letters for comment or investigation are these: the
case is typical, or else it is outrageous, or it is simply interesting as a
story, or else a crime is involved. The importance of purely journal-
istic criteria should not then be underestimated. The same informant
expressed the following view:

Any journalist, any editor of a newspaper, is interested in such
[critical] material. It is said that in the Soviet Union editors are
against sensational material, but in fact this is not so ... any editor
of a paper, within the limits that he can allow himself, naturally
wants to publish the sort of material that people will read ...[66]

But it is also clear that the criteria of selection are political. Certain
managers and officials are 'out of bounds' for a newspaper, unless the
editor has received special instructions or permission from a high
party authority (say the Central Committee at republican or All-
Union level). Who the paper can criticise will depend on the territorial
scope of the paper and the relative prominence of the manager or
official in question. One former journalist, who covered a variety of
assignments for a national daily, put it this way:

He [the head of the department] knows the level at which one can criticise. In the central Soviet press one can engage in criticism at any level ... excluding high-level party and komsomol officials. One can criticise the gorkom secretary, but not the obkom secretary ... For this one needs the permission of the central committee ... People simply know to which rung they can climb without further consultation ...

If a central paper gets some material about embezzlement at a machine tractor station, if the facts seem to be interesting then I may be sent on a trip in order to write something ... If the Ryazan provincial paper gets such a letter, it reacts quite differently, because the head of this station is a big figure in the context of the province, and it is enough for him to make a telephone call for the whole matter to die down.[67]

To judge from the sample of 70 reports (mostly from *Pravda*), it is unusual for an organisation of any size or prominence to be criticised in connection with a complaint, even in the most authoritative of Soviet newspapers. There seems to be no particular bias in the geographical coverage: all major regions of the USSR are covered (RSFSR: 48 stories; Ukraine: 12; Kazakhstan and Central Asia: 6; the Baltic republics: 2; the Transcaucasian republics: 1). But it is notable that the largest industrial centres are not well represented in the stories about whistleblowers. In the 70 reports, the following large cities[68] are mentioned: Moscow, Omsk, Sverdlovsk, Kuibyshev, Odessa, Gorkii. But in none of these cases does the report describe an organisation of any size or prominence (the Moscow stories deal with a garage and an electrical repairs shop). To some extent this bias must reflect differences in the incidence of law-breaking in different sectors and types of organisation. But it also shows the power of party and other officials in the major centres to avoid embarrassing press scrutiny. If there is any dirty linen, they can in general successfully protect it from public discussion.

Opposition to Press Criticism

Soviet editors and journalists work, then, within strict limits, which reflect the subordination of the press to the party, and the tendency of party officials to protect prominent people within their domain. This does not mean that editors and reporters never make 'mistakes', nor that they have a clear set of instructions about who is touchable and who is not. But if they step beyond certain limits they are likely to incur the wrath of management and local party officials. Journalists may face difficulties in trying to get hold of material for on-the-spot investigations, and even if a critical article does appear, this does not mean that the offending manager or official has lost political protection.

Soviet correspondents, and *Pravda* correspondents more than any others, have considerable authority to see documents and to question the people involved in a conflict that has reached the ears of the newspaper. But they may still encounter obstruction from management or local officials, and not receive the needed information.[69] This is partly a matter of the knowledge and experience of the journalist. If a reporter arrives, let us say, in Irkutsk, having been sent from Moscow to do a report, and if the reporter is shown around (and wined and dined) by local officials, then it becomes very difficult to write a report with any teeth in it.[70] But a locally based correspondent may find ways round this, as the informant from the republic party paper explained:

> I will take this letter (for example a letter of complaint against a director about a dismissal) and I will have to go and carry out an investigation at the factory. What will I do there? This is where the professional skill of the journalist comes in. It is difficult, because according to general Soviet norms I don't have the right to turn up at a factory without informing the director. Even supposing that they let me in because I produce a journalist's card, still this is considered unethical. On the other hand I can't come along to the director and say that I am investigating a complaint against him, because this will inhibit the investigation. So I arrive at the factory and say something to the effect that I would like to get acquainted with the work of, say, shop no. 2. Let's suppose that the person who sent the complaint works in shop no. 2. I'll go there and talk to the shop-head, and then have a general discussion with other people; after that I'll go up to the author of the letter, will have a talk, and then depending on what I discover, and depending on my experience and ability in these matters, I'll proceed ... [I will have spoken to the letter-writer's] comrades, to the shop-head, the trade union and party committees. And since there wasn't yet a director who didn't have any enemies, it can't be that everyone is lying. Some will tell the truth, some won't. In any case, before I speak to the director I will have collected sufficient material to get a rough idea of the situation ...[71]

There are problems of access, then, which may be more or less successfully tackled. But even if we set aside this aspect, the people who have had an accusing finger pointed at them may be able to fight back, before or after publication, because they have the support of key people within their own hierarchy or within the party apparatus. Editors may receive messages from party officials indicating that certain materials should not be published. This practice has been criticised in *Pravda* – though it would not of course reveal such problems in its own relationship with the Central Committee. One commentator remarked on this in the following terms:

> Sometimes, certain officials in the localities protect 'strong' managers from criticism. And journalists are 'forbidden' to publish material about the shortcomings of certain factories or even districts.[72]

Examples occasionally appear in the press. The director of a technical college who was guilty of 'gross violations of staffing regulations and financial discipline' was protected when 'the editor got phone calls from the gorkom secretary and from obkom instructors K. and S. They insistently suggested that the material should not be published.'[73] A story recently appeared in *Literaturnaya Gazeta* describing the case of a former student at the Odessa Nautical Academy, who later became a komsomol organiser there. He got into trouble because he was disturbed by the disappearance of several thousand rubles that had been earned by students when working on a farm. The administration found high-level support (the report does not say from where), and when it became known that *Literaturnaya Gazeta* was pursuing the case, intense pressure was put on them not to publish:

> With the support of these 'connections' attempts were made to influence the editors: in the course of six months telephones rang not only in the *Literaturnaya Gazeta* offices, but also at the author's home and at the homes of [the paper's] executives. They tried to demonstrate to us that this was a petty personal case from the life of one excessively ardent young man who had quite accidentally appeared at the centre of things, and that it did not merit public attention.[74]

The two cases above illustrate resistance to newspaper intervention before publication. Similar problems may crop up when a press report has already come out. For example, when a critical article was published in one republic party paper (concerning accusations of plagiarism by the dean of economics at an agricultural institute), the editors were carpeted by the propaganda department of the republic Central Committee. One of the editors said afterwards: 'If you want to make criticisms when these reveal defects in the position of the party committee, you had better ask permission first, or else you will bring unpleasantness on yourself.'[75] Such counter-attacks have been criticised in *Pravda* editorials. One such editorial, published in 1978, had this to say:

> It happens that after the appearance of criticism, the 'offended' begin to make the round of offices with complaints against the editors, or try to cast aspersions on the author; in short, they take all possible counter-measures ... Party committees are called upon to take incisive and effective measures to correct personnel who accept praise willingly, but do not want to listen to criticism or draw conclusions from it. Favourable conditions should be created for journalists to work with initiative and confidence ...[76]

A few years later, the same point was made in another leader:

> There are certain executives who try to turn their ... organisations into a zone free from criticism. There are attempts to get rid of press representatives who have made critical interventions ... There are cases when doubt is cast on businesslike and principled criticisms, which are greeted with dissatisfaction in local party and soviet organs, in ministries and establishments.[77]

The Effectiveness of Press Criticism

The power of local officialdom is reflected not only in the criteria of selection, and in opposition to press criticism when editors make 'mistakes', but also in the way the press itself comments on the effectiveness of its own interventions. Generally speaking some form of action will be taken once the paper, especially if it is a national paper, has spoken out. But, as one might expect from the earlier discussion of law enforcement, typically the minimum response is given. One gets the impression that replies to newspaper criticism by the managers of criticised organisations very often take a purely ritual form, and there are occasional follow-up reports saying that little if anything has been done in response to previous intervention. One such report, in *Sovetskaya Rossiya*, described the case of a director of a catering organisation in Krasnodar. He had previously been criticised in the paper for the 'widespread practice of giving customers short weight and shortchanging them, committing thefts and other abuses', with the protection of bribed police officials and auditors: 'Despite two *Sovetskaya Rossiya* articles, Borodkina [the director] felt she was unassailable. Small wonder! She was protected by Pogodin, first secretary of the city party committee at the time.'[78]

These problems are reminders of the limits to press power. True, national newspapers have considerable authority to investigate, can initiate action in relation to abuses up to quite a high level, and have a strong institutional interest in critical material because it makes for more interesting reading. Also, a lot of the critical writing is sharp and ironic in tone. But the press reports themselves give the game away: in their comments on the effect of press intervention they betray the limited ability of the paper to make managers and officials answerable for breaches of law. This comes through especially in the stories about whistleblowing. They make it clear that, despite press support, the whistleblowers very often get more penalised for their efforts than the offenders they are complaining about. These are *success* stories for the whistleblowers. They are drops in an ocean of complaints that do not get the privilege of press coverage. They are demonstrations that it is possible for the aggrieved citizen to gain support, through the media, from the highest reaches of state power. But even these success stories often betray the failure of the critics, who are often treated as the real culprits, while the penalties incurred by the offenders are typically very light. Out of 80 managers clearly identified in the sample of 70 reports, the following penalties are mentioned: none: 16; reprimands: 31; fines: 3; transfer: 5; discharge: 16; expulsion from the party: 7; court convictions: 2 (both of these were custodial sentences). Thus in only 11 per cent of cases, at the time of writing the report, was a serious penalty incurred, involving expulsion from the party or a court conviction. Another 20 per cent were discharged, but as the discussion in Chapter 2 suggested, this is not likely to be regarded as a very grave penalty. Meanwhile, out of 66 whistleblowers identified, 26 lost their jobs at some stage in the dispute, another 13 received some other penalty, and 4 left 'voluntarily'. A far higher proportion of critics were seriously penalised than the objects of their criticism. As a result one often finds, at the end of a press story, rhetorical questions like this: 'How did it happen that the person who was most punished over the years was the one who defended the law?';[79] 'Won't [the outcome of this case] strengthen the position of those who think that to take a principled stand is also a punishable matter?';[80] 'Why was it the dishonest person who came out of this [affair] clean and dry?';[81] 'When a person sees that so-and-so is dismissed because he told the truth ... then he will think: should I open my mouth or would it be better to keep it shut?'[82]

These remarks highlight the limits to press influence: it observes and comments, but its teeth are blunt. The informant from the republic party paper commented on this with a certain resignation:

> When a letter was written and the name of the letter-writer became well known, they started to take reprisals. The editors tried to do something, but this was very difficult. The paper sometimes spoke out two or three times in defence of a person. This hardly ever helped ... because the director was supported in the raikom, the gorkom, the central committee [of the republic] ... What could one do?[83]

A further point should be made in this discussion. While the press typically comes out as a defender of the whistleblower, this does not invariably happen. In five of the reports in the sample, journalists followed up the complaint, but then admonished the critics for wasting everyone's time with their groundless accusations. On these occasions the authors emphasise that some petitioners are using the complaints procedure simply to settle personal scores. In one such report the writer concluded:

> however much idlers and bad workers may try to defend themselves, whoever they may try to blame for their own sins, in the end each of them will get their deserts. And it ill becomes people in these cases to bombard every agency with their submissions ... We are not going to applaud and protect inveterate slackers ... however high they may go with their complaints ...[84]

In another case a complainant was described as 'a bad specialist, an irresponsible and undisciplined worker', and was castigated for 'abusing our democracy'.[85] In a third the author concluded: 'L. [the complainant] knows very well that not one letter should remain without a reply. And he is extremely pleased when he manages to drag state and social organisations into the orbit of his personal grudges ...'[86]

The effect of such reports, although they are quite rare, must be to dampen somewhat the enthusiasm of potential letter-writers. Even during the recent campaign against 'suppression of criticism' and against red-tape in the handling of complaints, a certain restraining influence could be noticed. A *Pravda* journalist observed that readers had been responding to the 'growing struggle against abuses and suppression of criticism', but he commented that 'some readers are one-sided in their approach, they demand excessively strict measures after every critical intervention by one or another newspaper: take them to court, they say, dismiss them from their posts, expel them from the party.' This, says the author, is not always an appropriate response, because the publication of criticism in the press is 'itself sometimes a sufficient moral punishment'.[87] Thus the press, while it gives the whistleblowers a chance, is itself afraid of the possible effects of an unrestrained call for 'criticism from below'. If such criticism were welcomed in an unambiguous fashion, it might encourage a flood of submissions which the current procedure would be unable to contain.

The factors I have discussed tend to reduce the power of the press in its role as defender of the critic from below. These limits are a reflection of the power of local interests and the unwillingness of the higher authority to enter into a serious contest with the local officials. But there is another important limit to the effectiveness of press intervention, which deserves comment. Every story is isolated from its social and political context. There is only the vaguest reference, if any, to the wider incidence of the abuses that are being commented on. The stories carry the assumption, ever-present in Soviet media discussions of social problems, that the problems are the result of the anti-social tendencies of particular individuals. The Soviet press fails to convey any sense of the normality of the 'anti-social' behaviour at which its criticism is directed. It was no doubt this that a reader quoted in *Pravda* was hinting at, commenting on press coverage of abuses: 'some articles are crowded with facts and names, but there are no generalisations, no thoughts or conclusions'.[88]

Because of this, the press cannot get to grips with the issue in a practical way. The problem is not that the narrative makes individuals responsible for social outcomes, but that it fails to trace the network of responsibility in such a way that viable solutions to the problem might emerge. It is true that we are often told that abuses only persist because the people who are supposed to be in control connive at them. But any detailed analysis of this relationship is always directed at manager so-and-so and party secretary so-and-so. To explore it further would lead to dangerous questions about the character of the political order itself.

6 CONCLUSIONS

The stories about whistleblowers are instructive in a number of ways. They are revealing both about responses from below to abuse of office and about the conditions which assist and impede management illegality.

Within Soviet organisations someone will often be found who is sufficiently perturbed by the practices they encounter to want to take a complaint about them outside the organisation, using well-established channels for this purpose. In most cases, it seems, the inspiration for this is a personal grievance that arises from what is felt to be the unjust result of management action. But a certain proportion of such complaints are sent by 'truth-seekers' whose motives are more disinterested.

Whistleblowing is not completely hopeless, because in breaking the law, managers and officials render themselves vulnerable. Their immunity from law enforcement remains fragile and dependent on changing political conditions at the central and local level. Critics can take advantage of that, and can take advantage of the fact that 'criticism from below' and petitioning are important elements of the Soviet ideological and political edifice. The whistleblowers have formal institutional support, and the press plays an important role as defender of the ordinary citizen against discrimination by managers and local officials. However, the critics find themselves in an extremely difficult position. They immediately make themselves unpopular with the management, and often (depending on the nature of the complaint) with a large part of the workforce, and come up against the entrenched networks of patronage and protection between local officials and managers, and between higher and lower levels of the political hierarchy. The fate of such a complaint betrays the strength of those relationships.

The role of the press in the whole process, especially the national party press, is particularly revealing. It criticises the offenders and defends the whistleblower, and thus testifies to the vulnerability that attends breaches of law, especially when they are made public. But the very partial and selective treatment that it gives, and the frustration that newspapers themselves express about the feeble consequences of press criticism, betray the severe limits to its power. The national party press is, in effect, an agent of the Central Committee, but is clearly unable or unwilling to take the matter very far when faced with the combined forces of local opposition to exposure. The upshot is that typically the whistleblower gets much rougher treatment than the offenders complained about. From the standpoint of hardened Soviet executives this is only natural. Organisations, and ambitious individuals, cannot survive in the Soviet environment without day-to-day breaches of law, and even if this allows one to gain a little extra personal reward as well, that too is part of the rules of the game. The critics appeal to law and to official values in pursuit of their claims, but this quickly marks them out as misfits in real life.

5 Soviet Law and the Security of Work

In the last two chapters I illustrated and discussed some of the problems that employees are likely to face if they indulge in criticism of management. It has become clear that one of the difficulties has to do with the ability of managers to penalise subordinates who have made themselves unpopular. For this reason a conflict which revolves around abuse of office will often also turn into a dispute within the terms of Soviet labour law. The position of the critic within the organisation will partly hinge, then, on the amount of protection offered by Soviet law to employees *as* employees. This is the issue on which I shall be focusing in the present chapter. My main purpose has been to get a fuller picture of the problems faced by the whistle-blowers. But the discussion also raises some general questions about the nature and extent of job security in the Soviet Union, which are worth commenting on.

On the general issue, the main line of argument can be presented as follows. There is in the USSR a highly codified and detailed framework of labour law which is designed, in part, to protect employees from arbitrary actions by management which threaten their interests, in particular the security of their jobs. It is often said that these legal guarantees give Soviet workers a high degree of protection. Indeed the guarantees cause considerable problems because in the Soviet Union a manager has the greatest difficulty getting rid of an unproductive worker. But this is a misleading image. It is true that jobs are secure in the USSR in a very important sense: there are widespread shortages of labour which tend to give Soviet workers a definite individual bargaining power. This security, arising from full employment, is also a major political fact which the Soviet Union can pride itself on in the face of the rapid growth of unemployment in the West. But Soviet *law* is not in practice a significant source of job security. If a manager sees fit to dismiss an employee, then it will not generally be difficult to do so.

Some dismissed employees – but not those in more responsible positions – have a fair chance of getting reinstated by appealing to the courts. But success will to a large extent depend on the same factors that have been discussed in the context of other forms of law enforcement. Success will be closely related to the position, prominence and political influence of the management of the organisation. Also, in appealing for reinstatement the employee suffers from a familiar handicap: acting as an individual in relation to a set of agencies that have a tendency towards mutual protection. These difficulties do not undermine the economic foundations of job security in the Soviet Union. But it is important to be clear about the source of that security, and not to confuse it with the question of legal guarantees.

1 SOVIET LABOUR LAW AND WORK DISPUTES

Soviet labour law is highly comprehensive and positive: that is to say, it specifies positively and in detail the rights and duties of the employing organisation and the employees, together with the functions of the trade unions and the courts, the two main agencies that have been given the role of defending the interests of Soviet workers. This provides a strong contrast with Britain, which historically has lacked a positive framework of legislation to define the functions of employer, employee and organised labour. The trade unions have established the right to exist and to engage in industrial action by gaining immunity from criminal prosecution and suits for civil damages, not by having their rights to exist and their functions positively defined in statute.[1] This state of affairs has tended to change in recent years. Corporatist trends have increased the arena of labour legislation, for example in the area of health and safety, in rules on unfair dismissal, and in attempts to delimit in statute the forms of permissible industrial action.[2] In this sense there has been a certain convergence. But Soviet labour law remains unusually comprehensive in scope. This has been especially true since 1970, when the Principles of Labour Law were adopted, followed in 1971 by the introduction of a new Labour Code.

I shall be concerned with only one part of this very large body of law: the part which relates to work disputes. Furthermore, I shall be focusing only on those disputes that affect the security of labour: disputes connected with disciplinary action by management and with dismissals.

In Soviet law, work disputes occur when either an employee or the management of an organisation wish to challenge the actions of the other side, on grounds laid down in the Labour Codes.[3] (There are codes for each republic in the USSR, but these vary only in minor ways.) Disputes can occur over disciplinary sanctions; termination of contracts; payment of wages, salaries and bonuses; holiday entitlements; compensation for damages; acceptance of technical innovations by employees. Disputes do not take the form of collective industrial action. They involve an individual (or an organisation acting as an individual) appealing to rights and duties and norms specified in law which are alleged to have been violated.

The main agencies responsible in law for the resolution of work disputes are the trade unions and the courts. Most disputes are subject to initial discussion within organisations by a Commission on Work Disputes, which is made up of half management and half trade union representatives. If the Commission fails to give satisfaction to the 'plaintiff', the matter passes to the trade union committee. The officially defined role of the trade unions gives them, even in principle, a radically different function in work disputes from their counterparts in capitalist societies. Trade unions are not defined in Soviet law as state organisations, but in the realm of disputes they are explicitly assigned a 'state' function, namely to defend workers against management action which contravenes the law. This function may now play some part in the activities of Western trade unions, as a result of the corporatist trends I have mentioned (for example, shop steward involvement in the supervision of health and safety). But the main role of trade unions in capitalist societies – to engage in collective bargaining over wages and salaries – makes no appearance in the Soviet Union, where basic wages and salary scales are established by administrative decision.

If the union committee of an organisation decides against the plaintiff in a dispute, the plaintiff can appeal to a People's Court.[4] As in criminal cases, the court comprises one presiding judge and two lay assessors. Both plaintiffs and defendants can have legal representation in work disputes, and in hearings on reinstatement it is obligatory for a procurator to be present and give her opinion on the legal aspects of the case. The decisions of the court are binding but can be appealed. As in criminal procedure, appeals through the courts can take two forms: either by means of an individual (the plaintiff or defendant) appealing to a higher court, or by means of judicial review of lower court decisions by higher courts. In the former case the appeal can go up to the level of the Republic Supreme Court. In the latter case reviews can occur at all levels, up to the USSR Supreme Court. The USSR Supreme Court is not an agent of appeal for plaintiffs or defendants, but it can quash the decisions of any other court. When deciding work dispute cases on appeal, the higher courts cannot change a decision, but they can demand a new hearing. In addition, both managerial and court decisions in work disputes can be protested (though not reversed) by the procuracy.[5]

For the purposes of my discussion the most important disputes are those arising from dismissals on disciplinary and non-disciplinary grounds, and from other disciplinary sanctions. The Commissions on Work Disputes do not play a significant role in this context, and are not entitled to discuss dismissals.[6] I shall therefore leave them out of this account, and focus on the trade union committees and the courts. In most cases the agreement of the trade union committee is necessary before issuing a dismissal notice. Thereafter one can appeal to a court for reinstatement. But before discussing the role of these agencies of labour law enforcement, it is important first to look at the effect of management attitudes towards the workforce on the security of labour.

2 MANAGEMENT ATTITUDES AND THE SECURITY OF WORK

The range of formal management powers in relation to the workforce, like other aspects of labour law, is defined in detail in the Labour Code and Principles of Labour Law. These specify all permissible disciplinary sanctions, and provide a complete list of grounds for dismissal.[7] The main disciplinary measures are (a) reproofs or reprimands, (b) withdrawal of bonuses for unsatisfactory work, (c) transfer to lower-paid work or demotion to a lower position for a period up to three months, (d) dismissal.

Dismissal for broadly disciplinary reasons is provided for on the following main grounds: (1) in the case of 'systematic non-fulfilment of work duties'. If this is to be applied, there must have been at least one other violation of discipline in the course of the past year; (2) in the case of 'absence without good cause'. This means absence for more than three hours, or appearing at work drunk; (3) there are additional disciplinary grounds for dismissal for people with special responsibility for money or goods (they can be dismissed because of 'loss of trust'), and also for people with educational functions, who can be fired for an 'amoral misdemeanour'.

In addition to these, there are certain non-disciplinary grounds for termination of contract. Thus (1) employees (usually administrative or technical staff) can lose their jobs because of 'staff reductions', which enterprises are on occasion instructed to carry out in the interests of economy and a more rational use of labour. It is, in the words of one authoritative source, 'one of the measures to improve the work of the enterprise, and also to staff it with more qualified cadres'.[8] In the event of such a dismissal, the management must offer the employee suitable alternative work in the same organisation, or be able to show that no other such work is available, or that the employee has refused a suitable offer. Also, managers must take into account qualifications and length of service in making the decision. (2) Employees can be declared 'unsuitable for the post' and dismissed if they cannot fulfil their duties for health reasons, or if they are judged to be no longer qualified for the job. In the case of non-manual personnel, this judgement may be reached on the basis of a periodical (every 3–5 years) certification test (*attestatiya*). The latter measure was introduced after a USSR Council of Ministers recommendation in 1973, 'with the aim of increasing the effectiveness and responsibility of the work of executives, engineering–technical workers and other specialists ...'[9] Decisions about implementation are made by individual ministries. Certification commissions, appointed by the administration, are staffed by managers and specialists, together with komsomol, party and trade union representatives.

These rules are intended *both* to protect Soviet workers from arbitrary action by management *and* to ensure that workers carry out their duties: that they come to work on time, stay sober, do a fair day's work, and where necessary keep their qualifications up to scratch. To what extent does managerial practice in the USSR conform to these rules, and what are the implications of these practices for the security of work?

It is commonly said by both Soviet and Western observers that the managers of Soviet organisations are inclined to tolerate behaviour by their workforces which according to law they should not tolerate. Soviet workers get away with an inordinate amount of drunkenness, shoddy work, absenteeism and bad time-keeping. Poor work discipline has been the source of constant critical comment in the Soviet press and in party, government and trade union resolutions. This has a long history, and the latest campaign by the post-Brezhnev leadership (early 1983) is only the last in a series of such efforts. To understand the reasons for this indulgence would need a lengthy analysis that would take me outside the scope of the book. But very briefly, it seems that the incentives built into the mechanism of directive planning encourage Soviet managers to hold on to labour, because a larger workforce means a larger wage fund and more financial flexibility, and because the rhythm of production tends to be very uneven: workers are underemployed in slack periods, but many hands are needed in 'storming' periods to meet the monthly plan. Furthermore, managers have no strong interest in increasing labour productivity by tightening work norms, because they want a relatively easy plan to meet. For these reasons, it can be argued that the shortages of labour arise from difficulties in the planning mechanism rather than from absolute constraints. But beyond this there are indeed demographic problems which have caused pressure on labour resources, and problems of implementing technical innovations have made it difficult for Soviet planners to reduce the overall demand for labour. The upshot of all this is that managers are not inclined to get tough with unproductive workers, with drinking on the job, with absenteeism and other forms of misbehaviour. The work regime is not authoritarian, but based on a type of informal agreement whereby employees will do what is necessary in order to fulfil plan targets (for example, turn up at the end of the month and do a lot of overtime), enjoying in return a definite laxity in relation to various forms of work 'indiscipline'.

I shall assume for the purposes of my discussion that this picture is accurate. The result, it seems, is that the behaviour of Soviet managers tends to create a greater security of labour than is intended in Soviet law. But it does not of course follow from this that Soviet managers are deterred by Soviet law from arbitrary action against their employees. Indeed it is clear that while managers are indulgent towards 'indiscipline', they are also often prepared to act in ways which undermine the security of jobs that the law is designed to protect.

According to some Soviet commentators, this is now less true than it was in the past. Labour law is now more codified, and managers are more law-conscious. In support of this one could point to a decline in recent years in the number of appeals for reinstatement coming before the courts. Between 1972 and 1979, according to a Supreme Court statement, the number of suits for reinstatement declined by 30 per cent.[10] It may well be that greater legal regulation and greater consciousness of law is part of the explanation for this decline. But there are other possible reasons. First, the range of people entitled to appeal to a court for reinstatement is now narrower than it was at the beginning of the 1970s (I shall return to this later), and this might make a significant impact on the figures. Second, it may be that the chances of reinstatement are now less than before (this is a speculative suggestion), so that fewer people are prepared to go to the trouble of disputing their case in court. Finally, it could be that, with greater labour shortages, the black mark of a dismissal in one's work book is less of an impediment in getting another job, and that this also deters people from pursuing a dispute through judicial channels.

Whatever the explanation for the decrease in dismissal cases in recent years, Soviet observers make it clear that contraventions of labour laws are still widespread. According to a recent statement by a USSR Supreme Court official:

> ... materials on court practice show that there are still cases of gross violation of the labour rights of citizens, in particular illegal transfers and dismissals, sometimes by way of retaliation for critical statements, signals about abuses by people in official positions.[11]

If one focuses on those parts of the law that impinge on job security, the main criticisms of Soviet management practice are these.

First, there is still not enough respect for some basic formalities when transferring, disciplining and dismissing employees. According to a USSR Supreme Court survey of more than 4000 claims for reinstatement coming before the courts in 1975, legal norms were most often violated when people were dismissed in connection with violations of discipline, and in connection with staff cuts. Together these made up a large proportion of the stated reasons for dismissal, as the figures in Table 5.1, based on the survey, indicate. (The commentary makes clear that 'disciplinary reasons' include 'systematic non-fulfilment' and 'absenteeism'.[12])

Looking in more detail at the kinds of formalities that were not respected, one finds the following comments. Managements were still frequently ignoring the requirement to get trade union agreement for dismissals, a requirement which has been described as one of the 'legal guarantees of the right to work'.[13] In the USSR as a whole, one out of three dismissals in the survey had been carried out without trade union agreement, and in Azerbaidzhan, Turkestan and Uzbekistan, about one in two.[14] Furthermore, employees were sometimes being fired for reasons and in ways not provided for in law:

TABLE 5.1   *Stated reasons for dismissal in cases before the courts, 1975*

	%
Staff cuts	16.9
Unsuitable for the post	5.6
Systematic non-fulfilment of work duties	13.5
Absenteeism (including drunkenness)	32.3
Loss of trust	9.5
Amoral misdemeanour	1.2
Transfer to other work	7.2
Other reasons	13.8

SOURCE   BVS SSSR 1977, 3, p. 29.

Contrary to law, employees were fired for systematic non-fulfilment of work duties for a single misdemeanour, or more than one month after the discovery of the misdemeanour, or sometimes even six months later. There were frequent dismissals for absenteeism when the reasons for the absence had not been checked, or dismissals for failure to carry out an illegal directive on transfer to different work.[15]

Finally, in carrying out staff cuts, measures were not always taken to transfer the dismissed employees to other work.[16]

Yet this aspect of the matter is not perhaps the most important. Even where management abides by certain formalities in penalising and dismissing people, this may provide only a thin veneer over practices which contravene the broader purpose of the law. The impression one gets is that serious disputes over penalties and dismissals very often arise out of a breakdown in personal relations of some kind, and that in such situations managers will be only too ready to discipline a troublesome employee. The law says that it is strictly impermissible to act against an employee for reasons of personal hostility – indeed it is defined as a criminal offence in article 138 of the RSFSR Criminal Code. This provides corrective labour of one year, or dismissal, for

The illegal dismissal of an employee out of personal motives, failure to carry out the decision of a court on reinstatement, and any other intentional serious violation of labour law by an official of a state or social enterprise or establishment.[17]

But to judge from a mass of anecdotal evidence, this carries little weight in practice. The problem emerges very clearly in the stories about the whistleblowers, and has already been touched on. But let us look at it more closely. There were 66 cases in the sample of 70 reports about whistleblowing, in which the outcome for the critics was mentioned. Out of these 66, 26 were dismissed at some stage during the dispute, 13 received some other penalty, 4 left 'voluntarily'. In 23 of the cases, the complainants did not seem to have incurred any special unpleasantness. Out of the 26 who were dismissed, 14 were later reinstated, 3 were reinstated and then dismissed again, and 9 were dismissed without apparently getting their jobs back. A further important point emerges from a scrutiny of these stories, if one is entitled to rely on such a small sample: if the complainants are in managerial or technical positions, they have considerably *less* chance of getting away with a complaint about abuse of office. They are more likely to suffer a successful counter-attack from management. Whistleblowers are safer if they are manual workers or political activists, or if the complaint is signed by several people within the organisation. Table 5.2 sums up the information on which these suggestions are based. (It should be remembered that the information is based on press reports, and that in a few cases the dispute may not have been finally decided – a whistleblower may later have been penalised, dismissed or reinstated. Also, it should be noted that the labels describing the position of the complainants are simply the descriptions used in the press reports, and are not necessarily mutually exclusive. For example, someone in a managerial or technical position might also be an activist (e.g. a People's Control volunteer or party activist), and an activist might be a manual worker.)

The picture that emerges from the reports is that members of the intelligentsia are least able to bring off a successful complaint. This is not surprising, since people in responsible positions are less protected by law, and have weaker sources of support in the event of unfair dismissal. I shall return to this point later.

We have seen that the majority of whistleblowers incurred some form of penalty for their efforts, penalties that might include transfer, loss of bonus, reprimands or dismissal. Here are a few examples of disciplinary measures that were used by management against trouble-makers:

(1) A shop manager who made himself unpopular with the director of a wine plant was held responsible for some defective products, received a reprimand and was deprived of his bonus. Later he was

TABLE 5.2 *Management response to complaints by employees about abuse of office*

Penalty	Position of complainant				
	Manag.–tech.	*Activist*	*Manual worker*	*Collective complaint*	*Customer*
Dismissal	8	1	—	—	—
Dismissal and reinstatement	6	2	6	—	—
Dismissal, reinstatement and dismissal	2	—	1	—	—
Other penalties	5	3	1	4	—
Left voluntary	—	3	1	—	—
No penalty	4	6	4	8	1
Total	25	15	13	12	1

SOURCE Soviet press reports, 1979–83.

dismissed after being held responsible for a batch of products that were defective because 'some of the labels had been put on skew'.[18]

(2) A non-cooperative legal consultant working for a building organisation, who wrote a critical article in *Pravda*, encountered heavy opposition from his superiors, who contrived to have him expelled from the trade union, and then dismissed him after he had 'arrived late for work' (in this case, the management made use of an article in the Labour Code which permits dismissal after a 'single serious violation of work duties').[19]

(3) A trade employee who wrote to the city party committee to express concern about losses of goods and embezzlement received three reprimands for poor work in the space of nine days.[20]

(4) A doctor working for a sanitary–epidemiological station, who was resisting false reporting, was given three reprimands in the space of a month, and then demoted.[21]

(5) A pig minder on a state farm had incurred hostility by protesting that the director was trying to improve the economic position of the farm by illegal means. She was offered a transfer which it was pretty certain she would refuse, and having got the refusal, the director fired her.[22]

(6) A research engineer G., who did design work for automated machine tools, fell out with the head of his department, and left his research institute. G. led a group in the department and one of the designs was refused by a commission, apparently a common occurrence. The department head took advantage of this situation:

> He told me openly that he would find the first suitable moment to dismiss me ... what does this mean? He would not simply write an order. In Russia, if they tell you they're going to dismiss you, it means that they're going to start something up against you. Let's say today you were late for work, it will be written down, something else – again it will be noted, you'll get a reprimand, gradually a certain material is accumulated, and then a lawful dismissal can occur.[23]

In addition to the use of these disciplinary clauses in the Labour Code, a director can also make use of other grounds for discharge. 'Staff cuts' seems to be the most popular tactic in the case of administrative and technical personnel who fail to cooperate.[24] But 'unsuitability for the post' is also sometimes used. An employee in a construction organisation, who was discharged after failing a certification test (*attestatsiya*), took the view that certification was being used as a 'new form of dismissal of employees'.[25] Specialists are vulnerable in this situation since it is difficult, in the face of another opinion, to prove that one is still sufficiently qualified for the job. One informant, who had worked as an engineer in a radio plant, put it this way:

> If he [the director] had wanted to dismiss me, he could have done it very simply. He would have written a note ... that I wasn't coping with the work ... It is impossible to prove [that you are working well] ... with a lathe operator, you can see what he has done ... but with a designer you can always say that he's not coping, that he's not suitable, etc. ... You can say that his level used to be high, but has become lower than two years ago ...[26]

It is possible, then, to use the formal provisions of the labour law in order to dispose of unwanted employees. A final dismissal notice may be indeed unnecessary, since they may choose to leave of their own accord. Life will be especially difficult for someone who has taken a complaint outside the organisation, and strong pressure is likely to be put on such a critic to leave 'voluntarily', or, to use an ironic Soviet expression for it, 'by the voluntary decision of the bosses' (*po sobstvennomu zhelaniyu nachal'stva*). This is no doubt the preferred option for management because it avoids possible legal complications, and it seems that this is what a liberal sprinkling of reprimands is often designed to achieve. A farm manager implicated in a letter of protest about the theft of milk was reported as saying to the 'culprits': 'So you're writing anonymous letters about me? Well, I'll teach you a lesson. I'll make things so hard for you that you'll leave of your own accord.'[27] In another instance, the management of a furniture factory, when confronted with a troublesome engineer, decided to put him in his place, and 'used the slightest excuse to "reward" this trouble-maker with punishments: perhaps he would get the idea and give notice himself'.[28]

The following picture emerges from this discussion. On the one hand, managers are all too reluctant to impose sanctions on employees who break the official rules that define labour discipline. On the other hand, they are all too willing to penalise subordinates who are not prepared to play by the informal rules, and who get in the way of the task at hand as understood by their superiors. There is no conflict between these elements. They are two sides of the same coin, which reflect the dominant role of informal and personal relationships in organisational life. In his book on Soviet managers, Andrle (1976) aptly describes the Soviet manager as a 'benevolent boss', who can dispense favours to selected employees, strengthen loyalties and thus hold on to needed members of the workforce. But the same benevolent boss can turn 'malevolent' when people fail to play the game. The critics who have taken the centre of the stage in this book found this out to their cost. It should not be concluded from this that there is anything especially vindictive about Soviet managers. It is just that the culture and practice of labour relations have been established to a large extent without reference to the law. The law plays a part in those relationships, but far less than the immensely detailed – and admirably fair – body of legal regulation would suggest.

3 THE ROLE OF THE TRADE UNIONS

In the stories recounted in Chapters 3 and 4, the trade union organisers and committees at enterprise level appear as defenders of management, as part of the inner circle, closing ranks against troublesome employees. Officially and in law the trade union organisations are supposed to defend workers from arbitrary action by management. In particular, they are instructed to withdraw their agreement to a dismissal if it contravenes the law. But this seems to happen rarely. The general impression one gets is that union officials are either unable or unwilling to speak up for employees in the case of serious disputes leading to disciplinary sanctions and dismissal. In saying this I am not suggesting that the trade unions are powerless in relation to work disputes in general, and still less that they perform no useful functions.[29] It may well be that in less contentious matters union organisers and committees are less ready to jump to the defence of management. Dismissals are not frequent events in the life of a single organisation, and will not often appear on the agenda of trade union meetings. The bread and butter of union activity, in so far as it relates to *disputes*, is connected with matters of pay and bonuses – not with basic wages and salaries, but with whether payments have been correctly made. On these issues there will be many arguments where the outcome will be less loaded, and where the union may have a greater leeway to defend employees.[30] Also, the strength of the union committee seems to be much greater in some sectors than in others. In the view of one informant, who had long trade union experience in machine tool plants, the amount of influence was likely to depend greatly on the 'professional level of the workers' and 'the strength of the collective'.[31]

Union officials within the organisation may then have some room for manoeuvre in less contentious matters. But where the management is intent on disciplining or dismissing an employee, the trade union is unlikely to be willing to do much about it. One informant, a former legal consultant with a variety of different organisations in Kiev, stressed that dismissals were surrounded with formalities, and noted that dismissal directives might be changed on the advice of a legal consultant, but added: 'if it was necessary to dismiss a person, this was done without any discussions. They found a pretext, got the agreement of the trade union committee and dismissed them ...'[32] Another interviewee, who had experience as a union official, made a similar observation:

> Formally, by law, the administration could not dismiss a person without the agreement of the trade union organisation. As a rule ... the trade union organisation gives its agreement automatically, it was rare that the union did not give its agreement.[33]

The weakness of enterprise union committees has been criticised by some Soviet observers as well. One such comment, which was focusing on the question of dismissals, ran as follows:

> ... many trade union committees, which are called on to provide supervision and control over observance of labour law by the administration, at times fail to enter deeply into the substance of the labour conflict that has arisen, do not check in an all-sided, and most important, in an objective way the materials presented by the administration on the dismissal of a worker and often simply blindly sanction the decision taken by the administration. In a number of cases they do not abide by the rule that meetings of the committee are only competent with the participation of at least two thirds of the committee ... the workers to be dismissed are not always invited to the meeting.[34]

In the sample of 70 stories about whistleblowing, there were two cases in which, so far as one could tell, the trade union failed to support the management in their efforts to dispose of an unwanted employee. In one of them, a serious rift had developed in the organisation between supporters and opponents of the director, collective letters of complaint had been written to the city party committee, and the party secretary had also come out against the director.[35] The other case was about a building organisation in which a worker had publicly criticised the boss for his 'immodest style of life': he already had a posh establishment but was now, among other things, building a 'huge detached home with a garage and a bath', when there was a long queue of workers for housing. The worker was offered a transfer to the job of night guard, which it was clear he would refuse because his wife was ill, and was then given his notice. But the trade union chairman refused to sanction this.[36]

These examples show that not all trade union officials can be relied on to support management in firing employees. But they are interesting as atypical situations. It seems clear that in the great majority of cases, a Soviet manager will have no reason to fear trade union resistance when the question of disciplinary sanctions and dismissals comes up.

The reluctance of the unions to defend employees in the more serious disputes over disciplinary matters and over dismissals is not surprising, but it deserves some comment. One should bear in mind, in the first place, that trade union officials bear joint responsibility with management and the enterprise party committee for the results of the organisation's activities. One of their tasks is to assist the enterprise in meeting targets. Union organisers will therefore, broadly speaking, share the management's definition of the situation. For example, if safety requirements lose out in the struggle for the plan, the enterprise union officials are not likely to make a fuss. They 'know', as managers and party secretaries know, that long-term problems of safety must come second to the pressing task of meeting immediate targets. Similarly, if the administration has defined an employee as troublesome to the organisation, union officials are scarcely likely to quarrel with that judgement.

Secondly, although members of a trade union committee are formally elected, in practice it seems that nominees for the committee are usually selected by the administration in alliance with the party secretary, and that such nominees are rarely turned down at annual trade union meetings when elections are held. The nominees are therefore beholden both to the administration and to the party secretary. If the director has the support of the party secretary, which is usually the case, the trade union official will have very little room for manoeuvre.[37]

Finally, union organisers have something to gain materially from their positions. Being a union official brings a number of material privileges and career advantages which incumbents may not want to forgo by making themselves unpopular. If they fall out of step, they may fail to gain reelection the next time round.

In sum, trade union officials at enterprise level simply do not have the independence from management that they would need in order to offer any serious challenge when conflicts develop and an employee needs support from within the organisation.

4 THE ROLE OF THE COURTS

Since the trade unions are weak sources of support for aggrieved employees, and tend to rubber stamp management decisions on disciplinary penalties and dismissals, considerable weight is put on the Soviet courts to defend people against unfair dismissal and other illegal managerial decisions. What is the effect of judicial intervention in civil law cases involving disputes at work, and in particular, what are the chances of reinstatement if one appeals to a Soviet court against illegal dismissal? These questions are difficult to answer in the absence of any systematic published data on court decisions. The problem is similar to the one that came up in Chapter 2. But by gathering together some scattered pieces of information it is possible to draw a rough picture and to make some inferences.

The possibility of defending yourself in court against arbitrary action by managers or officials is now a constitutional right of Soviet citizens. Article 58 of the 1977 Constitution says that 'The actions of officials committed in violation of law, in excess of their powers and impinging on the rights of citizens, may be appealed to a court in accordance with the procedure established by law.' In similar vein, article 57 states that 'Citizens of the USSR shall have the right to judicial protection against infringements on their honour and dignity, life and health, personal freedom and property.'[38]

In the light of these provisions it is important to note that people in certain categories of jobs are *not* entitled to appeal to a court for reinstatement or for redress of other grievances under labour law. They must appeal to administrative superiors. The most important of these categories are defined in a 'List No. 1' and 'List No. 2', which were appended to the Regulations on Work Disputes drawn up in May 1974.[39] List No. 1 covers a wide range of people in responsible positions at higher and lower levels. The defining feature appears to be that a post involves administrative responsibility over a group of subordinates, though whether this is consistently applied I am not sure. It includes heads of enterprises, shop-heads and their deputies; heads of departments and chief specialists (chief engineers, accountants, designers, mechanics, etc.) and their deputies; foremen; heads of administrative divisions and subdivisions in ministerial departments down to city level; staff working for elected bodies and social (e.g. party and trade union) organisations. A variety of other posts in state agencies are also mentioned. 'List No. 2' has a more limited reference. It prohibits the staff of scientific research and educational institutions from appealing to a court if they have been dismissed on the grounds of 'unsuitability for the post', where these grounds have been decided on the basis of a certification procedure.[40]

People in these positions and circumstances must then rely on a complaint to a superior within their own administrative hierarchy, a process which by all accounts is highly unlikely to succeed. The resulting problems have led to some discussion by Soviet legal specialists. It has been said unambiguously that it is now unconstitutional not to give the categories in these lists the right of judicial defence, and that the law should be brought into line with the Constitution. Two writers from the Institute of State and Law in Moscow have this to say:

> At present there is a large group of employees deprived of judicial defence ... We are speaking of those employees whose positions are listed in the appendices to the Regulations on Work Disputes, together with those falling under special disciplinary regulations. When dismissed for violations of labour discipline and for other stated reasons which infringe upon their honour as workers, and when disciplinary penalties are imposed on these employees, they do not have the right to turn to the courts. Their honour as workers can be defended only by higher administrative organs. Practice has shown how weak this form of defence is. Yet at present the exclusion of these employees from the sphere of judicial defence has no constitutional justification.[41]

Writing on the same theme, another legal specialist notes the contrast between the Constitution and the law, and observes:

> In Soviet labour law ... the examination of disputes by administrative superiors was always regarded as an exception. But

in the recent period the list of cases excluded from the jurisdiction of the courts has increased to such an extent that the exception has spread to quite a wide circle of employees. This is surely incorrect. The new Constitution of the USSR allows the problem to be decided from a fully democratic standpoint . . .[42]

This position has been given some support also from the USSR Procuracy. According to the head of the department of general supervision:

Every citizen must have the opportunity to appeal to a court in the event of an infringement of his work rights. This does not mean, of course, that the administrative apparatus is not able correctly to resolve this or that work conflict. However, the examination of such cases . . . is often unjustifiably drawn out. There are cases where particular officials, in order to defend their illegal actions, try by any means to discredit unjustifiably dismissed employees . . .[43]

These observations show that there is now some awareness in establishment circles of the difficulties that face people who are dismissed and have to rely on administrative intervention – though as far as I know this discussion has not yet resulted in legislative changes. This was a serious problem for many of the people who blew the whistle; as we saw, they were often people in responsible positions, and some of these, if dismissed, would have been unable to appeal to a court for reinstatement. If one considers too that administrative and technical staff are more likely to be affected by 'staff cuts' than manual workers, and that 'unsuitability for the post' is a provision applied to specialists, the upshot must be that the jobs of the intelligentsia, broadly defined, are less protected in law than the jobs of manual workers. It is not therefore surprising to find that among the whistleblowers it is the people in intelligentsia positions who are least able to protect themselves from management counter-measures.

If we now set aside this problem and consider those who are entitled to appeal to a court for reinstatement, what are the chances of getting a decision in one's favour, and what will that decision depend on? Information on the extent and pattern of reinstatement is scarce, and no general data seem to have been published very recently. But global figures have on occasion been given. The most recent relate to 1975: the USSR Supreme Court reviewed a sample of more than 4000 claims for reinstatement in the Soviet courts in that year. Some 55 per cent of the plaintiffs were successful in the USSR as a whole, with a higher figure in some republics: more than 70 per cent of plaintiffs were successful in Uzbekistan, and more than 60 per cent in Armenia, Kirgizia, Kazakhstan, Georgia and Azerbaidzhan.[44]

Soviet commentators do not regard a high rate of reinstatement as a good thing in itself. If large numbers of management decisions are being reversed in the courts, it means that managers are showing far too little respect for labour law. This is logical enough, and it may well be that the management attitude to these matters is more casual in Central Asia and Transcaucasia than in the RSFSR and European republics. With these criteria in mind, one local party secretary pointed with pride to the fact that in Ivanovo province, in 1974, 102 out of 207 claims for reinstatement were successful, whereas in the first half of 1981, only 1 out of 35 such claims had succeeded.[45]

Following this line of thought, one would have to say that the lower the rate of reinstatement, the better. But the issue takes on a different significance in the light of a good deal of criticism of the Soviet courts for their failure to give an adequate response to claims against illegal dismissal, and thus to ensure that the legal right to job security is fully observed. Given this criticism, which I shall discuss presently, one wants to know more about what lies behind these general figures on reinstatement. The important thing is not just the general chances of success, but what the chances depend on. For example, what kind of organisations were involved (how big a fish was the director)? What were the reasons given for dismissal? What kind of jobs did the plaintiffs occupy? What reasons were given for accepting or rejecting the claim? Did the court consider the possibility that the management was 'taking reprisals for criticism'? Given the absence of detailed published information, these questions cannot be answered in anything like the way that one would ideally like. But a few suggestions will be offered that may at least begin to answer them.

In the event of blatant disregard of correct procedure by management, the chances of reinstatement are probably very high, because when considering dismissal cases the Soviet courts seem to put a heavy emphasis on procedural correctness. A former legal consultant, with experience of several organisations in Kiev, put it this way:

> If a dispute occurred and the matter got to a court, then ... the representative of the procuracy had to participate in every hearing ... if the administration wanted to dismiss an employee and ... drew up the documents so that everything was according to the law, then no court could reinstate that person. [But] often the

enterprise administration made all kinds of mistakes, and then the court quickly reinstated this employee ... you see, on the one hand the laws were broken by everyone how and when they wanted, on the other hand ... the courts and the procuracy formally stood guard over the observance of law, including labour law.[46]

However, the amount of care and objectivity that the courts bring to work disputes seems to vary greatly. One can point to contrasting pieces of evidence on this score.

Over the past ten years or so USSR Supreme Court resolutions and reviews of court practice have recurrently noted an improvement in the 'role of the judicial organs in strengthening socialist legality in the sphere of labour relations'.[47] In support of such statements, Soviet commentators have pointed to a general decline in the number of work disputes coming before the courts, and in particular a decline in the number of dismissal cases. This change, according to one resolution, is 'to a certain extent a result of the activity of the courts in the struggle against violations of labour law'.[48] I have already suggested that the reduction in the number of work disputes dealt with by the courts might be explained by factors other than those that relate to the level of observance of law. But I see no reason to doubt that the general level of observance has indeed increased, and the role of the courts in reinstating people may have had something to do with it.

I would add to this that some personal experience listening to cases dealing with dismissals in Moscow and Leningrad courts suggested that the court procedure, at least in principle, allows room for a quite thorough, informal and fair investigation of the claim, with plenty of scope for the plaintiff and the plaintiff's lawyers to defend their case.[49]

But against this there is a lot of criticism by the USSR Supreme Court of the handling of work disputes, and dismissals in particular. Recurrent references have been made to 'serious shortcomings' and violations of procedure by the lower courts.[50] The main complaints are the following:

(1) The most frequent criticism is that the courts examine dismissals and other work disputes in a superficial way. It is also clear from USSR Supreme Court judgements that this superficiality generally works against the interests of the plaintiffs. It is true that the courts have also been instructed to 'eliminate from their practice cases, where, in deciding work disputes, they show a liberal attitude to gross violations of labour discipline by some employees',[51] and it has been

said that 'cases of unjustified reinstatement of absentees and other violators of labour discipline are still not rare'.[52]

But the great bulk of critical comment is reserved for illegal dismissals in which employees' rights have been violated, and focuses on the failure of the courts to offer an adequate response to this. In almost all the dismissal cases reviewed on appeal by the USSR Supreme Court, the plaintiffs are defended against superficial or prejudicial decisions by lower-level courts, and are sent down again for a new hearing.[53] As one resolution put it, 'the most widespread reason for incorrect decisions on claims for reinstatement . . . is the lack of a thorough investigation by the court of the actual circumstances of the dispute'.[54] In a review of court practice in 1973, these observations are spelt out. The courts are criticised for sometimes failing to examine properly the arguments for reinstatement in cases of dismissal on grounds of staff cuts, unsuitability for the post, systematic non-fulfilment of work duties and absenteeism. For example, the courts did not always check properly that there were no alternative jobs for 'reduced' staff, nor that those dismissed under a certification procedure were indeed 'unsuitable'; they sometimes failed to check that violations of discipline had been 'systematic', or to investigate the real reasons behind somebody's failure to appear at work. On occasion, too, the courts ignored the lack of prior agreement to a dismissal from the trade union.[55]

(2) Another failing of the courts is that although they are obliged by law to take action against managements that have dismissed an employee in clear violation of the law (for example, if trade union agreement was not given for a dismissal), they seldom do this in practice. In such cases the courts are instructed to recover from individual managers some of the damages incurred by the enterprise in paying for the involuntary absence of the plaintiff. But 'the courts rarely [do this] even when the dismissal occurs without the agreement of the trade union committee'.[56] In 1975, in only a quarter of cases where this agreement was lacking, were any damages recovered at all, and in only 14 per cent were managers personally penalised.[57] Problems of this kind led to the following Supreme Court statement:

> Despite many directives by the Plenum of the USSR Supreme Court, courts do not yet ensure the adequate implementation of article 93 of the Principles of Labour Law . . . providing for the imposition of material responsibility on officials guilty of obviously illegal dismissal or transfer of an employee to other work.[58]

(3) The courts are instructed, as in criminal cases, to issue Special Rulings where clear violations of labour law have taken place. The purpose of the rulings is to comment on the conditions giving rise to illegal management decisions, and to help managers to mend their ways. These too, it is said, are issued all too rarely.[59] In 1975, Special Rulings were issued in 16 per cent of cases where it would have been appropriate, and it was lower than this in many republics.[60]

In addition to these problems, all raised by the higher judicial authorities, it is worth asking also to what extent the courts consider the possibility that the formal grounds on which a person has been dismissed are simply pretexts, and that the real reason has to do with personal animosities, perhaps as a result of 'criticism from below'. This is an important general point in considering appeals for reinstatement, because it is likely that a high proportion of dismissals are basically due to soured personal relations, rather than formal infractions of work discipline by employees. But it is especially relevant, as we have seen, to the whistleblowers, who are typically penalised for specious reasons.

In law, the courts are supposed to consider the possibility that the plaintiff has been disciplined or dismissed for personal reasons, since it is regarded as a serious offence. If this is revealed during the court hearing, the court is instructed to issue a Special Ruling, and if necessary to raise the question of bringing a criminal charge.[61] On occasions the courts do comment on this aspect of dismissals. One report ran as follows:

It happens that a manager out of personal hostility throws down one punishment after another on a subordinate. And even, ignoring the law, dismisses a person.

The Chairman of the Matchinsk voluntary fire service (Leninabad province, Tadzhikistan) dismissed two of his subordinates ... They were accused of every sin: absenteeism, shoddy work and even extortion. The Matchinsk People's Court established that the administration of the fire service, in the person of K.S. who had issued this directive, was guided not so much by the paragraphs of the labour law as by personal hostile relations ... [The two workers] were reinstated by the court.[62]

But my impression, both from a reading of legal sources and from some experience listening to dismissal cases in Soviet courts, is that judges are not generally prepared to enter into a discussion of motives, and tend to stick strictly to procedural matters. Special Rulings are rare in this connection, and I have come across no case in which a manager was dismissed (under the provisions of article 138 of the RSFSR Criminal Code) as a result of a violation of this kind. In 1981 the USSR Supreme Court reviewed a sample of 327 cases on reinstatement. It noted that in 153 of these, the plaintiffs had indicated that the reason for dismissal had to do with criticism. But in only 12 cases did the court issue a Special Ruling, and in no case raised the question of a criminal charge, although there were grounds for doing so.[63]

All this is understandable. It is difficult to sort out rights and wrongs when there is a breakdown in personal relationships. It is difficult to sort out the origins of personal animosities. But it is also clear that the court cannot do its job of understanding the real reasons for the dispute unless it is prepared to examine this aspect of the matter. The high degree of codification of Soviet law is here ambiguous in its effects. In one sense it favours employees, because managers cannot simply get rid of an employee without finding some formal pretext. But it also makes it easier for the administration superficially to abide by the rules, while obscuring the real basis of its behaviour.

These appear to be the main procedural transgressions by the courts in dealing with claims for reinstatement, which in the eyes of the higher judiciary have led to an unacceptably high level of decisions being annulled. In 1973, 22 per cent of decisions on such claims were annulled, and in 1975, 20 per cent. In six non-European republics the figure ranged from about 25 per cent to about 37 per cent.[64] These figures seem very high in the light of statements from several sources that judicial decisions are rarely reversed on appeal, because of the view that such decisions must remain 'stable'. A former Moscow advocate commented on this:

> In Moscow the People's Court ... feels a complete lack of responsibility ... [because] it is not at all afraid of the city appeal court ... As a rule, it confirms the sentence. Why? There is the view that sentences and decisions must remain stable ... In Moscow, for example, 0.3% of decisions are changed. In the Moscow province court it is a bit higher, because it is considered that in Moscow province judges are less qualified.[65]

Another informant, a former Moscow judge who specialised in labour law cases, now a lecturer in the Faculty of Law at Moscow University, quoted the following figures for reversals in work dispute cases: 1½ per cent through the courts and 1½ per cent through the procuracy.[66] If all the figures are roughly right, I am not sure how they can be squared. The explanation could be that the level of reversals is much higher in some republics than in others, or much higher in relation to courts outside the big cities, or much higher in certain types of judicial decision – or some combination of these factors. It seems unlikely, though, that the middle-level (city and province) courts are responsible for many of the reversals in disputes over dismissals. It is probable that most of the annulments come from the higher reaches of the judicial system. Since it is difficult to believe that the higher courts can review more than a certain proportion of cases, one may guess that many unsatisfactory decisions pass through this net.

Court Decisions and Managerial Power

This review of court practice suggests that the chances of reinstatement are quite good, if one considers simply the general proportion of successful claims. But it also emerges that Soviet judges, though they put great emphasis on procedural matters, often fail to observe the requirements laid down by the highest judicial authorities, and are not over-concerned to get to the root of a dispute. There are no doubt quite wide variations in this respect between different republics and regions of the USSR. But this is not the only issue. The attitude of the court will depend upon the size and importance of the organisation and the prestige and influence of the director. In the case of a smaller enterprise, where the director will be low on the party *nomenklatura*, the court will be less likely to worry about offending the director or his supporters within officialdom by reinstating an employee. This observation is not easy to demonstrate conclusively, but it is plausible on *a priori* grounds, and is compatible with other evidence. The *a priori* grounds are simply these: if the courts did not act in this way, then their behaviour would be significantly different when dealing with work disputes than their behaviour in the kind of criminal cases discussed in Chapter 2, where it seemed clear that court policy had a lot to do with the importance and prestige of the enterprise. It is inherently implausible that this consideration would cease to play a part when the courts are considering claims for reinstatement.

But there are more concrete things that one can point to in this context. First, all the detailed descriptions of successful claims for reinstatement published in Soviet legal sources are apparently about relatively small and unprestigious organisations. I am referring in particular to the cases reviewed by the USSR Supreme Court and published in its Bulletin (42 dismissal cases were examined, within the years 1971–82). In principle this could be simply because far fewer disputes over dismissal occur within large organisations in priority sectors, because the managements are more law-abiding. This may be part of it. But the explanation is also that the court will want to avoid decisions in favour of reinstatement if this is going to reflect badly on a 'big fish'. Such a big fish will typically have the support of the local party secretary, whom the judge cannot lightly ignore. One informant, a former legal consultant, had a comment about this:

Undoubtedly this [i.e. the prominence of the enterprise] had a significance. This was not blatant, it was not emphasised, but it was significant ... for example, the director of Z. [an agricultural procurements organisation], where I worked to begin with, was a small figure in the district ... [On the other hand] the director of the ship-building factory ... was a member of the raikom buro. The judge who examines cases involving this factory ... will not usually be a member of the buro. He might be a member of the raikom, but even that not always. But he is unfailingly a party member. From this point of view, from the point of view of one's position within the party, the director stands five heads higher than the judge ... And, of course, the judge feels this all the time when he is examining cases concerning this factory.[67]

A very similar observation was made by another informant, a former journalist, who was familiar with cases in which, even when an employee had been reinstated by a district People's Court, the management refused to reinstate or procrastinated. In this event the court could in theory start criminal proceedings against the manager, but there were difficulties:

There is of course another possibility, to bring a criminal charge against [such a director]. But this is another and complex matter ... connected with the Soviet *nomenklatura*. A district judge is, let's say, in position no. 8 on the *nomenklatura*, whereas the director of a big factory is, say, no. 6. This means that the chairman of the court cannot simply start criminal proceedings. He must ring up a district party secretary, usually the third, and tell him that this swine is not carrying out my decision. But the district party secretary will say: no, no, that's not how to settle such things ... such cases are so normal that anecdotes cannot convey their typicality.[68]

The importance of the director's position and influence is strongly suggested also by the fact that in some cases an enterprise administration reinstates an employee on a court order, only to find the next suitable pretext to issue another dismissal notice. If a management can regard legal intervention as only a temporary setback, and continues with its efforts to get rid of an undesirable employee, this must mean that the director has the necessary support or indulgence of his own superiors or of local party officials.

A few examples of this came up in the press accounts of whistle-blowing: as we saw, some of the critics endured more than one dismissal and reinstatement before being finally defeated, or in exceptional circumstances getting support from the higher authorities or from the national press. A particularly striking illustration of this kind of 'ping pong' match between the judiciary and management came up in one of the reviews by the USSR Supreme Court, and is worth describing in some detail. The story is about one Salikhova, a nurse employed by a sanatorium in Kazakhstan. In 1972 she was dismissed for absenteeism, and reinstated by a district People's Court in Alma Ata. This decision was annulled on appeal and at a new hearing by the city court, in 1973, the reinstatement was refused. That decision was allowed to stand by the Kazakhstan Supreme Court, and Salikhova was again dismissed. (The course of events here is unusual, suggesting that the management lacked political support in the immediate locality, but found it higher up.) The Deputy Procurator of the USSR then issued a protest to the Kazakhstan Supreme Court and asked for a new hearing, because 'the circumstances of the dispute were not adequately examined'. The protest was turned down. The General Procurator of the USSR now brought a protest to the USSR Supreme Court, which granted it, annulling the decision of the Alma Ata city court and all subsequent decisions, and asking for a new hearing by the Kazakh Supreme Court (that was in 1974). It would not be appropriate to go into all the details, but it was clear from the review by the highest court that the management of the sanatorium had forged Salikhova's work rosters and had produced the most specious reasons for her dismissal, while the Kazakh courts had displayed gross bias.

Salikhova was reinstated, but even after this intervention at the highest level, the management did not abandon its efforts. In 1982 a *second* USSR Supreme Court review appeared about the same Salikhova. In 1979 she had been dismissed for 'systematic violation of labour discipline'. She had appealed for reinstatement and the case was heard 'several times' in the Kazakh courts, without success. The same protests from the USSR Procuracy were again issued and the USSR Supreme Court again annulled the previous decisions, on the grounds that 'the alleged violations of labour discipline did not take place ... the penalties were given as a result of the prejudicial attitude towards her on the part of the head doctor and some other employees of the sanatorium'.[69]

I have described this case at some length not in order to suggest that such obstruction is an everyday occurrence but to illustrate the resilience of management and local interests, and the limits to judicial power, when political factors intervene even in a perfectly mundane and 'non-political' case of dismissal.

5 OTHER CHANNELS OF APPEAL

The weakness of the enterprise trade union bodies and the limited power of the courts help to explain the frequent pursuit of claims for reinstatement through other channels – through the higher trade union agencies, the procuracy, the party and the press. The role of the party and the press in the complaint procedure has already been discussed, so I shall restrict myself here to some brief remarks about the unions and the procuracy.

The higher trade union bodies (the central or local trade union councils) receive a vast number of submissions on a wide range of matters relating to labour law, including disputes. Employees can appeal to the higher body if they are dissatisfied with the handling of a dispute, and higher union officials are obliged to respond. In certain circumstances they have the authority to demand that management meet the complaint, and to impose penalties on management for failure to observe the law. However, in the case of complaints about illegal dismissal, it is stressed that higher trade union officials are not to 'substitute' themselves for the agencies responsible for resolving disputes.

Trade union agencies, along with the party, press and soviets, evidently get very large postbags. In July 1981, at the Eighth Plenary

Session of the All-Union Central Council of Trade Unions, the Secretary discussed the 'letters and suggestions of the working people' at some length. During the Tenth Five-year Plan period, he said, the All-Union Council had had more than 225 000 letters and more than 60 000 people were personally received. The Central Committees and councils of the individual trade unions had received nearly 2 million letters and oral statements. This state of affairs indicated 'pressing problems connected with the development of the national economy', and was a sign of the trust that the working people hold towards the trade unions, their 'confidence that their legitimate demands will be met'. But the Secretary also expressed great disquiet about the fact that 'our trade union organs, our papers and journals receive a great flow of statements about serious violations of the lawful interests of the working people and about weak control on the part of trade union organisations in defending those interests'. He listed, in particular, complaints about violations of the rules on allocation of housing, and on distribution of social security and pensions, together with submissions about payment of wages and bonuses, safety conditions and illegal dismissals.[70]

I do not know how effective higher trade union intervention is in dismissal cases. This needs a separate study. But this type of intervention does not get much mention in press reports about dismissals, and given the difficulties that even the judiciary can experience, it would be surprising if the higher union bodies had much clout in this domain.

The procuracy is another possible source of appeal for employees with claims under labour law. The procuracy can review management decisions on this as on other matters and issue protests. Procuratorial intervention in cases of illegal transfer and dismissal is not uncommon, and offers, at least potentially, an important alternative source of support for those categories of employee who cannot appeal to the courts for reinstatement. In the stories about whistleblowing there were indeed a few cases where the procuracy came to the defence of people who were judged to be illegally transferred or dismissed.[71] But the same problem arises here as the one that emerged from the discussion in Chapter 2. The procuracy does not have sufficient political independence to defend a dismissed employee, if such an intervention works against local party interests.[72] Also, one encounters the same problem of managerial resistance to procuratorial intervention, as sometimes occurs with court decisions. An instructive example appeared in a story in *Literaturnaya Gazeta*. The gist of it was this. In

January 1976 the acting director of the Enakiev metallurgical plant dismissed the head of the enterprise nursery, Ch. This was after an inspection of the nursery's storerooms, which revealed a shortage of 14 rubles 77 kopeks worth of fruit juice. The nursery head was charged with 'gross violation of work duties', because of her failure to 'control the work of people with financial responsibilities and the work of employees in the food bloc'. She was told that she could not appeal to a court, and would have to go to her superiors. However, she got the support of the city and Donetsk province procuracies, both of whom sent protests to the factory administration. In both cases the procurators got the firm reply that Ch. would not be reinstated. The deputy procurator of the Ukraine then intervened, turning to the Ukraine Ministry of Ferrous Metallurgy. In the words of the reporter:

> The procurator set out the essence of the case thoroughly and in detail. He explained that the procuracy, having invited specialists to participate, once again had checked all the accusations ... It was established that she was not to blame. Meanwhile the actions of the factory administration showed glaring prejudice and lack of objectivity.
>
> It seems to me that this letter should have evoked a certain embarrassment and indignation amongst the republican leaders ... towards their stubborn subordinates. There they were settling personal scores, breaking Soviet laws in the most flagrant way, so the ministry must surely feel some shame on their behalf ...? Alas. There was no indignation ... the republican ministry replied to the republican procuracy coldly and succinctly: Ch. will not be reinstated ...
>
> I suppose it happened this way. They got a protest, they made a note of it. Against whom is the complaint made? The directors of the Enakiev factory? OK, that means the ball is in their court. Let them prepare their reply to the procuracy. Afterwards in the ministry they would put it in order, put a stamp on it ... It seems that another significant circumstance should be taken into account. This letter, although signed by a procurator, even the first deputy procurator of the republic, was not in the eyes of certain people in the ministry a dangerous document. Now if it had been a matter of some major abuse of office on the part of subordinate officials, if it had been a question of a black mark that would threaten to spoil the reputation of the ministry ... well, that would be a real procuratorial piece of paper. But what was this? Someone had got

angry, someone was dismissed not quite in the right way, an illegal note was written in her workbook. Nothing serious. We'll manage.[73]

The matter did not stop there. The USSR Procuracy eventually intervened, sending a protest to the Ministry of Ferrous Metallurgy. A big commission was sent down to the factory, which decided that Ch. was indeed a 'gross violator of discipline', a decision that was backed up by the minister himself.

In the event, this hapless nursery head was reinstated through another channel. She was encouraged to go back to a court, and this time it was discovered that she was in fact eligible to pursue her claim through judicial channels. The court reinstated her. But the story vividly illustrates the manner in which a management can ignore a legal intervention if it has sufficient support from its superiors, as well as showing some of the extreme limitations one faces when an appeal to a court is blocked off.

6 CONCLUSIONS

The main points that come out of this discussion can be summarised as follows. It is important, first, to distinguish the different sources of work security in the USSR. The Soviet law on disputes seems admirably fair and well worked out, and legal guarantees of job security are strong on paper. But in practice these guarantees impinge much less on work relations than appears on the surface. The formalities required by the Labour Code in relation to dismissal and disciplinary penalties must be taken into account, but it is not difficult to get around them. Nobody is perfect and pretexts can be found for penalising subordinates. This is clear from the briefest examination of the consequences of blowing the whistle. Soviet labour relations are heavily based on informal relationships and reciprocal favours. It may be that this is up to a point no different from labour relations in capitalist economies. But the contrast between the detailed legal prescriptions and actual practices is great. The effect of this is that on the one hand employees are more protected than the legislation intended – the management acts indulgently towards the workforce in return for needed services performed by employees. On the other hand, people are less protected than was intended. They are highly dependent on the good or ill will of the boss. One can break the written rules and get away with it. But the whistleblowers have broken the unwritten ones, and cannot expect indulgence.

The trade unions are supposed to defend employees in the event of arbitrary actions by management, but simply lack the independence they would need to develop a view of the situation different from the administration, and to impose that view. This gives the courts, which are the second main institutional source of support for employees, a correspondingly important role to play. They do indeed act in the defence of people who are in dispute with management. But this defence is likely to be selective and partial. This is suggested by numerous criticisms of the courts by the higher judicial authorities themselves. The basic problem here is the same as the one that emerged from the discussion in Chapter 2 – the subordination of law to immediate political considerations. Where the organisation is small and the management relatively uninfluential, one can expect the courts to act objectively. The procedure itself allows full scope for a thorough examination of the case. But in other situations the outcome is much less certain. Just the same sort of obstacles arise with appeals to other sources of support – the higher trade union bodies and the procuracy.

The difficulties are especially great for non-manual workers. There are more provisions in law itself allowing for their dismissal, and a significant proportion of such employees cannot appeal to the courts for support. The intelligentsia is less protected in the Soviet Union than the working class. This is important for understanding the fate of the whistleblowers, because they are very often members of the administrative or technical staff, and in this event are especially dependent on the benevolence of management.

6 Conclusions

In this concluding chapter I would like to summarise again, very briefly, the main issues that have guided and emerged from the research, and then to look at some possible political reactions to them. The idea of this final exercise is not to pretend to offer solutions to Soviet policy-makers, which would be very presumptuous, but to draw out the broader implications of the study and to allow readers to choose between a variety of responses to the issues that have been raised.

1 A BRIEF SUMMARY

I began with the general problem of law and lawlessness in relation to abuse of office. In order to secure effective political control, law and legality are vital, and become more important the greater the complexity of the socioeconomic structure to be managed. Yet the same structure and the same form of political management which seem to demand more legal regulation, also constantly inhibit the ostensible efforts of the authorities at the centre to implement it. This is manifested in the pattern of law enforcement. Partly, that pattern reflects the greater opportunities for abuse of office in some sectors than in others. But it also reflects the power and political connections that managers in some sectors and organisations are able to establish. Law enforcement is subordinated to political considerations even when the offences are not 'political'. To some extent, this is due to the recognition by political and legal agents that organisations must be given some leeway if they are to meet their targets or to create the appearance of success. In this connection, one could point to the fact that production organisations have far greater immunity from serious sanctions than organisations in distribution and services. But there is more to it than that, since the forces of patronage make themselves felt even where the abuses could not plausibly be explained as 'necessary evils'. It would be more accurate to say that managers in

177

distribution and services are more vulnerable *both* because they are in a more crime-prone environment *and* because they have less political clout.

In any event, the pressures of patronage tend constantly to impede central law enforcement initiatives in relation to abuse of office. As a result, one has to question whether the concept of a political centre makes sense at all, if by this one means a central source of power able or willing to press the local authorities in order to break through the 'family circles'. The party leadership can launch periodic campaigns and produce, at least for a time, a shift in the investigative and sentencing policy of the procuracy and courts. There have indeed been signs recently of greater concern by the party leadership about abuse of office as one law and order problem. But the experience of the past suggests that unless the offence is particularly outrageous, or political tensions between centre and locality have built up to an exceptional degree (as happened in Georgia in the 1970s), such campaigns will be selectively directed at relatively small fry.

The picture that emerges is one of symbiosis between higher and lower levels of political authority, which tends seriously to blunt the effect of central policies and resolutions. This can be clarified further by looking at the consequences of whistleblowing, which is one source of information for law enforcement, and forms part of the broader and very important phenomenon of individual petitioning. Complaints about abuse of office are of interest in their own right as an indication of reactions from below to management and official illegality. But they also enable one to highlight the character of the political relationships in which this illegality becomes embedded.

There has been some evidence recently of increasing official worries about the volume of complaints arising from abuse of office – though one is forced to speculate about the full reasons for the spate of party propaganda in support of the letter-writers and complainants. But just the same problem arises in this context, since there is no central source of power able or willing to mobilise the agencies that might come fully to the whistleblowers' defence. Indeed the whistleblowers, although they assist in law enforcement and play a key role in maintaining the ideological link between the concerned citizen and the state, also quickly become a menace to the authorities at the centre if their complaints get too persistent. One is thus compelled to conclude that although the resolutions from the top will mean that coverage is given to this matter in the press and elsewhere, campaigns against the victimisation of the letter-writers will continue to serve a mainly moral purpose. They will create the climate for selective sanctions against 'official', 'economic' and 'socialist property' offences. But the gap between abstract statements of intent and the ability to act will remain very wide. It seems that this has a double effect. On the one hand, it encourages a thoroughgoing cynicism about the relevance of law to social behaviour. In this sense it may reinforce the popular sanction given to unofficial networks of production and distribution. But on the other hand, those same networks give rise to considerable popular grumbling, which is expressed in but not satisfied by the complaints procedure.

Abuse of office thus becomes an important issue not just because it undermines the perceived requirements of legal regulation but also because it tends to erode the social unity which gives strength to the whole political edifice. This does not mean, as I stressed at the beginning, that the Soviet political order is about to collapse under the strain of the gulf between legal norms and actual practice. But that gulf is one source of some stubborn social tensions.

One of the effects of this gulf is the problem of arbitrary treatment of troublesome employees through the specious use of provisions in the Labour Code. These were designed as weapons against unproductive employees, not against people who had become an embarrassment to the organisation. But that has not prevented their arbitrary use. None of this detracts from the fact that there are powerful economic sources of job security in the USSR. But it highlights the importance of informal bargains as against legal regulation in Soviet labour relations. The law is in practice not a significant source of the security that has been established.

2 ABUSES AND COMPLAINTS: A ROUND-TABLE DISCUSSION

I have summarised the main lines of thought that arose from the different but connected lines of investigation in the book. What political conclusions might one draw from all this? It is not the job of this study to offer solutions to issues that can be confronted in a practical way only within the Soviet Union itself. But it may be instructive to consider some possible political reactions to the whole matter. I shall set up a brief round-table discussion with five participants. They are called *Champion of Soviet Socialism, Enemy of Legal Rationality, Truth-seeker, True Socialist* and *Radical Reformer*.

The discussion is imaginary, but some of the arguments are based on statements I have heard or seen. Some conceivable responses are not represented, and the views that are expressed are not necessarily mutually incompatible in every respect. This is how the discussion goes, with each participant saying only one piece:

Champion of Soviet Socialism

The Soviet complaints procedure is an important topic of investigation. It shows the great and developing strength of Soviet socialism, the ability of the Soviet system to handle and respond to the many submissions that Soviet citizens make. The growing number of written and oral statements by individuals to the authorities and the press testifies to the strong bond between the citizens and the state, a bond which enables the party and other agencies to listen to suggestions, to learn from people and to rectify problems when they arise. No other political system in the world has such well-developed channels of appeal and complaint as the USSR.

So far as complaints about abuse of office are concerned, that too is an important issue. It is quite correct to say that a certain category of submissions deals with just this problem, and that it is often the most principled and law-abiding citizens who take up their pens in the search for justice. That is why the Soviet press devotes much space to an investigation of citizens' complaints of this type. The publicity given to such questions in Soviet newspapers shows clearly that genuine complaints about law-breaking will get the fullest support from the media and from party and state organisations. We should note that the present book simply could not have been written but for the excellent investigative efforts of Soviet reporters in uncovering breaches of law by some managers and local officials.

But let us turn now to certain very dubious aspects of the book, which, despite protestations to the contrary, is in serious danger of falling into the camp of anti-sovietism. What could be the purpose of the lengthy discussion of illegality in Chapter 2, except to show that socialism leads inherently to lawlessness and arbitrariness? The author admits that there are no precise estimates of the extent of law-breaking, yet insists on vague generalisations about the widespread character of embezzlement, bribery, false reporting and other abuses in the USSR. Furthermore, he explicitly links these to the foundation of Soviet socialism: the planned economy. What else is this but an attempt to discredit socialism as such? The author disclaims any intention of making a comparative analysis. But this is a serious omission given the overall implications of his approach. If a comparative study were carried out, it would undoubtedly be shown that the scale of the problem is far greater in the capitalist countries and in the Third World than in the USSR. How can one seriously compare the phenomenon of false reporting, or the theft of a few hundreds or thousands of rubles, with the massive losses caused to the capitalist state by large-scale tax frauds, or compare the Soviet phenomena with the corrupt practices of many capitalist corporations when pursuing contracts with local government officials or with governments of Third World countries?

Now this is not to say that all is perfect in the socialist system. There are many problems yet to be overcome. Of course there are still cases of corruption and abuse. There are still unscrupulous people who take advantage of the continuing deficit of certain goods and services. They line their own pockets with the 'rewards' of theft and bribe-taking, and thus encourage the morally unstable part of the population to adopt a nihilistic attitude towards socialist laws. Also, there are, undoubtedly, certain difficulties with the fulfilment of plans that are frequently used as a justification for irregular practices by the executives of various organisations. All these are significant problems, and they cannot be solved overnight. But they are not a product of Soviet socialism. They are deviations which can be confronted through the constant improvement in the planning mechanism and in the supply of consumer goods and services, and by making law enforcement more effective.

As for the assertions about the security of labour in the Soviet Union, these are simply difficult to take seriously when capitalism has thrown millions on to the dole queue in recent years, when even school-leavers have no guarantee of a job, and when governments in the Western world have cynically used unemployment as a way of forcing the working class to submit to a decline in living standards. It is true that some Soviet managers act in an arbitrary fashion and ignore the requirements of labour law. Too many people are still illegally dismissed. But consciousness of law among managers has increased over recent years and will continue to do so. Like the other problems referred to in the book, this will gradually be overcome with the strengthening of Soviet democracy and socialist legality.

Enemy of Legal Rationality

Champion of Soviet Socialism has said everything one would expect
of an official apologist, and denies or ignores the main issue: namely,
that lawlessness is thoroughly ingrained in the Soviet system, that for
Soviet managers and officials the law is a quite secondary matter.
They sometimes get into trouble for 'breaking the law'. But the basic
reason is that they have lost political support. Since managers do not
lose support *because* they have acted illegally, they have little to fear
from the law as such. The life of Soviet organisations is a world apart
from the legal rationality that Max Weber spoke about in connection
with bureaucracy. It is far removed from a system in which officials
are bound by a set of formal rights and duties and are restrained by a
service ethic. No such service ethic can be found in the USSR. But
what conclusions should we draw from this? That the whole system
should be overturned? Not at all. There is no guarantee whatever that
the alternative would be any improvement. The system functions
moderately well just because it does deviate from official norms,
values and resolutions. It *must* constantly deviate in order to exist,
and the result is not so bad for the inhabitants. Abuses are a social
mechanism for maintaining equilibrium, they help to balance supply
of and demand for goods and services. They allow poorly-paid
employees to increase their earnings to a level at which they can
sustain at least a half-way decent standard of living, and provide
goods and services that would not otherwise be available. Furthermore, the system gives people a definite security, so long as they don't
do anything 'political', and don't ask too many embarrassing
questions about the gulf between official norms and actual practices.
To rock this boat is not doing anyone a favour.

So who are the real culprits in this book? The real culprits are those
who choose to make a fuss about 'crimes' which are by and large
necessary to keep the wheels of Soviet production and exchange
turning. Nobody is harmed by these activities and everybody gains. So
the whistleblowers must really not be surprised if they get penalised
for their quixotic attempts to get the law enforced. Such efforts may
be well-meant – though not always, by any means – but they are mis-
conceived, because they undermine the delicate balance of forces
which gives everyone a quiet life. After all, what principle do the
'truth-seekers' represent? They represent a world of thorough and
cold-blooded state control. The whistleblowers are the totalitarians of
the piece, spying on their colleagues and fellow workers and setting

themselves up as agents for the prying eyes of the state. Life is more or less tolerable in the Soviet Union only because and to the extent that the plethora of controlling agencies *fail* to do the job they are assigned to do. The personal relationships and mutual protection which neutralise the efforts of the state to control everything that everyone does, make for a far less objectionable world than the imagined alternative of complete bureaucratic rationality.

Everyone, then, gains from the 'loss of control' by the Soviet political authorities – not just the managers. The workers too benefit from the pervasive presence of informal rules that undermine the efforts of the would-be controllers. So the whistleblowers are not to be thanked. Besides, 'truth-seeking' can become a real illness. People start writing and they can't stop – this becomes a life purpose, and turns into scandalmongering or graphomania. Some of these people need a medical cure. Isn't it crazy to appeal to Soviet laws all the time and expect them to be observed?

Truth-seeker

Enemy of Legal Rationality has made a clever speech, but it is cynical and irresponsible, and offers no hope whatever of any improvement in the working of the socialist system. The statement completely ignores the corrosive moral effects of the type of law-breaking described in the book. What are these effects? First, people are constantly encouraged, at least when they are acting in a public capacity, to dissimulate in order to get by or to 'succeed'. False reporting by enterprises about plans is just part of a wider and deep-seated mendacity. This lie is not just a matter of the yawning gap between what official ideology says and how people actually live. It is also a question of the pervasive pressure to present yourself as something that you are not. It is a form of institutionalised schizophrenia, which has crippling moral effects on citizens even if they are not aware of them. Most often, the split between public and private responses manifests itself in a thorough cynicism – though sometimes it is coped with by means of a less hopeless type of irony. But in any case its debilitating consequences are clear.

That is one problem. Another is that the fruits of abuse of office are arbitrarily shared out. It is all very well to talk about abuses as a mechanism of social equilibrium. But bribery and embezzlement also artificially magnify the shortages. They thus hit especially those people who don't have the necessary 'connections'. This creates a sense that there is no justice, that there are no clear rules about who is entitled to what and why. There are only personal relations – you scratch my back and I'll scratch yours. But what if some people are unable or unwilling to scratch, just want to do an honest day's work, don't want to drink with the management, don't want to demean themselves by asking favours from the 'benevolent boss', don't want to partake of illegal earnings based on theft from the state or bribes from customers? Illegal types of exchange between different organisations – that is a different matter. Here there are all kinds of difficulties with supplies which even the most well-meaning of managers could not possibly tackle without breaking the law. That is ABC. But even here the answer is not to become cynical about the relevance of law to social behaviour. The answer is to search for a more rational planning structure, for conditions in which managers are allowed to comply with the law.

Do not, then, pour scorn on the whistleblowers who, for once, choose to stand up for the official values, but regularly get penalised for doing so. The party organs are constantly appealing to citizens, and especially party members, to expose illegal actions when they encounter them. How, as an honest citizen and a good party member, can you not respond to these appeals? To be sure, there are many people who use the complaints procedure just to settle personal accounts. They don't do it because they want to do a service for the party and the people, they are simply exploiting the situation. But there are many others, many honest people who do it with good faith and in the expectation that things will improve. It is easy to call names, to say that this is quixotic at best and at worst, spying on fellow workers, that it is akin to informing for the police. But if you want to combat lawlessness, what other forms of action are open to you? The alternative is to shut up and to encourage a time-serving atmosphere in which nobody takes responsibility for anything. It is moral death.

The fate of the critics shows that although criticism from below is welcomed in principle, in practice the whole business is an extremely tough struggle. Managers and officials are beholden to those who stand above them, not to those below. The important thing is to ingratiate yourself with superiors, and if you rub the faces of your subordinates in the dirt, nothing serious will happen. The support for the whistleblower turns out to be, to a large extent, a sham. If someone at the top seriously wanted improvements, they would not send brush-off replies to letters and would not refuse to see you. The resolutions are all very fine, but they are too vague to be fulfilled and don't really oblige anyone to do anything. So what is required? What is needed is not a change in the basic system of central planning and management, but a much more thoroughgoing support of criticism from below and a set of leaders who will take law enforcement seriously and will not allow campaigns to fizzle out through the obstruction of the local bureaucracy. There is no law of nature that says that people can't take criticism or responsibility, and it is simply not true to say that all forms of abuse are necessary. It is a question of finding the political will to create a political and moral climate in which managers and officials take the consequences for their actions, and critics are thanked and not penalised for their efforts. In the last analysis it is people's attitudes and expectations that have to be changed.

True Socialist

Truth-seeker is full of indignation about the collapse of moral values in Soviet society, and has given us a lot of fine phrases. But it is not enough to get into a moral stew, and not enough to ask simply for more political will or for a moral regeneration, or for tighter law enforcement. The problem cannot be confronted on this level. The issue is a structural one which can only be resolved by a radical trans-formation of the Soviet system in which the real meaning of Soviet democracy, derived from the classical Marxist tradition, will be retrieved and put into effect. The actors in the Soviet drama are no more wicked or venal than the rest of us. Soviet managers and officials are responding to the pressures of their environment in a quite understandable way. If there is a moral problem, then it can only be confronted by offering an alternative set of social arrangements that will have different consequences.

The problem is clear. The Soviet political elite has appropriated the slogans of socialist democracy but has emasculated them in practice. The Soviet Union has failed to fulfil its promise to establish a society democratically controlled by the associated producers. Instead of a society of fundamental harmony, which is what socialism is all about, it has created a society which for all its trumpeting about social unity is riven with competitiveness and conflict, creating a maze of atomised yet mutually protecting bureaucracies and a mass of atomised individuals. What kind of 'planning' can there be in an environment in which each economic agent is responsible only to higher economic agents or to political officials? Since these agents are not responsible to the masses, they become concerned only with getting a bigger slice of the cake, or getting an easier plan, or presenting a good image if things go wrong. In short the bureaucratic atomisation inspires the constant pursuit of individual bureaucratic interests at the expense of wider social consequences. The anarchy of Soviet socialism is just as pernicious in its own way as the anarchy of capitalism.

The atomisation of citizens is no less damaging in its results than the atomisation of organisations. What chance can there be of democratic control from below when the only course of action open to citizens is individual petitioning? The bureaucrat to whom the whistleblower makes appeal has no basic interest in making another bureaucrat accountable for illegal practices, because neither of them is answerable to the people. It is hardly surprising that whistleblowers will appear naive, quixotic and perhaps plain mad if they think that they can have any effect on this bureaucratic colossus through an individual 'proposal or complaint'. But this 'madness' is, so to say, built into the petitioning relationship, which compels the citizens to spend enormous amounts of time and energy to create the smallest chance that someone will pay attention. The impact of a complaint is the impact of a pinprick in the skin of an elephant. Admittedly, a sufficient mass of pinpricks might make even an elephant feel uncomfortable. But this is no substitute for socialist democracy. The point is that there is no possibility of collective political action by citizens independently of the existing degenerated state institutions. Such collective action could alone create the conditions in which managers and officials would feel a greater sense of responsibility and in which socialist legality could be really practised.

Radical Reformer

True Socialist has pointed the finger in roughly the right direction, towards certain basic structural defects in Soviet socialism, and towards the need for greater democracy. But this kind of diatribe is of little help if we are trying to construct real and practicable alternatives, and not just indulging in the utopias of middle-class intellectuals. *True Socialist* continues to cling to the classical Marxist image of democracy which projects an image of complete social harmony based on democratic control by the 'associated producers'. But this is dangerous because it is just the myth of a golden social unity which has contributed so much to the authoritarian character of the Soviet political system. If a single party takes on itself the task of representing that unity, it can in practice achieve only a pseudo-unity based on political *diktat*. The unity exists in the heads of a political elite which rules in the name of the working class and the whole people, but ceases to be responsible to them. It is transformed into a system based on patronage and loses accountability to the mass of the citizens. This is the basic source of the whistleblowers' problems, of the systematic tendency towards protection of 'official' offenders. The Soviet political system is founded on elaborate networks of patronage – it is only when cracks appear in these networks that law enforcement can take its course. *Enemy of Legal Rationality, Truth-seeker* and *True Socialist* all understood this. But the first simply abdicated all responsibility as far as any improvement was concerned; the second appealed for a strong leadership and thus begged the question of *how* the conditions for such a new political will could be created; the third went back to the hoary old image of the Paris Commune and of Lenin's *State and Revolution*. But one must learn from experience. The Soviet experiment has shown that socialism in the classical Marxist image does not work. The classical conception leads to a heavily centralised form of political management which produces fundamental problems for the planning system and which systematically reproduces widespread lawlessness, with all the attendant conflicts and demoralisation. The Soviet Union must therefore learn some lessons from capitalism and from bourgeois democracy – if that is what you want to call it. The unsavoury features of abuse of office and the disputes that surround it are the outcome of an unsuccessful attempt to do away with the market, which has returned through the back door, except in a distorted form. The way to establish the conditions of social morality as well as economic rationality is to expand the arena of legitimate market activity and to decentralise the Soviet planning mechanism – without in either case abandoning the political guidance needed to ensure that certain priority goals are met. Admittedly, people have been grappling for a long time with the problem of how you combine the virtues of central direction with the virtues of a market mechanism – but that does not lessen its importance or rule out its feasibility.

Further, the lesson could be learned from 'bourgeois' political systems that some form of parliamentary democracy is the best way of achieving at least some representation of a complex set of economic and political interests which no single party can claim to encompass. In addition, and this is of the greatest importance in the light of the main theme of the book, it is essential to give far more independence to those agencies which have the job of upholding the law. The task is to free the law from political subordination, since this alone could meet the demands of the whistleblowers that the rules should be the same for everyone.

In all these ways the conditions can be met for loosening the grip of patronage and protection, for removing a major part of the economic foundation for lawlessness, and for ensuring that the law will be enforced. Complaints would remain, and it would be very important to make the complaints procedure effective. But it would cease to be used to the extent that it is within the present political arrangements.

Having considered these perceptions, readers may find that there is more than a grain of validity in each of them. They can be left to grapple with that. But it would be an evasion of responsibility if the author were to end by simply withdrawing from the scene of this discussion without saying something about his own responses. It has to be admitted that this format – a presentation of different views – is one way of dealing with one's own uncertainties, a way of confronting a definite element of sympathy with each view. Acknowledging that, my own reactions can be stated as follows:

The trouble with both *Champion of Soviet Socialism* and *Enemy of Legal Rationality* is that neither is prepared to admit that there is any serious issue at stake. Each position in its own way is complacent about the existing state of affairs and neither wishes to rock the boat. The difference is that while the first denies that there is any special problem about lawlessness, the second emphasises this lawlessness, yet is content that nothing should be done about it.

The virtue of the last three views is that they recognise that there is an important political and moral issue to discuss, an issue which the stories about whistleblowing throw into clear relief. *Truth-seeker* is right that major moral questions are raised and that it is not good enough for *Enemy of Legal Rationality* to say that personal relationships are cosy, and that illegality is functional for the workings of the economy. *Truth-seeker* is also right that the whistleblowers need defending and need more solid institutional support.

But both *True Socialist* and *Radical Reformer* are surely right to suggest that the appeal to moral norms and/or tougher law enforcement, which is *Truth-seeker*'s tendency, is not enough. This is not to say that political leadership and the moral climate can make no difference, nor is it to deny that individuals should take responsibility for the outcome of social practices. In that I am in agreement with *Truth-seeker*. But there are deep-seated structural problems which *Truth-seeker* tends to skate over, because pondering on these too long might make the prospects of change rather gloomy.

Both *True Socialist* and *Radical Reformer* emphasise these structural problems, and both point the finger towards lack of political *accountability* as the key to the lack of *responsibility* which so angers *Truth-seeker*. I agree with them on this point, but it is only *Radical Reformer* who has a set of proposals that seem at least half way politically realistic – though even these more modest proposals have foundered on many occasions in the postwar Soviet Union and in Eastern Europe. However, that does not mean that given sufficiently serious internal problems, and given a less paranoid response to the Soviet Union on the international plane, renewed efforts at reform might not be made and get off the ground, so that the virtues of central guidance would be retained within a much more flexible and less monopolistic set of political arrangements. *True Socialist* offers nothing positive except a harking back to the images of 1917 – images which were very powerful in one political conjuncture but which are now to a large extent played out. What's more, *Radical Reformer* is right that the image of a golden social harmony has its dangers. It is better replaced by a more modest idea of the possibilities of political representation.

Exploring the problem of abuses and complaints leads, then, to far-reaching and difficult political issues. To do research on the Soviet Union is hard, but it is a lot easier than to make concrete proposals about the problems that one comes up against. But there is, perhaps, just a chance that such laborious academic efforts as this book will find their way into somebody's more practical thinking.

Appendix

INTERVIEWS

1. Journalist with a major national newspaper
2. Engineer in machine-tool plant (Ukraine)
3. Chief engineer in organisation for installation of heating systems (Azerbaidzhan)
4. Legal consultant in various organisations (Moldavia)
5. Legal consultant in trade organisation (Ukraine)
6. Advocate (Moscow)
7. Head doctor of a sanatorium (Leningrad province, RSFSR)
8. Advocate (Estonia)
9. Engineer in construction organisation (Novgorod province, RSFSR)
10. Manager in radio plant (Belorussia)
11. Journalist with a republic newspaper
12. Legal consultant in trade organisation (Leningrad province, RSFSR)
13. Lathe worker in experimental sewing plant (Moscow)
14. Legal consultant in various organisations (Ukraine)
15. Advocate (Moscow)
16. Supply manager in various organisations (Novosibirsk province, RSFSR)
17. Legal consultant in trade organisation (Leningrad province, RSFSR)
18. Advocate (Ukraine)
19. Manager in local industry knitwear factory (Ukraine)
20. Designer and university teacher (Latvia)
21. Manager in construction organisation (Ukraine)
22. Manager in transport organisation (Azerbaidzhan)
23. Group leader in scientific research institute (Leningrad province, RSFSR)

Notes and References

CHAPTER 1

1. *Pravda*, 23 November 1982, p. 1. For some other statements appealing for more discipline, see *Pravda*, 17 December 1982, pp. 1 and 3; 25 December 1982, p. 2; 27 December 1982, p. 1.
2. See M. Clarke (1983) for a selection of pieces that give some idea of the state of current work on corruption in capitalist and Third World countries as well as the Soviet Union. In his introduction, Clarke very effectively draws the threads of these pieces together, and offers a starting point for a comparative analysis. But he also highlights the difficulties involved in such a project in the present state of research.
3. For a translation and comment on all the Soviet legal codes, see W.B. Simons (1980). For a discussion of the publication of the first volume of the new general Code of Laws, see *Sots. Zak.*, 1981, 3, p. 5. In this connection, there has been pressure from some quarters for a separate code of economic law (dealing with 'horizontal' relations between enterprises, and 'vertical' relations between economic organisations and economic administrators), in order to increase the legal autonomy and responsibility of economic units. See P. Lavigne, 'Economic Law', in F. J. M. Feldbrugge (ed.), *Encyclopedia of Soviet Law* (Leiden: Sijthoff, 1973).
4. See e.g. articles on education in law in *Pravda*, 8 April 1972; 25 May 1978; 19 July 1981. For a review of Soviet academic literature published in the 1970s, see *Lichnost i uvazhenie k zakonu* (1979), Introduction.
5. Cited in *Pravda*, 3 July 1981, pp. 2–3.
6. Ibid.
7. *Pravda*, 6 May 1979.
8. Such a picture may be compared with the analysis in V. Andrle's *Managerial Power in the Soviet Union* (1976), a first-class work that has influenced the thinking in the present book about the relationship between central and local power in the Soviet Union, perhaps to an even greater extent than I have been aware in writing it. Andrle argues that, given an imperfect system of planning, enterprise directors have acquired a factual autonomy in relation to the higher organs of management: directive planning is informed by a central dialectic between 'plan discipline' and unplanned initiative. This area of autonomy is enlarged and made more secure where directors strike personal bargains with individual state and party officials charged with supervising plan implementation, thereby gaining immunity from law enforcement and party campaigns. Local power elites are formed which serve to integrate two structures of action belonging to plan discipline and unplanned initiative. The former 'needs' the latter, but limits to managerial power are set by the fact that local officials must appear responsive to centrally initiated campaigns, and cannot lose themselves entirely in the web of local interests. The

191

present work arrives at a similar picture, but from a different vantage point, focusing on the role of law enforcement agencies and on the mechanism of complaints arising out of managerial breaches of law.

9. See, for example, W. Gellhorn, *Ombudsmen and Others* (Cambridge, Mass: Harvard University Press, 1967).

10. A particularly dramatic case involved Stanley Adams, who tried to expose unlawful trading practices in the Swiss-based drug company, Hoffman–La-Roche, and paid heavily for it. See *New Statesman*, 7 March 1980, p. 345. A more recent report in the *New Statesman* (23 July 1983, pp. 8–10) has described the cases of Britain's first 'nuclear dissidents', who lost their jobs after expressing doubts about nuclear safety. Meanwhile, an editorial in the *New Scientist* has called for whistleblowing to become a recognised role, and for some protection to be offered: 'corporate solidarity isn't the most important thing in life. When it is punctured for the good of society, the person with the pin needs our protection', *New Society*, 23 June 1983, p. 838. (I am grateful to Bob Davies for drawing my attention to this comment.)

11. See, for example, the remarks of S. Hall *et al.* about the significance of crime reporting in Britain: 'Crime ... is "news" because its treatment evokes threats to, but also reaffirms the consensual morality of society: a modern morality play in which the devil is both symbolically and physically cast out from the society by its guardians – the police and the judiciary.' S. Hall *et al.*, *Policing the Crisis* (1978) p. 66.

12. These were conducted in January 1983. A list of the people interviewed is provided in an appendix, stating their occupations and giving a rough indication where they worked. For obvious reasons, more detailed information is not provided.

CHAPTER 2

1. See RSFSR Criminal Code, article 99 (Criminally negligent use or storage of agricultural machinery), and article 152 (Output of poor quality, substandard or incomplete production) in *Ugolovnyi Kodeks* (1978).

2. The question of the scope of Soviet criminal law is discussed in Pomorski (1978). The same author, in another article, also provides a detailed and very useful account of changing Soviet legal perceptions of state and personal property. He points out that early Soviet legislation did not include crimes against state or cooperative property as a separate category. The watershed in this respect, presenting socialist ownership as a distinct value, was the notorious law of August 1932, which contained the preamble: 'social ownership (state, kolkhoz, cooperative) constitutes the foundation of the Soviet system, it is sacred and inviolable, and persons who infringe on it shall be deemed enemies of the people'. In the post-Stalin period the distinction between petty and non-petty theft was introduced, petty theft was decriminalised and penalties generally reduced. But socialist property remained sacrosanct in law. See Pomorski (1977).

3. *Entsiklopedicheskii Slovar'*, p. 500.

4. *Entsiklopedicheskii Slovar'*, pp. 379–80.

5. BVS SSSR 1981, 1, p. 35.

6. USSR Supreme Court Plenum resolution, 12 January 1973 (with modifications of 25 February 1977), in *Sbornik*, part 2, p. 195.

7. *Ugolovnyi Kodeks*, p. 59.
8. Ibid., p. 58.
9. *Sots. Zak.*, 1980, 3, pp. 5–9.
10. *Ugolovnyi Kodeks*, p. 53.
11. BVS SSSR 1981, 6, p. 42.
12. *Sots. Zak.*, 1980, 3, pp. 5–9.
13. *Kommentarii*, p. 325.
14. *Ugolovnyi Kodeks*, p. 52.
15. *Ugolovnyi Kodeks*, p. 57.
16. For details of permitted penalties, see *Ugolovnyi Kodeks*, articles 92, 138, 153, 156, 170, 173, 174.
17. D. K. Simes, 'The Soviet Parallel Market' in *Economic Aspects of Life in the USSR* (1975) p. 91.
18. G. Grossman, 'The "Second Economy" of the USSR', *Problems of Communism*, Sept–Oct 1977.
19. G. Grossman, 'Notes on the Illegal Private Economy and Corruption' in *The Soviet Economy in a Time of Change* (Washington, 1979) vol. 1, pp. 834–55.
20. G. Ofer, A. Vinokur, *Private Sources of Income of the Soviet Urban Household* (Rand Publications, 1980).
21. See, especially, V. Andrle (1976), J. Berliner (1957), D. Granick (1954).
22. Interview 7.
23. *Entsiklopedicheskii Slovar'*, p. 148.
24. Interview 22.
25. Hadden (1982) draws attention to a similar distinction in relation to corruption in capitalist firms. 'Corporate' corruption might involve, for example, salespeople being encouraged to use bribes to secure contracts, or managers being encouraged to ignore health and safety rules to reduce costs. Embezzling company funds or defrauding its clients would be examples of 'individual' corruption.
26. *Sots. Ind.*, 9 October 1979, p. 2. This was a story about a beer plant, in which the management was exchanging beer for spare parts with another enterprise.
27. See Shenfield (1983), and comments by Hanson appended to Shenfield's paper.
28. *Sots. Zak.*, 1980, 3, pp. 29–30.
29. *Pravda*, 18 April 1982, p. 3. It was a factory for electrodes in Rostov.
30. Soviet legal decisions often assert that *pripiski* are especially prevalent in construction and agriculture. For a typical statement, see BVS SSSR 1981, 1, p. 35.
31. Interview 10.
32. Interview 12.
33. Interview 21.
34. Interview 22.
35. Interview 9.
36. Interview 9.
37. Interview 12.
38. For a legal comment to the effect that 'writing off' is especially prevalent in agriculture and construction see e.g. *Sots. Zak.*, 1980, 1, pp. 17–20.
39. See Ofer and Vinokur (1980) p. vi.
40. S. Pomorski (1977) pp. 238–45.
41. For a more detailed analysis of the conditions facilitating bribery, see Pomorski (1983). Katsenelinboigen (1983) presents a typology of 'corrupt' relationships, based on Soviet experience, which helps to identify the main possible sources of

bribery and to make comparisons with other systems. It involves nine permutations of relationship between individuals, enterprises and government agencies.

42. *Pravda*, 26 June 1976, p. 4. The source of this remark is not specified. The article is a description of a 'round-table discussion' with supply agents from different enterprises, who had been having problems in getting supplies from the Novolipetsk metallurgical factory.

43. A. Kirpichnikov in *Sots. Zak.*, 1975, 12, p. 42.

44. *Pravda*, 1 August 1979, p. 2.

45. On the importance of family obligations, and extravagant displays of wealth in Georgian culture, see G. Mars and Y. Altman (1983).

46. For a discussion of chief accountants and other internal controllers, see J. Berliner (1957) ch. 13.

47. Interview 12.

48. *Sots. Zak.*, 1980, 1, pp. 17–20.

49. *Sots. Zak.*, 1980, 5, pp. 74–5.

50. *Sots. Zak.*, 1980, 2, p. 60.

51. *Pravda*, 4 February 1982, p. 3.

52. *Sots. Zak.*, 1980, 3, p. 60.

53. *Pravda*, 14 July 1979, p. 3.

54. *Pravda*, 24 August 1979, p. 2.

55. *Pravda*, 30 January 1980, p. 3; CDSP vol. 32, 4, p. 22; *Pravda*, 18 December 1980, p. 3; CDSP vol. 34, 51, p. 25. The Vice-Chairman of the USSR State Committee was reprimanded, and the head of the commission was given a corrective labour sentence. Several other officials were given suspended sentences, and the fledgling plant's director got four years' imprisonment. The second report on this affair described it as rare if not unique in Soviet legal history: the members of a state commission were on trial for forgery.

56. *Sots. Ind.*, 4 October 1981, p. 2; CDSP vol. 33, 41, p. 9.

57. See e.g. the statement by S. Gusev, first deputy chairman of the USSR Supreme Court, *Sots. Ind.*, 28 September 1979, p. 3.

58. *Pravda*, 24 January 1980, p. 3.

59. *Pravda*, 24 January 1980, p. 3.

60. There is a reference to these experiments in *Pravda*, 22 November 1979, p. 3.

61. *Pravda*, 1 December 1979, p. 3; CDSP vol. 31, 50, p. 12.

62. On paper, there were 9½ million volunteer inspectors in 1977. See J. S. Adams (1977) p. 1.

63. *Pravda*, 1 December 1979, p. 3. CDSP vol. 31, 50, p. 12.

64. *Pravda*, 2 December 1979, pp. 3–4. CDSP vol. 31, 51, p. 7.

65. For a detailed description of the structure and functions of the procuracy, see G.B. Smith (1978).

66. See articles on the Procuracy, Appellate Procedure, and Res Judicata in F.J.M. Feldbrugge (1973).

67. 'On improving work to safeguard law and order and on intensifying the struggle against violations of law', *Pravda*, 11 September 1979, pp. 1, 3.

68. *Sots. Zak.*, 1980, 9, p. 9.

69. BVS SSSR 1981, 1, p. 32.

70. See, for example, directives by the Plenum of the USSR Supreme Court from the

1960s and 1970s under the sections on economic crime, official crime and socialist property offences, in *Sbornik* (1981) part 2.

71. *Sots. Zak.*, 1980, 9, p. 9. Statement by deputy General Procurator of the USSR.
72. BVS SSSR 1981, 5, pp. 18–20; 1982, 1, pp. 8–11.
73. BVS SSSR 1981, 5, pp. 18–20; 1982, 1, pp. 8–11.
74. BVS SSSR 1981, pp. 35–41.
75. BVS SSSR 1981, 1, pp. 35–43.
76. BVS SSSR 1981, 5, pp. 18–20.
77. BVS SSSR 1982, 1, pp. 8–11.
78. *Sots. Zak.*, 1980, 3, pp. 5–9.
79. BVS SSSR 1981, 1, pp. 35–43.
80. BVS SSSR 1982, 1, pp. 8–11.
81. *Sots. Zak.*, 1980, 3, pp. 5–9.
82. BVS SSSR 1981, 1, pp. 35–43 (on report-padding); BVS SSSR 1981, 5, pp. 18–20 (on embezzlement); BVS SSSR 1982, 1, pp. 8–11 (on embezzlement).
83. BVS SSSR 1981, 5, pp. 18–20.
84. BVS SSSR 1982, 1, pp. 8–11.
85. BVS SSSR 1981, 5, pp. 18–20.
86. BVS SSSR 1982, pp. 8–11.
87. BVS SSSR 1981, 1, pp. 35–43; 1981, 5, pp. 18–20; 1982, 1, pp. 8–11; *Sots. Zak.*, 1980, 3, pp. 5–9.
88. See pp. 51–9.
89. Interview with Aliev, first secretary of the Azerbaidzhan republic Central Committee, *Pravda*, 1 August 1979, p. 2.
90. *Pravda*, 30 June 1981, p. 2.
91. *Pravda*, 21 June 1981, p. 2.
92. *Pravda*, 16 May 1981, p. 3.
93. *Ustav Kommunisticheskoi partii*, pp. 32–3.
94. *Lit. Gaz.*, 31 January 1979, p. 12.
95. *Pravda*, 14 January 1980, p. 2.
96. Interview 10.
97. *Pravda*, 15 November 1979, p. 2.
98. These 56 reports are part of a bigger sample of 70 reports that I shall be analysing further in Chapter 4. For the purposes of the present discussion, I selected only those that clearly specified both the offences and the penalties.
99. Sample (b) included a wide range of Soviet periodicals: *Izvestiya, Pravda, Nedelya, Kommunist* (Armenia), *Sovetskaya Rossiya, Kazakhstanskaya Pravda, Sotsialisticheskaya Industriya, Trud, Bakinskii Rabochii* (Azerbaidzhan), *Vechernaya Moskva, Zarya Vostoka, Literaturnaya Gazeta, Byulleten Verkhovnogo Suda SSSR.*
100. See CDSP vol. 27, 21, p. 9; vol. 30, 4, p. 22; vol. 32, 37, p. 15; vol. 32, 38, p. 14.
101. Interview 21.
102. *Pravda*, 30 June 1981, p. 2; 11 August 1981, p. 3.
103. BVS SSSR 1976, 5, pp. 23–4; 1978, 3, pp. 31–4; 1976, 4, pp. 24–5.
104. *Sots. Zak.*, 1980, 3, pp. 5–9.
105. BVS SSSR 1973, 2, pp. 15–18.
106. BVS SSSR 1974, 5, p. 21.
107. BVS SSSR 1976, 1, pp. 26–8.

108. *Zarya Vostoka*, 2 August 1980, pp. 1–2, CDSP vol. 32, 39, p. 13.
109. *Pravda*, 25 March 1981, p. 3.
110. Several Soviet émigrés interviewed in Israel spoke about this campaign, which affected mostly Jews, and impressed those who had encountered it as a particularly horrific episode. One informant, who had participated in some of the trials as a defence lawyer, was making a detailed study of the campaign. According to her figures, covering the period 1960–6, there were 1138 convictions for embezzlement, 576 for bribe-taking and 496 for foreign currency offences. Some 801 people got up to 10 years, 720 up to 15 years, and 162 were shot (interview 15). After one major arrest in January 1962, according to another interviewee, the first secretary of the Lvov city party committee shot himself. The same informant said that the chairman of the Lvov party–state control committee got the death sentence during the campaign (interview 18). Interviewee 19, who worked as a manager in a local industry textile factory in Lvov, was caught in this campaign and spent 15 years in camps.
111. *Bakinskii Rabochii*, 30 July 1978, p. 4. CDSP vol. 30, 32, p. 20.
112. On the Georgian campaign, see Menabde (1977). *The Current Digest of the Soviet Press*, which translates many articles from the Georgian, Armenian and Azerbaidzhani republican press, is a good source on law enforcement in Transcaucasia.

CHAPTER 3

1. BVS SSSR 1980, 3, p. 38.
2. Ibid., p. 40.
3. Ibid., pp. 41–2.
4. *Pravda*, 4 April 1981, p. 1.
5. *Trud*, 30 July 1981.
6. S. White (1983) p. 54.
7. According to one Soviet report, complaints account for 'at least half' of the letters received by most Soviet newspapers. G.S. Vychub, *Pis'ma trudyashchikhsya v sisteme massovoi raboty gazety* (Moscow, 1980) p. 8, cited in White (1983) p. 52.
8. A much earlier study by Inkeles and Geiger (1968) threw some light on this point in a survey of letters to the press in the late Stalin period, based on a content analysis of 270 critical letters to 8 Soviet newspapers in 1947. Some 64 of the letter-writers were acting in an 'occupational' capacity, and 127 'organisational relationships between critics and targets of criticism' were identified in the 64 letters. There were only 12 cases where critics focused criticism on the work of their own organisation. An article by Adams (1981) tries to replicate the Inkeles and Geiger study, examining 240 critical letters to the Soviet press in 1977. But it does not touch on this particular question.
9. On this see for example G. Rittersporn (1978).
10. *KPSS v rezolyutsiyakh* (1972) vol. 9, pp. 369–73.
11. *Vedomosti Verkhovnogo Soveta SSSR*, no. 17 (1415) 24 April 1968.
12. B. Yakovlev (1979) p. 23.

13. For a translation, see *Collected Legislation of the USSR and the Constituent Republics*, Release 2, August 1980.
14. S. White (1983) p. 47.
15. BVS SSSR 1980, 5, pp. 8–10.
16. *Pravda*, 4 April 1981, p. 1.
17. The remarks that follow can be compared with the discussion in J.S. Adams (1981) and S. White (1983). I am in broad agreement with what they say about the significance of the petitioning process in the USSR.
18. Central Committee resolution, 29 August 1967, *KPSS v rezolyutsiyakh*, vol. 9, pp. 369–70.
19. BVS SSSR 1980, 3, p. 38.

CHAPTER 4

1. Interview 11. A similar view was given by another journalist in interview 1.
2. *Pravda*, 6 July 1981, p. 3 (report by staff correspondent about a timber organisation, Novokuznetsk, RSFSR).
3. *Pravda*, 14 July 1981, p. 2 (letter from an engineer working on the railways in Elets, Lipetsk province, RSFSR).
4. *Pravda*, 7 January 1981, p. 2 (report by staff correspondent about Primorsk province, RSFSR – the factory was in Vladivostok).
5. *Pravda*, 29 August 1981, p. 3 (report by staff correspondent from Vasil'kov, Kiev province, Ukraine).
6. *Pravda*, 11 April 1981, p. 3 (report by staff correspondent about a farm in Orenburg province, RSFSR).
7. *Pravda*, 15 March 1982, p. 3 (letter from the complainant).
8. *Pravda*, 13 April 1982, p. 3 (report by a party control committee official and a staff correspondent, about a construction organisation in Saratov province, RSFSR).
9. *Pravda*, 4 February 1982, p. 3 (People's Control page).
10. *Pravda*, 14 August 1981, p. 2 (letter from brigade leader, from Kirovakan, Armenia. The author was also a member of the Kirovakan city party committee).
11. *Lit. Gaz.*, 1 January 1979, p. 10 (letter from N. Sokoreva).
12. *Lit. Gaz.*, 1 July 1981, p. 13; CDSP vol. 13, 40, p. 17 (article by A. Rubinov, abstracted statement).
13. These remarks are quoted from cases 1, 2, 3, 6 and 8 in Chapter 3, and from *Lit. Gaz.*, 19 January 1983, p. 15.
14. A. Gel'man, 'Protokol odnogo zasedaniya', *Teatr*, 1976, 2.
15. *Pravda*, 21 August 1981, p. 3 (report by staff correspondent, Adlersk district, Krasnodar province).
16. *Pravda*, 17 October 1981, p. 3.
17. Ibid.
18. *Pravda*, 9 July 1981, p. 3 (People's Control page, about Novo–Gorlovsk engineering plant, Ukraine).
19. *Pravda*, 26 February 1980, p. 3 (report by staff correspondent about a mink farm in Irkutsk province).

20. See for example *Pravda*, 21 August 1981, p. 3; 3 October 1981, p. 2.
21. *Sots. Ind.*, 14 June 1979, p. 3 (report by staff correspondent about a construction trust in Kremenchug, Ukraine).
22. *Pravda*, 8 January 1983, p. 2 (article by deputy party secretary at a collective farm in Tel'shyaiskii district, Lithuania).
23. *Pravda*, 28 March 1981, p. 3.
24. *Pravda*, 8 August 1981, p. 3 (report by staff correspondent, about construction in Ryazan RSFSR).
25. *Pravda*, 13 December 1982, p. 2 (report by staff correspondent about a research institute in Krasnodar).
26. *Sots. Ind.*, 13 June 1979, p. 2 (report by staff correspondent about a pressure-pipe factory, Volgograd, RSFSR).
27. E.g. *Pravda*, 28 March 1981, p. 3 (report by staff correspondent about a factory for semiconductor instruments in Kabardino–Balkarskaya ASSR).
28. E.g. ibid; *Pravda*, 21 August 1981, p. 3 (report by staff correspondent about a wine factory in Adlerskii district, Krasnodar province, RSFSR); *Pravda*, 17 October 1981, p. 3 (report by a staff correspondent about a transport enterprise in Sumskaya province, Ukraine).
29. E.g. *Sots. Ind.*, 12 June 1979, p. 2 (report by staff correspondent about a mining repair works, in Shakhty, RSFSR); *Sots. Ind.*, 18 November 1979, p. 3 (report by staff correspondent, from Kirgiz SSR, sector not mentioned).
30. *Pravda*, 20 July 1981, p. 3 (report by staff correspondent about a state farm in Khabarovsk province, RSFSR).
31. *Sots. Ind.*, 4 September 1979, p. 2 (report by party control committee official about a construction institute in Omsk).
32. See, for example, reports in *Pravda*, 10 August 1979, p. 3; 5 October 1979, p. 3; 12 October 1979, p. 2; *Sots. Ind.*, 12 June 1979, p. 2; 14 June 1979, p. 2.
33. *Pravda*, 30 August 1981, p. 2 (a general article on the problem of criticism, citing several cases of official indifference at the local level to 'suppression of criticism').
34. *Pravda*, 28 March 1981, p. 3 (report by staff correspondent about Prokhladnyi, city party committee, Kabardino–Balkarskaya ASSR, RSFSR).
35. *Pravda*, 29 August 1981 (report by staff correspondent on a transport organisation in Vasilkov, Ukraine).
36. *Pravda*, 18 September 1979, p. 3 (report by staff correspondent on a trade organisation in Kuibyshev, RSFSR).
37. *Pravda*, 8 August 1981, p. 3 (report by staff correspondent, Ryazan, RSFSR).
38. *Pravda*, 26 August 1981, p. 3 (quoted in a report by a staff correspondent, about Kameshkirskii district, Penza province, RSFSR).
39. *Pravda*, 15 October 1979, p. 2 (report by staff correspondent about a dairy farm in Dagestan SSR, RSFSR).
40. *Pravda*, 7 January 1981, p. 2 (report by staff correspondent on Primorskii province, RSFSR).
41. *Sots. Ind.*, 29 May 1979, p. 2 (report by staff correspondent).
42. See Introduction to Chapter 3.
43. E.g. *Pravda*, 14 April 1981, p. 1; 18 May 1981, p. 1; 17 June 1981, p. 1; 29 August 1981, p. 1.
44. *Pravda*, 4 April 1981, p. 1 (editorial).
45. *Pravda*, 14 April 1981, p. 1.

46. *Pravda*, 11 December 1982, p. 1. See also a *Pravda* editorial of 28 December 1982, p. 1.
47. *Pravda*, 12 October 1978, p. 1; CDSP vol. 30, 41, p. 22.
48. *Pravda*, 4 April 1981, p. 1.
49. *Pravda*, 17 June 1981, p. 1.
50. *Pravda*, 18 May 1981, p. 1.
51. *Pravda*, 29 August 1981, p. 1 (editorial).
52. *Pravda*, 4 April 1981, p. 1 (Central Committee resolution).
53. *Pravda*, 14 April 1981, p. 1 (editorial).
54. *Izvestiya*, 25 January 1983; CDSP vol. 35, 4, p. 25.
55. BVS SSSR 1980, 5, pp. 8–10.
56. *Pravda*, 11 December 1982, p. 1.
57. *Pravda*, 17 June 1981, p. 1 (editorial).
58. Cited in *Workers Against the Gulag* (1979) p. 23.
59. *Pravda*, 7 September 1981, p. 2 (discussion with 1st secretary of Ivanovo obkom). The offender was deputy director for services at the Krasnovolzhsk combine, Ivanovo province.
60. BVS SSSR 1981, 5, pp. 28–35. The reference was to the Torez city executive committee, Donets province, Ukraine.
61. *Pravda*, 30 August 1981, p. 2 (article by A. Chernyak). The two provinces were Tatar and Gorkii.
62. According to a statement from the letters department of *Komsomol'skaya Pravda*, petitioners who had written in were assisted in the following ways by the paper's interventions during 1982: 46 were reinstated in their previous jobs; 78 had illegal penalties removed; 21 young specialists got work in accordance with their assignments; 44 returned to *vuzy* and *teknhikums*; 28 students had their stipends returned. As a result of signals sent on the initiative of readers, the following penalties were handed out: 240 criminal cases were started; 215 protests were issued against decisions by the People's Courts and decisions of procuratorial organs; 127 were dismissed from their posts; 48 were demoted; 67 were deprived of bonuses; 545 got administrative and disciplinary penalties; 262 got party or komsomol penalties. *Komsomol'skaya Pravda*, 22 January 1983, p. 2.
63. This is not a strict formula, but editors stick to a rough proportion, and local papers use national papers as a guide (information provided in interview 11).
64. Interview 1.
65. Interview 11. A similar picture was given in interview 1.
66. Interview 11.
67. Interview 1.
68. 'Large cities' here refers to cities with more than 1 million population in 1977. See *SSSR: Administrativno-territorialnoe delenie* (1977).
69. See e.g. *Pravda*, 25 June 1979, p. 3; 5 July 1981, p. 2.
70. Interview 1.
71. Interview 11.
72. *Pravda*, 30 August 1981, p. 2 (article by A. Chernyak).
73. *Pravda*, 15 November 1979, p. 2 (the paper in question was *Sotsialisticheskaya Osetiya*); see also *Pravda*, 21 June 1981, p. 2 describing an attempt by the Ashkhabad gorkom to prevent publication of material about abuse of office.
74. *Lit. Gaz.*, 19 January 1983, p. 15.

75. *Pravda*, 25 June 1979, p. 3 (the paper was *Kommunist Tadzhikistana*).
76. *Pravda*, 12 October 1978, p. 1; CDSP vol. 30, 41, p. 43.
77. *Pravda*, 27 January 1983, p. 1.
78. *Sovetskaya Rossiya*, 22 March 1983, p. 2; CDSP vol. 35, 12, p. 5.
79. *Sots. Ind.*, 14 June 1979, p. 3.
80. *Pravda*, 15 May 1981, p. 2.
81. *Pravda*, 25 August 1981, p. 2.
82. *Pravda*, 30 August 1981, p. 2.
83. Interview 11.
84. *Pravda*, 29 February 1980, p. 3.
85. *Pravda*, 21 October 1979, p. 3.
86. *Sots. Ind.*, 18 October 1979, p. 3.
87. *Pravda*, 3 July 1981, p. 3.
88. *Pravda*, 3 July 1981, p. 3.

CHAPTER 5

1. See e.g. Kahn-Freund (1977).
2. This drift has in no way lessened in Britain under the Thatcher governments, which have extended the scope of law in relation to trade union affairs. Ironically, 'right-wing' policies on the trade unions make appeal to an image which is very close to the Soviet image of responsible industrial relations.
3. The term 'work disputes' is a translation of the Russian *trudovye spory*. Up until 1957, the term used in Soviet legislation was *trudovye konflikty* (work conflicts). 'Disputes' is held to be a more appropriate term because the problem does not arise out of 'antagonistic relations'. See V.I. Smolyarchuk (1966) 1f. In theory disputes can arise not only out of individual claims but also in connection with the signing of collective agreements (about conditions of work) between the enterprise administration and the trade union committee. But in practice the vast majority of disputes are claims by individuals for the implementation of existing rules and agreements. See Smolyarchuk (1966) p. 9.
4. Court review of work disputes is just one kind of case in which a court may review administrative action. Others include: complaints about incorrect information on voters' registration lists; collection of tax arrears from citizens; imposition of administrative fines; complaints about errors in records of acts of civil standing; complaints about the activities of notaries, court executors and bailiffs; requests to countermand decisions about occupancy of housing and refusal to permit change in housing; suits about the origin of inventions and technical improvements; complaints about incorrect inventory of property; complaints against the orders of the State Automobile Inspectorate. See G.B. Smith (1978) p. 38.
5. Among many Soviet commentaries on work disputes and dismissals in particular, see *Sovetskoe Zakonodatel'stvo* (1980); Smolyarchuk (1966); Shlemin (1966); Nikitinskii and Panyugin (1973); Skobelkin (1977).
6. The Commissions on Work Disputes seem to be in general ineffective and very often set up in only a half-hearted way. For some comments on this see *Postanovlenie* (1976) and *Postanovlenie* (1979).
7. See article 56, All-Union Principles, and *Sovetskoe Zakonodatel'stvo*, pp. 71–93.

8. *Sovetskoe Zakonodatel'stvo*, p. 71.

9. Ibid., p. 77.

10. BVS SSSR 1980, 6, p. 3. Between 1966 and 1975, according to another statement, there was a decline of 31 per cent in the number of suits for reinstatement. *Sov. Gos. i Pravo*, November 1978, pp. 63–7 (editorial); CDSP vol. 31, 8, p. 15.

11. BVS SSSR 1980, 6, p. 3.

12. A similar picture emerged from a survey of dismissal cases in 1973, when 52 per cent of such cases in the RSFSR were for disciplinary reasons (systematic non-fulfilment of work duties and absenteeism), and 42 per cent (on average) for disciplinary reasons in 7 other republics (Lithuania, Armenia, Uzbekistan, Azerbaidzhan, Latvia, Estonia, Belorussia). BVS SSSR 1974, 4, p. 34.

13. *Sovetskoe Zakonodatel'stvo*, p. 66.

14. BVS SSSR 1977, 3, p. 30.

15. Ibid., p. 29.

16. Ibid.

17. *Ugolovnyi Kodeks*, p. 48.

18. *Pravda*, 21 August 1981, p. 3 (wine factory in Adlerskii district, Krasnodar province).

19. *Lit. Gaz.*, 12 September 1979, p. 12. He was working for an organisation under the Moldavian SSR Ministry of Construction.

20. *Pravda*, 2 October 1979, p. 2 (fruit and vegetable organisation in Irkutsk; see case 4 in Chapter 3).

21. *Pravda*, 8 August 1981, p. 3 (Ryazan).

22. *Pravda*, 23 July 1979, p. 3 (state farm in Kuibyshev province, RSFSR).

23. Interview 23.

24. See e.g. *Pravda*, 6 July 1979, p. 3; 5 October 1979, p. 3; 15 October 1979, p. 3; 15 August 1981, p. 2; *Sots Ind.*, 14 June 1979, p. 2.

25. *Sots. Ind.*, 15 August 1979, p. 4.

26. Interview 9.

27. *Pravda*, 7 January 1980, p. 3.

28. *Sots. Ind.*, 27 June 1979, p. 3.

29. For a general discussion of Soviet trade unions, see Ruble (1981). From the point of view of the membership, the most important role of the trade union seems to be in the allocation of benefits. As one informant who had been a union organiser put it: 'A person on whom you depend for getting a holiday trip, such a person is respected' (interview 23). Admittedly this is an administrative function, but a function none the less.

30. It is noted in *Postanovlenie* (1976) that 'most disputes' involving the trade unions are about 'correct payment of wages, payment of rewards on the annual results of the work of the enterprise, withholding of workers' pay'. One former trade union official at a scientific research institute stressed the importance of trade union agreement for the distribution of bonuses and noted: 'There was no case in my experience, in all my work ... when after bonus payments there was not a definite flow of complaints. Everyone thinks that he got less ... There are very many complaints about bonuses.' (Interview 23).

31. Interview 2.

32. Interview 14.

33. Interview 23.

34. *Sots. Ind.*, 26 September 1979, p. 4.

35. *Pravda*, 28 March 1981, p. 3 (electronics factory, Prokhladnyi, Kabardino-Balkarskaya ASSR).
36. *Pravda*, 13 April 1982, p. 3 (Inter-kolkhoz mobile mechanised column, Saratov province, RSFSR).
37. A former trade union committee chairman at a large scientific research institute described the procedure of elections as follows:

> Before the elections at the annual general meeting, the present trade union organisation meets for the last time, and discusses a report about past work and possible candidates ... As a rule, the same people remain, because they have experience, unless there are people who want to step down ... At this meeting a representative of the party organisation and of the administration are unfailingly present. They participate in the discussion of candidates and sometimes support their own. If they have no objections to existing people, then they don't suggest anything, but if someone is to be replaced, they will nominate their candidate ...
>
> [At the general union meeting] a list is drawn up with more people than are needed, that is, you can cross somebody off. Let's suppose that the administration has singled you out for the position of chairman of the union committee. If you are being nominated for the first time, you are included in a list which is then read out at the meeting. 'In the name of the party and trade union organisations, the following candidates are nominated' ...
>
> Once the administration has chosen its own person [to go on the list] the work begins ... The heads of departments are called out, together with trade union representatives of departments. You are told: 'The party and trade union organisations and the administration consider that so-and-so ... has the following services to his credit, and should be promoted as a member of the trade union committee. You do the work with your people, explain it to them.' In every department, before the meeting, discussions are held. The department heads say that such and such a person is a good worker, he should be supported ... When the union committee for the institute is elected, votes are taken. At the general meeting not all employees are present, only representatives of departments. These representatives are already briefed in the appropriate way, discussions have been held with them, and so on. And so 15 people are elected to the committee. These 15 people choose a chairman from their own ranks ... Once the 15 have been elected, a personal discussion is held with each of them, in which it is recommended that such and such a comrade be elected chairman ... as a rule, whoever the administration and party organisation choose, is the one elected (interview 23).

Another informant, the head doctor of a sanatorium, explained that he did not interfere in union elections, but he made it sound like an exceptional state of affairs. In general, he said, he tried not to order the trade union about, and 'even when there were elections to the trade union committee, I didn't try to ensure that they would elect my nominees ... so at the trade union committee I had to argue my case' (interview 7).

38. See *Collected Legislation of the USSR*.
39. For a full discussion of the legal provisions on this, see *Sovetskoe Zakonodatel'stvo*, pp. 420–8.
40. Ibid., p. 426.
41. S.A. Ivanov and R.Z. Livshits, *Sov. Gosud. i Pravo*, 1978, 4, pp. 14–24. The 'special disciplinary regulations' involve certain categories of employee in some

types of work where violation of regulations may have especially dangerous consequences, e.g. on the railways and in the navy. See *Trudovoe Pravo*, pp. 474–5.

42. A.D. Zaikin, one of the commentators quoted in 'Delo ob uvolnenii', *Lit. Gaz.*, 10 January 1979, p. 11.
43. Ibid.
44. BVS SSSR 1977, 3, p. 29. The overall rate of reinstatement was similar in the early 1960s: 'Summaries of court practice show that more than half of claims for reinstatement are satisfied by the courts'. A.M. Shlemin (1966) p. 17, citing *Sots. Zakonnost'*, 1964, no. 8, p. 27.
45. Discussion with first secretary of the Ivanovo province party committee, *Pravda*, 7 September 1981, p. 2.
46. Interview 14.
47. E.g. USSR Supreme Court Plenum resolutions of 1971, 1974 and 1976 in *Sbornik postanovlenii* (1980) pp. 236–9; 239–42; 256–8; review of court decisions in BVS SSSR 1977, 3, pp. 29–37.
48. USSR Supreme Court Plenum resolution 1971, *Sbornik postanovlenii* (1980) p. 236.
49. The cases were heard in Leningrad in 1979 and Moscow in 1981.
50. *Sbornik postanovlenii* (1980) USSR Supreme Court Plenum resolutions 1974, 1976, pp. 240 and 256; BVS SSSR 1974, 2, pp. 45–6.
51. USSR Supreme Court resolution 1971, *Sbornik postanovlenii* (1980) p. 237.
52. BVS SSSR 1977, 3, p. 33. The courts were similarly warned by the USSR Supreme Court against any indulgence towards violators of labour discipline in BVS SSSR 1980, 3, pp. 9–14.
53. For a few examples, see BVS SSSR 1971, 4, pp. 7–9; 1971, 6, pp. 26–7; 1973, 2, pp. 26–8; 1974, 4, pp. 21–2; 1974, 6, pp. 3–5.
54. USSR Supreme Court Plenum resolution 1974, *Sbornik postanovlenii* (1980) p. 240.
55. BVS SSSR 1974, 4, pp. 33–9; similar criticisms were made five years later in BVS SSSR 1980, 6, p. 3.
56. USSR Supreme Court resolution 1974, *Sbornik postanovlenii* (1980) p. 241.
57. BVS SSSR 1977, 3, p. 35.
58. 1976 resolution, *Sbornik postanovlenii* (1980) pp. 256–8.
59. USSR Supreme Court Plenum resolution 1974, *Sbornik postanovlenii* (1980) p. 24.
60. BVS SSSR 1977, 3, p. 37.
61. USSR Supreme Court Plenum statement, quoted in *Pravda*, 30 August 1981, p. 2.
62. *Pravda*, 29 February 1980, p. 3.
63. USSR Supreme Court Plenum statement, quoted in *Pravda*, 30 August 1981, p. 2.
64. BVS SSSR 1974, 4, p. 38; 1977, 3, p. 30.
65. Interview 6.
66. Discussion on 15 April 1981.
67. Interview 14.
68. Interview 11.
69. BVS SSSR 1974, 6, pp. 3–5; 1982, 4, pp. 27–30.
70. *Trud*, 30 July 1981, pp. 1–2.
71. E.g. *Pravda*, 2 October 1979, p. 2; *Sots. Ind.*, 12 June 1979, p. 3; 14 June 1979, p. 3.
72. For an illustration of the problem, see case 3 in Chapter 3.
73. *Lit. Gaz.*, 22 November 1978, p. 12.

Bibliography

I PERIODICALS

Bulleten' Verkhovnogo Suda SSSR
Literaturnaya Gazeta
Pravda
Sotsialisticheskaya Industriya
Sotsialisticheskaya Zakonnost'
Sovetskoe Gosudarstvo i Pravo
Trud

II BOOKS AND ARTICLES IN RUSSIAN

Bor'ba s dolzhnostnymi prestupleniyami: sbornik nauchnykh trudov (Moscow, 1977)
Entsiklopedicheskii slovar' pravovykh znanii (Moscow, 1965)
A. Gel'man, 'Protokol odnogo zasedaniya', *Teatr* (1976) no. 2
Kommentarii k ugolovnomu kodeksu RSFSR (Moscow, 1971)
KPSS v rezolyutsiyakh i resheniyakh, vol. 9 (Moscow, 1972)
Lichnost' i uvazhenie k zakonu (Moscow, 1979)
A. Menabde, *Protektsionizm i bor'ba s nim* (Tbilisi, 1977)
V.I. Nikitinskii, V.E. Panyugin, *Dela ob uvol'nenii rabochikh i sluzhashchikh* (Moscow, 1973)
Postanovlenie VTsSPS: O nedostatkakh v rabote po rassmotreniyu trudovykh sporov na predpriyatiyakh, v uchrezhdeniyakh i organizatsiyakh Kalininskoi oblasti (Moscow, 13 July 1979)
Postanovlenie VTsSPS: O rabote KTS i FZMK profsoyuzov predpriyatii i organizatsii Bryanskoi oblasti po rassmotreniyu trudovykh sporov (Moscow, 25 June 1976)
Sbornik postanovlenii plenuma Verkhovnogo Suda SSSR, parts 1 and 2 (Moscow, 1980 and 1981)
A.M. Shlemin, *Otvetstvennost' dolzhnostnykh lits za nezakonnoe uvol'nenie* (Moscow, 1966)
V.M. Skobelkin, *Kak rassmatrivayutsya trudovye spory rabotnika s predpriyatiem* (Voronezh, 1977)
V.I. Smolyarchuk, *Zakonodatel'stvo o trudovykh sporakh* (Moscow, 1966)
Sovetskoe zakonodatel'stvo o trude (Moscow, 1980)
SSSR: Administrativno-territorialnoe delenie (Moscow, 1977)
Trudovoe pravo (Entsiklopedicheskii slovar') (Moscow, 1979)
Ugolovnaya otvetstvennost' za khishcheniya gosudarstvennogo ili obshchestvennogo

imushchestva, khozyaistvennye prestupleniya i vzyatochnichestvo (Moscow, 1967)
Ugolovnyi Kodeks RSFSR (Moscow, 1978)
Ustav KPSS (Moscow, 1971)
B. Yakovlev, 'Vazhnaya forma svyazi s massami', *Partiinaya Zhizn'*, 17 (1979) 22–37.

III BOOKS AND ARTICLES IN OTHER LANGUAGES

J.S. Adams, *Citizen Inspectors in the Soviet Union: the People's Control Committee* (New York: Praeger, 1977)
J.S. Adams, 'Critical Letter to the Soviet Press' in D.E. Schulz and J.S. Adams (eds.), *Political Participation in Communist Systems* (New York: Pergamon Press, 1981)
All-Union Principles of Labour Legislation (July 1970) in M. Matthews (ed.), *Soviet Government* (London: Cape, 1974)
V. Andrle, *Managerial Power in the Soviet Union* (Westmead: Saxon House, 1976)
D.D. Barry *et al.* (eds.), *Soviet Law after Stalin*, vols 1–3 (Alphen aan den Rijn: Sijthoff & Noordhoff, 1977, 1978, 1979)
J.S. Berliner, *Factory and Manager in the USSR* (Cambridge, Mass.: Harvard University Press, 1957)
M.C. Clarke (ed.), *Corruption* (London: Frances Pinter, 1983)
Collected Legislation of the USSR and the Constituent Republics, Release 2, August 1980 (Translation of the Soviet Constitution) (New York: Oceana Publications Inc.)
F.J.M. Feldbrugge (ed.), *Encyclopedia of Soviet Law* (Leiden: A.W. Sijthoff, 1973)
W. Gellhorn, *Ombudsmen and Others* (Cambridge, Mass.: Harvard University Press, 1967)
D. Granick, *Management of the Industrial Firm in the USSR* (New York: Columbia University Press, 1954)
G. Grossman, 'The "Second Economy" of the USSR', *Problems of Communism* (Sept–Oct 1977) 25–40
G. Grossman, 'Notes on the Illegal Private Economy and Corruption', *The Soviet Economy in a Time of Change* (Washington DC: Economic Committee, US Congress, 1979) pp. 834–55
T. Hadden, 'Corporate Corruption', unpublished paper for conference on corruption, Birmingham, June 1982
S. Hall *et al.*, *Policing the Crisis* (London: Macmillan, 1978)
A. Inkeles and H.K. Geiger, 'Critical Letters to the Soviet Press' in A. Inkeles, *Social Change in Soviet Russia* (Cambridge, Mass.: Harvard University Press, 1968)
O. Kahn-Freund, *Labour and the Law* (London: Stevens & Sons, 1977)
A. Katsenelinboigen, 'Corruption in the USSR: Some Methodological Notes' in M. Clarke (ed.) (1983)
G. Mars and Y. Altman, 'How a Soviet Economy Really Works' in M. Clarke (ed.) (1983)
G. Ofer, A. Vinokur, *Private Sources of Income of the Soviet Urban Household* (Santa Monica: Rand Publications, 1980)
S. Pomorski, 'Criminal Law Protection of Socialist Property in the USSR' in D.D. Barry *et al.* (1977)

S. Pomorski, 'Crimes against the Central Planner: "Ochkovtiratel'stvo"' in D.D. Barry *et al.* (1978)

S. Pomorski, 'La corruption de fonctionnaires devant les tribunaux sovietiques', *Revue d'Études Comparatives Est–Ouest*, vol. XIV, no. 1 (March 1983) 5–22

G. Rittersporn, 'L'État en lutte contre lui-même', *Libre*, 4 (1978) 3–38

B.A. Ruble, *Soviet Trade Unions* (Cambridge University Press, 1981)

S. Shenfield, '*Pripiski*: False Statistical Reporting in Soviet-type Economies' in M. Clarke (ed.) (1983)

D.K. Simes, 'The Soviet Parallel Market' in *Economic Aspects of Life in the USSR* (Brussels: NATO Directorate of Economic Affairs, 1975)

K.M. Simis, *USSR: Secrets of a Corrupt Society* (London: J.M. Dent, 1982)

W.B. Simons (ed.), *The Soviet Codes of Law* (Alphen aan den Rijn: Sijthoff & Noordhoff, 1980)

G.B. Smith, *The Soviet Procuracy and the Supervision of Administration* (Alphen aan den Rijn: Sijthoff & Noordhoff, 1978)

S. White, 'Political Communications in the USSR: Letters to the Party, State and Press', *Political Studies*, XXXI (1983) 43–60

Workers Against the Gulag (London: Pluto Press, 1979)

Index

Abuse of office 1–2, 3, 4, 19–20, 43, 177, 179
  agencies of appeal 122–7
    see also under Soviet labour law
  bribery 17, 22, 27, 31, 33–4, 44, 110, 114–15
  deceiving customers and clients 17–18
  embezzlement 14–15, 31–4 passim, 45, 110, 114–15
  false reporting 3, 15–16, 22, 57–8, 114; 'dead souls' 16; illegal wage payments 16, 24, 29–30, 119; report padding 15–16, 27, 28–9, 45, 47, 57, 110; understating resources to cover waste or theft 16
  favouritism 19, 24, 110
  forgery 16–17
  in Soviet criminal law 13–14
  'organisational' 26–7, 30, 31–2
  penalties for 20, 52–9
  press coverage 10
  pressures leading to 21–3; keeping up appearances 27–30; meeting targets 23–7; public office and private gain 31–5
  private enterprise 18–19
  problem of official immunity 7
  scale of problem 21–3
  using resources illicitly 19–20, 31
All-Union Ministry of Machine-building 38
Andropov, Yuri 132
  introduces law and order campaign, 1982 1
Andrle, V. 158
Armenia 35, 59, 164
Azerbaidzhan 34, 35, 52, 58, 59, 152, 164

Brezhnev, Leonid 59, 65, 66, 106, 132
  on importance of 'renewal of Soviet law' 5–6

Cherkassov, V. 101
Criminal Code of the Russian Republic (RSFSR) 14, 130, 168
Current Digest of the Soviet Press 52

Danilov, V. 69

Ermolaev, V. 86

Free Trade Union Association 132–3

Gelman, Alexander
  The Bonus (play and film) 116
Georgia 164
  abuse of office in 35, 59, 178
Grossman, G. 21

Institute of State and Law 162
Izvestiya
  letters received annually 64

Kazakhstan 52, 164
  case of victimisation of nurse in 171–2
KGB 42, 133
Kiev 155–6
Kirgizia 164
Krushchev, Nikita 58, 65

Lenin
  State and Revolution 187
Literaturnaya Gazeta 139, 173

Ministry of Chemical Industry 38
Ministry of Finance 36, 39, 40

Ministry of Forest and Timber 38
Ministry of Internal Affairs 42
Ministry of Petroleum Industry 54
Mukimov, Yu. 92

Novikov, I. 73

Ofer, G. and Vinokur, A.
on Soviet 'second economy' 27

Pomorski, S. 33
Pravda 52, 64, 108, 128, 138, 139,
143, 153
complaints reported by correspondents 69–72, 73–7, 78–85,
86–91, 92–5, 101–4, 105–7
letters received annually 64
on misapplication of material and
manpower 47–8
on 'suppression of criticism' 129,
140
quotes Aliev on consumerism 34–
5

Simes, D. K. 21
Simis, K. M. 48
Solidarity, in Poland 133
Sotsialisticheskaya Industriya
reports dispute over rights under
labour law 95–100
Sovetskaya Rossiya 141
Soviet Communist Party 35, 36, 46–
51
agency of appeal over abuse of
office 122–7
Central Committee 139, 145;
Letters Department 65, 128,
131; on importance of
people's letters 67, 128–9;
petitions to, 1971–5 63
concern with image 47, 50, 125
expulsion of members before
criminal proceedings 49, 51
leadership's response to
complaints 127–34;
advocation of 'open letter'
days 129; condemns sup-
pression of criticism 129;
exhortations to deal with

complaints fully and quickly
128–9; reminder to law
agencies of duties concerning
129–30; viewed as
constructive criticism 128;
viewed as uncovering law-
breaking 128
local reluctance to act on
complaints 123–5
members' near immunity to law
46–7, 49, 59; examples of
49–50, 55–6
misapplication of materials and
manpower by members of
47–8
role of reprimands in 50–1
Soviet controllers 35–6
chief accountants 36
control from above 37–9;
examples of 'eyewash' 39
control from outside 39–41
control from within organisations
36–7
legal consultants 37
Soviet labour law 146–7
appeal procedure 148–9; sources
of appeal for workers 172–5
see also role of courts and
role of trade unions *below*
Commissions on Work Disputes
148, 149
dealing with work disputes under
147–9
decline in suits for reinstatement
151–2
Labour Code 147, 148, 149, 156,
175, 179
management attitudes under 149–
58; contraventions of law
152–3; desire to keep large
workforce 150–1; dismissal
149–50, 153, 154; response to
complaints 155; use of disciplinary clauses of Labour
Code 154, 156, 157
Principles 147, 149
role of courts 161–9; concen-
tration on letter of law
167–8; court decisions and

Soviet labour law—*continued*
managerial power 169–72;
failure to uphold employees'
rights 166; leniency towards
management violations of
code 166, 167; reinstatement
cases 163–5, 169, 170–1;
reversals of decisions by
higher judiciary 168–9;
workers deprived of appeal
to 161–3
role of trade unions 148, 149,
158–61, 176; privileges of
organisers 161; support for
management 158, 159, 160;
workers' appeals to higher
bodies in 172–3
Soviet law
defeated by political structure
3–4, 6, 7, 24, 177, 178, 182–3
'law and order' propaganda 6,
131, 132, 178
petitioning 8, 62–8, 131, 133; few
penalties for ignoring 133–4;
press coverage 134–44
regulating social behaviour 1
Soviet labour law, *see* separate
entry
Soviet legal apparatuses 35, 36, 41–6
courts 42, 129–30; criticisms of
44–5; labour law and 161–75;
People's 42, 168, 171
Department for the Struggle
against the Theft of Socialist
Property 42
law enforcement 51–9
People's Control 36, 40–1, 63, 64,
66, 113, 114, 130
procuracy 41–4, 129–30, 163, 172;
as source of appeal for
workers 173–5; criticisms of
44; Procurator's Office 130
restraints on 59–60
Soviet Union
approaches to system; cynical
view of 182–3, 188; demand
for return to socialist
democracy 185–6, 189;
socialist defence of 180–1,

188; suggestions for radical
reform 186–8, 189; wish to
improve working of 183–5,
188
centralised system 2–3
Constitution of 1977 5, 62, 65,
128, 161
full employment 146, 181
'second economy' in 21–2, 23
tolerance of illegality 5, 145
'unofficial' practices 3, 24–6;
example of running sana-
torium 24–5
Stalin, Josef 65
State Bank 36, 39

Tbilisi, Georgia 52, 54
trade unions
All-Union Central Council 173
see also under Soviet labour law
Trud
letters received annually 64
Turkestan 152

USSR Supreme Court 42, 43, 65–6,
163, 165, 170, 171, 172
condemns 'suppression of
criticism' 130
Criminal Chamber 43
on abuse of office 43
on bribery 17, 44
on contraventions of labour law
152
on false reporting 15, 16, 45
on illegal levies from citizens 18
reviews of lower courts' decisions
57, 58, 165–7
USSR Supreme Soviet
decree on 'Procedures for
examining citizens'
proposals, statements and
complaints', 1980 67
Uzbekistan 152

Weber, Max 182
whistleblowing 8, 9, 65
approach to investigation of 11–
12
complaint of lack of safety

Whistleblowing—*continued*
  provisions in excavator plant
    92–5
  complaint of victimisation and
    abuse of office 78–85; effect
    of 86; *Pravda* comment 82
  defined 2
  disclosure of report-padding 73–7
  dispute over rights under labour
    law 95–100
  encouragement of ordinary
    citizens to undertake 7–8, 61
  exposure of bribery in victimis-
    ation in school 105–7
  exposure of graft in health service
    101–5
  housing complaint from
    electrician 69–72; action
    against plaintiff 70, 72;
    partial success of 72
  management response to 116–22;
    counter-accusations of
    malpractice 121–2; imposing
    penalties 121; mobilising
    party secretary against
    plaintiff 119–20; mobilising
    workforce against plaintiff
    118–19; nervousness 117;
    self-justification 117
  motives for 111–16;
    conscientiousness 111, 112,
    114–15, 144; individual
    concerns 112–14, 144
  official worries about increasing
    volume 178
  organisations subject to complaint
    109–10
  party leadership response to 127–
    34
  party response to 122–7
  press coverage of 12, 134–5, 144–
    5; effectiveness of press
    criticism 140–4; investigation
    of complaints 138; limits to
    press power 141, 142, 143;
    occasional admonishment for
    whistleblower 142–3; official
    resistance to 139–40; problem
    of selection among letters
    135–40
  sources for 9–11
  types of complaint 110
  used by Communist Party as
    safety valve 132
  whistleblowers' occupations 109
White, S. 64